500
toys to make

500 toys to make

adorable projects to crochet, knit, felt & sew

Nguyen Le

NEW HOLLAND

A Quintet Book

First published in Australia in 2013 by
New Holland Publishers (Australia) Pty Ltd
Sydney • Auckland • London • Cape Town

Unit 1, 66 Gibbes Street, Chatswood, NSW 2067 Australia
218 Lake Road, Northcote, Auckland, New Zealand
86 Edgware Road, London W2 2EA, United Kingdom
Wembley Square, First Floor, Solan Road Gardens, Cape Town 8001, South Africa

www.newholland.com.au

ISBN: 978 1 74257 357 1
QTT.FHSB

This book was conceived, designed and produced by
Quintet Publishing Limited
6 Blundell Street
London N7 9BH
United Kingdom

Photographer: Sussie Bell
Designer: Rod Teasdale
Art Director: Michael Charles
Editorial Assistant: Hazel Eriksson
Editorial Director: Donna Gregory
Publisher: Mark Searle

10 9 8 7 6 5 4 3 2 1

Printed in China by 1010 Printing International Ltd.

contents

introduction

Handmade toys are so special, whether they're made as gifts or simply for yourself. They are cherished and enjoyed by all ages. We remember our favourite toys as children, and sometimes even get to pass them onto the next generation to be played with and loved again and again. They spark creativity and imagination, and even offer comfort when needed. This book is the perfect companion for knitters, crocheters, stitchers and felters who are looking for patterns and inspiration for making toys. It uses a variety of techniques and often combines them to create more interesting pieces.

I love the feeling of excitement I get when I find a new project to make – I just want to get started right away so I can have the finished piece in my hands. The beauty of this book is that the majority of the projects are small and can be completed in just a few hours. It's perfect for instant gratification, and for those last-minute crafters like myself!

The patterns in this book use basic knit and crochet stitches, and basic sewing instructions. They're great for beginners, but the projects are so cute that more advanced crafters will enjoy making them as well. This book includes general instructions on how to make five variations of each toy. They serve as ideas and inspiration, and I hope that they will help you to be creative in putting your own twist on the projects as well.

The toys chosen for this book are classics, although the crocheted mobile phone may beg to differ. The rest of the toys though, are timeless pieces that each generation will enjoy. Whether you're looking to make a baby shower gift, a birthday gift, or something for yourself or your little one, this book will help you create something sweet and memorable.

Happy crafting!
Nguyen

METHUEN

essential tools & materials

knitting needles

Knitting needles are usually made of lightweight metal, wood, bamboo or plastic and come in a range of sizes, both in diameter and length. The size of the needles required for any project is determined by the thickness of the yarn and the number of stitches the project requires.

needle gauge and ruler

A needle gauge with a ruler is useful if you own knitting needles without size markings or are converting sizes from metric to US or vice versa. Simply slide a needle through successive holes until you find the correct size. One side has a ruler, while the other side shows the needle gauge. I like a 150-cm (60-in) tape marked with inches and centimetres on either side. Some of these sewing patterns call for measuring and marking out a square or rectangle, so a ruler helps to draw a straight cutting line.

crochet hooks

Similar to knitting needles, crochet hooks are made of various materials, such as lightweight metal, wood, bamboo, or plastic, and also come in a range of sizes. They differ from knitting needles in that there's a hook at the end, and you only need one hook to crochet. The size of the needles required for any project is determined by the thickness of the yarn and the number of stitches the project requires.

row counters

Row counters are used to help you count the number of rows you have worked in knitting or crochet.

scissors

A pair of small, sharp scissors is an essential tool for trimming loose yarn and thread ends. Larger, sharp fabric shears are essential for cutting out patterns from fabric.

stitch markers

Stitch markers are useful for counting stitches and pattern repeats as well as marking the beginning of a round in circular knitting or crochet. There are different stitch markers used in knitting and crochet. A knitting stitch marker is a closed ring. It can be placed over the knitting needle when working in the round. A crochet stitch marker has a opening for slipping on and off the first stitch of the round.

tape measure and ruler
Some projects call for knitting or crocheting for a certain length, and tape measures come in handy for measuring your progress.

straight pins
Straight pins are used for knit, crochet, or sewing projects to hold pieces together while sewing up. Choose pins with brightly coloured tips, as they are much easier to see.

tapestry, sewing, and embroidery needles
Tapestry needles come in various sizes. The eye needs to be large enough to accommodate the yarn, and the point should be relatively blunt. Embroidery needles have a larger eye than sewing needles, and both come in different lengths and sizes for different fabrics and projects. The needle should glide right through the fabric and not tug at it. You don't want to leave any holes in the fabric.

felting needles and felting foam pad
There are a few different sizes of felting needles. The smaller-gauge needles such as 40 and 42 are fine-tipped, and used for finer wool and detail work. And the larger-gauge needles such as 36 and 38 are for coarser wools. I like to use a size 38 needle, which is a medium gauge. It works well for fine and coarse roving. A foam pad is used to protect your work table and your felting needle. It is where you place your project to work on. You can buy specific needle felting foam, but you can also use the same foam used in making cushions, and found at most craft supply shops.

sewing machine
There are many different models of sewing machines, but they do the same basic stitches. The sewing patterns in this book call for making straight stitches and zigzag stitches. Sewing machines are a great help for sewing larger projects, but not absolutely necessary for creating the projects in this book. If you have one, use it, if not, sew by hand.

fabric tailor's chalk

Fabric chalk comes in light and dark colours so you choose which one will show up best on your fabric. They'll disappear with washing or by rubbing the fabric together.

water-soluble fabric marker

These markers are great to use on light-coloured fabric when marking out sewing patterns. The lines will disappear when washed.

point turner

A point tuner is a piece of plastic or wood used to help push out a corner or a curved seam. You can buy a specifically made point turner, or you can use a chopstick or knitting needle tip to do the trick in a pinch.

iron

An iron is an essential tool for flattening fabric, pressing seam allowances and hems for sewing patterns.

cotton fabric

Most of the sewing patterns in this book call for 100 percent cotton fabric. There are different weights of cotton fabric, but the ones mainly used here are a light- to medium-weight cotton. If you have other fabric in your stash, feel free to use it, and don't worry so much about the fabric content. Toys are small projects, and are perfect for using up scraps.

felt fabric

There are two main types of felt fabric – craft felt and wool felt. I also use a wool and rayon blend felt for a few projects. Feel free to use whichever felt you like. Craft felt is much less expensive than wool felt, and wool blends are a good in-between price range.

yarn

Yarn is available in a multitude of fibres, colours and weights. Most of the yarn used for the projects in this book are wool or cotton blends, but feel free to substitute yarn from your stash for any of the projects. Be sure to use the corresponding size needle or hook for your yarn. (See knit and crochet tension). Different weights of yarn call for different-sized needles or hooks.

roving

Roving is an unspun mass of fibres. It's the stage of fibre before being spun into yarn, so it's fluffy, like cotton wool balls. The projects in this book call for wool roving, and coarser roving, such as Corriedale, is better for needle felting.

thread

Like yarn, thread comes in different varieties. A cotton or an all-purpose polyester thread will work well for the projects in this book.

embroidery thread

Embroidery thread is thicker than sewing thread, and comes twisted in six strands. You split the strands to use it in different thicknesses as you like. I usually use embroidery floss double stranded when stitching facial features and back stitching.

knit and crochet tension

Because the projects in this book are toys and not garments, it's ok if the finished piece is a little bigger or smaller than the ones here. When substituting yarn, you want to make sure your stitches are tight enough so that the stuffing doesn't show through. This usually means going down one or two needle or hook sizes from normal for that particular yarn. A swatch will always be able to help you figure out the needle or hook size to obtain the necessary tension. Stretch your knitted swatches to see how it will look when stuffed, and keep in mind how much you'll be stuffing. Crochet is stiffer than knitting, so you'll be able to see any holes without stretching.

essential techniques

knitting

making a slip knot

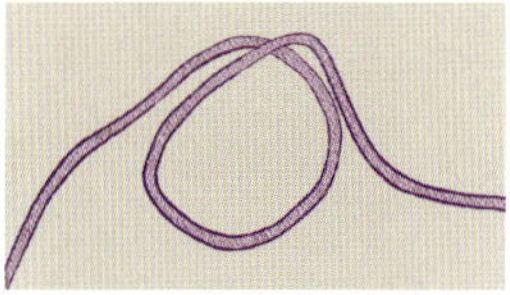

1 Holding the yarn in both hands, make a small loop in the yarn. Take the piece that you are holding in the right hand underneath the loop.

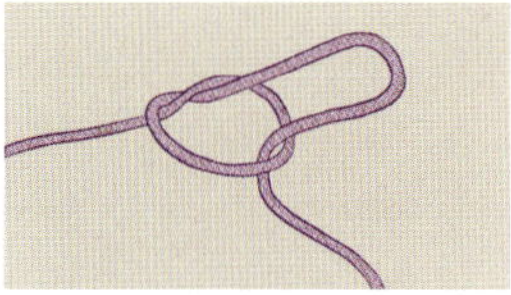

2 Pull this piece of yarn through the original loop, to create a knot. Do not pull the short end of the yarn through the loop.

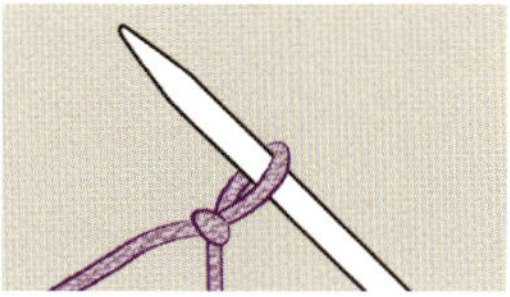

3 Place the slip knot onto the knitting needle.

holding the needles

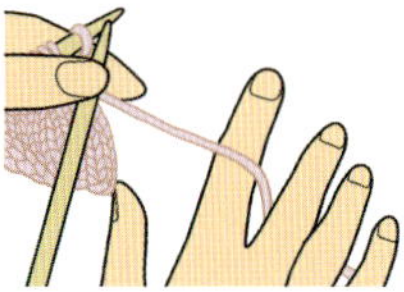

english method
The left hand takes the weight of the needles while the stitch is being made. The yarn is held in the right hand and wraps around the right needle.

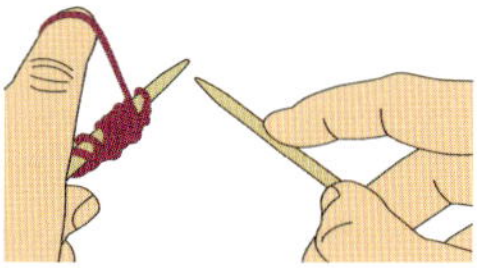

continental method
The yarn is held in the left hand and the right needle 'picks' the yarn from the left hand.

casting on

Casting on is the first step in hand knitting and it provides the first row of loops on the needle. The diagrams below show the cable method, but if you prefer another method, use that instead.

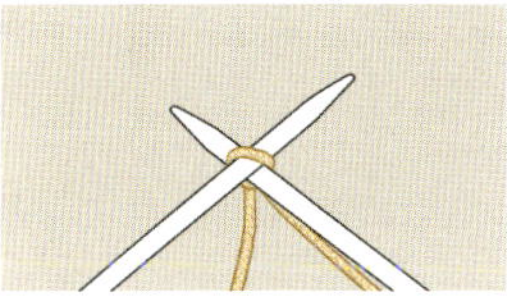

1 Place the slip knot onto a knitting needle and hold the needle in your left hand. Slide the right knitting needle through the loop created by the slip knot from front to back.

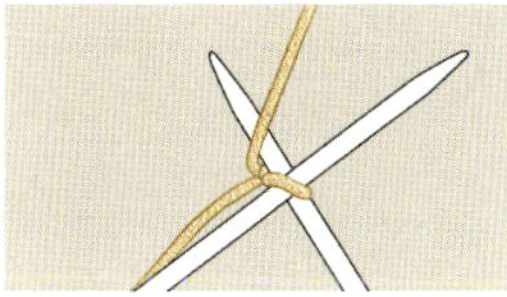

2 With your right hand, wrap the yarn around the right knitting needle anticlockwise from back to front.

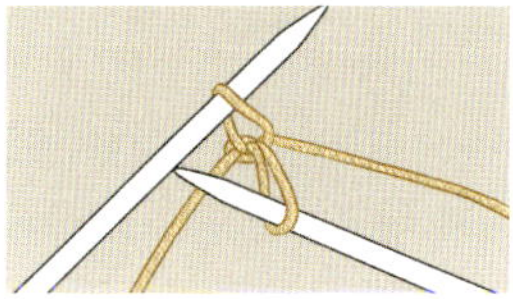

3 Slide the right needle through the loop on the left needle, catching the wrapped yarn and bringing it through the loop to create another loop.

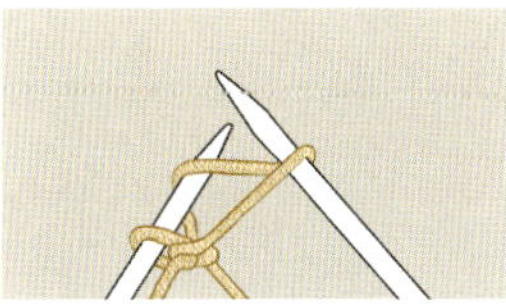

4 Pass the left needle over the top of the new loop, placing the tip of the needle through the loop on the right needle. Remove the right needle, thus transferring the stitch to the left needle.

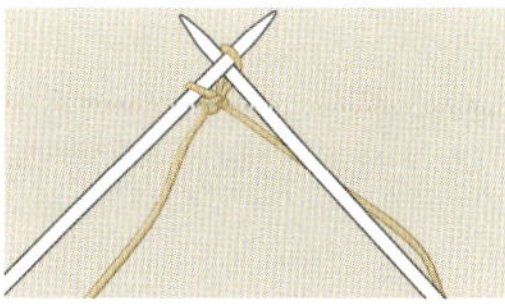

5 Make each subsequent stitch by placing the right needle between the last two stitches made on the left needle, and repeating steps 2–4.

knit and purl stitches

Most knitting is based on combinations of just two basic stitches – knit stitch and purl stitch.

knit stitch

1 Hold the needle with the stitches to be knitted in the left hand with the yarn behind the work.

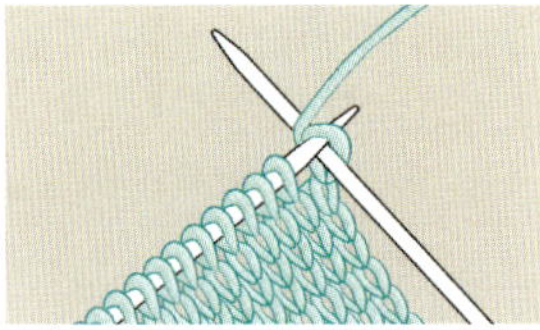

2 Insert the right-hand needle into a stitch from front to back. Take the yarn over it, forming a loop.

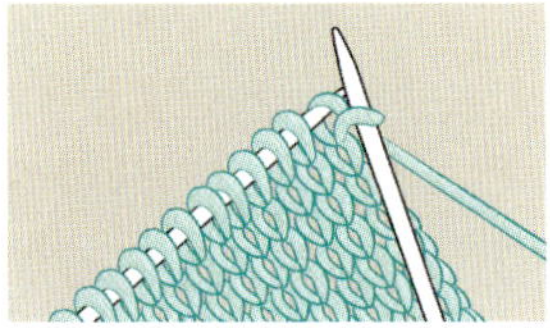

3 Bring the needle and the new loop to the front of the work through the stitch, and slide the original stitch off the left-hand needle.

purl stitch

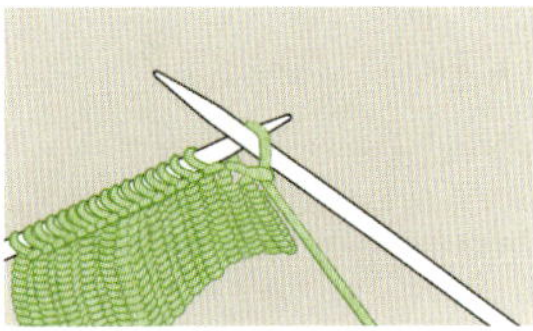

1 Hold the stitches to be purled in the left hand, with the yarn at the front of the work.

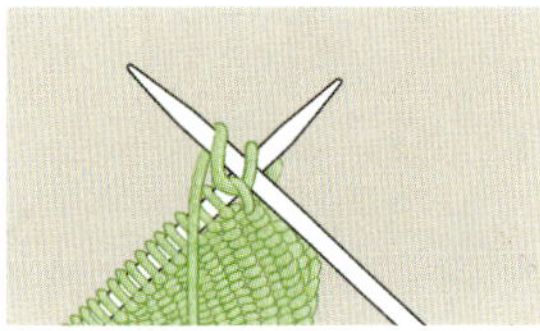

2 Insert the right-hand needle through the front of the stitch, from right to left. Take the yarn over and under, forming a loop.

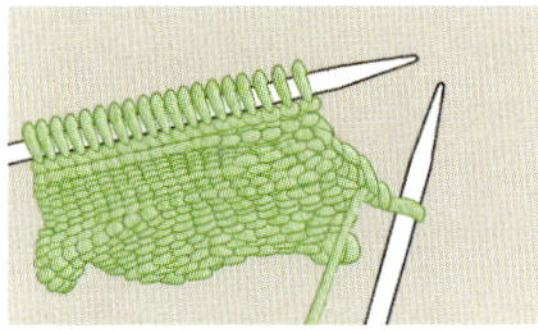

3 Take the needle and the new loop through the back and slide the stitch off the left-hand needle.

casting off

1 At the point where you are ready to cast off, knit the first two stitches.

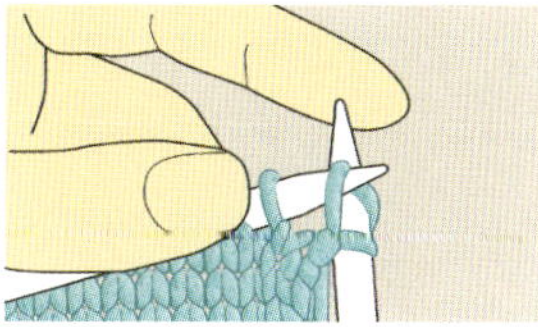

2 Slip the left-hand needle into the first stitch on the right-hand needle, and lift it over the second stitch and off the needle.

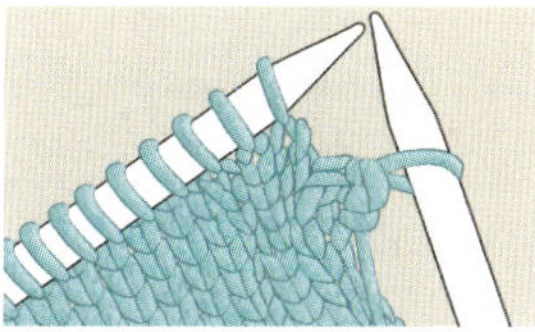

3 Knit the next stitch so that there are two stitches on the right-hand needle again.

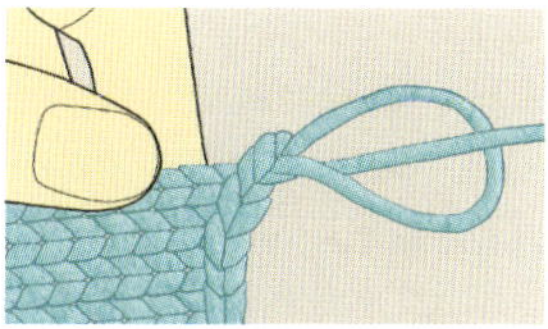

4 Repeat steps 2 and 3 until all stitches are knitted from the left-hand needle and one stitch remains on the right-hand needle. Make the last stitch loop larger, break the yarn, and draw firmly through the last stitch to fasten off

basic knitting stitch variations

garter stitch

If you were to work rows of just knit, or rows of just purl, stitches in succession you would create a knitted fabric known as garter stitch. This looks the same on both sides of the fabric.

stocking stitch (or stockinette stitch)

To make a fabric using stocking stitch, work rows of knit stitches and rows of purl stitches alternately.

Stocking stitch fabric is different on both sides. The right side is smooth, and you will be able to see that the stitches create a zigzag effect. The wrong side is bumpy and looks a little like garter stitch.

moss stitch (or seed stitch)

Moss stitch fabric looks like tiny little seeds across the fabric. It is made by knitting one stitch and purling the next stitch alternately across the right side of the fabric. On the wrong side, you'll knit the purls and purl the knits, and continue doing so for every stitch.

make one increase (m1)

This is usually done by knitting into the back of the bar between stitches. It is a neat increase worked between two stitches.

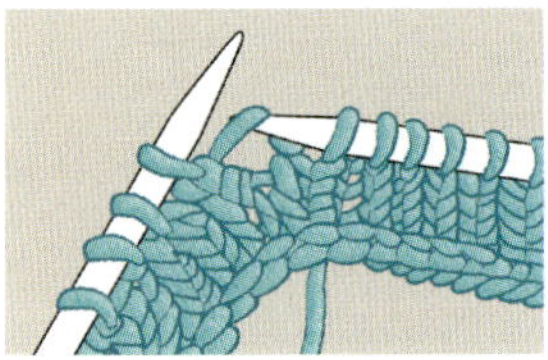

1 Pass the right knitting needle underneath the 'bar' of yarn between two stitches from front to back.

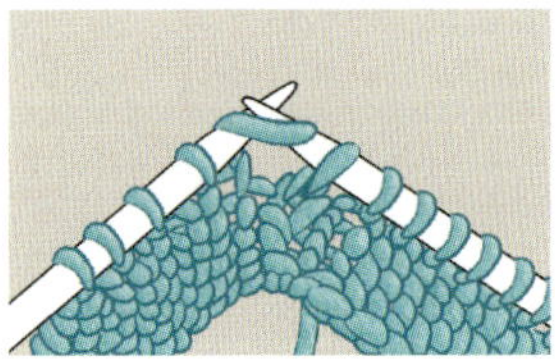

2 Slip the loop onto the left needle and remove the right needle.

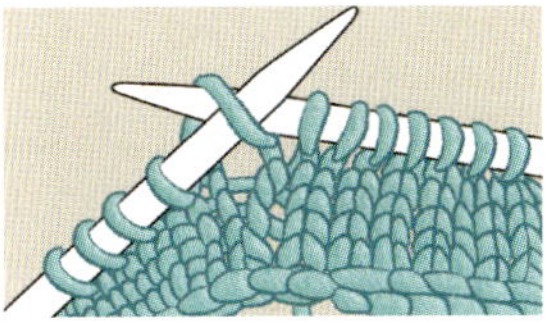

3 Knit into the back of the loop to twist it, by inserting the right needle behind the yarn on the left needle from right to left.

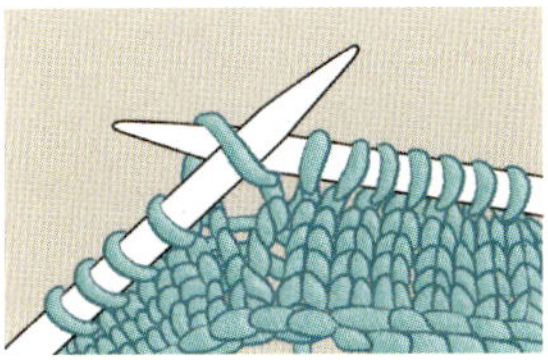

4 Finish the stitch as a normal knit stitch, and remove the left needle, passing the new stitch onto the right needle.

knit two together (k2tog)

Decreasing is most commonly done by working two or more stitches together to form one stitch. On a knit or right-side row this creates a slope to the right.

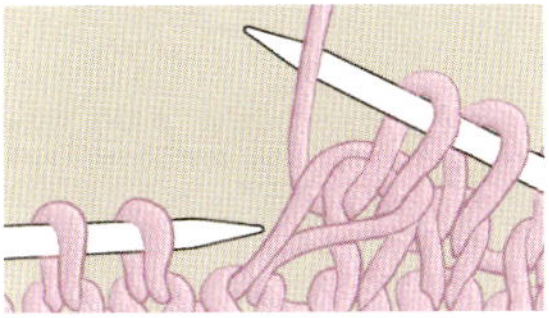

1 Slide the right needle through the second and then the first stitches on the left needle from front to back. Wrap the yarn around the right needle as a normal knit stitch.

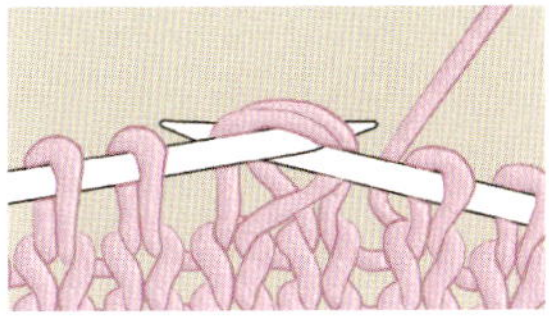

2 Knit the two stitches together as if knitting normally and slide both from the left needle.

purl two together (p2tog)

Working two or more stitches together on the wrong side of the knitted piece creates a slope to the right on the right side.

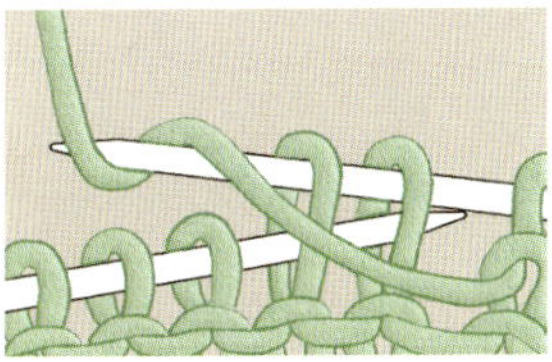

1 Slide the right needle through the first two stitches on the left needle 'purlwise'.

2 Purl the two stitches together as if purling normally and slide both from the left needle.

slip slip knit (ssk)

This is simply slipping the next two stitches, then knitting them together – it is a left-slanting decrease.

duplicate stitch

This stitch is a way to add a bit of colour into a piece.

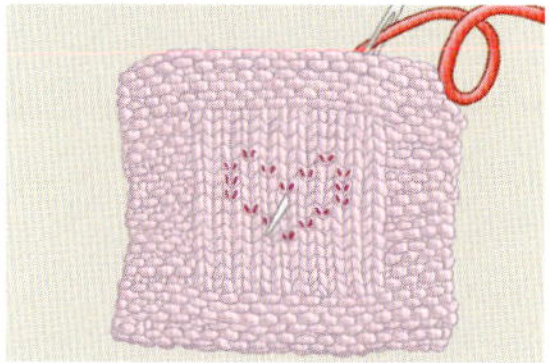

1 Thread a length of yarn through a tapestry needle and pull the needle up from back to front through the centre bottom point of a knit V stitch.

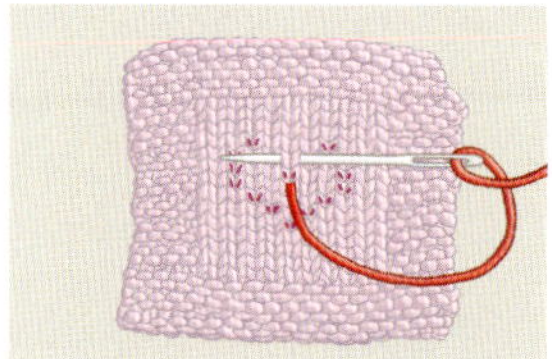

2 Pull the needle from right to left under the bottom legs of the stitch above the one you're duplicating. Pull the yarn through gently so it sits right above the stitch below it.

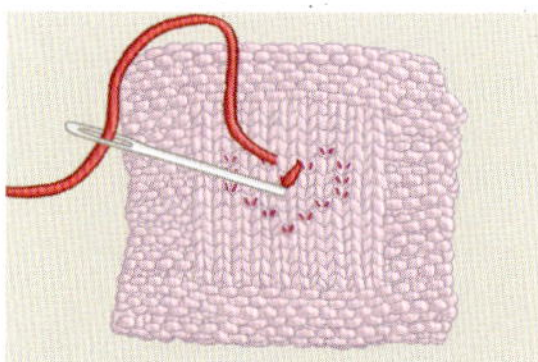

3 Pull the needle back down into the first hole from front to back. You've completed one duplicate stitch.

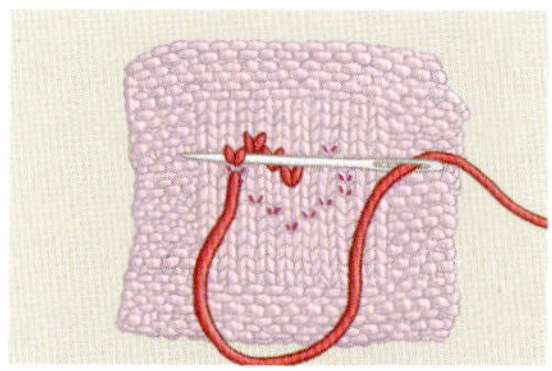

4 Continue stitching as stated into the next stitch you want to duplicate, until you've finished duplicating all that you wanted.

i-cord

The I-cord is an easy way to knit a small tube of cording.

1 Cast on three stitches (or as many as your pattern calls for) onto a double-pointed needle and knit those stitches.

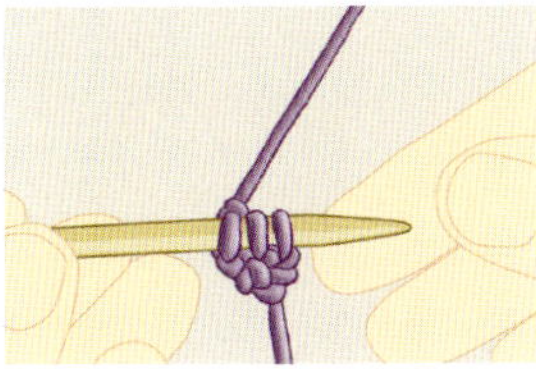

2 Slide your knitting to the other end of the needle (right end) without turning it, and switch needles in your hands.

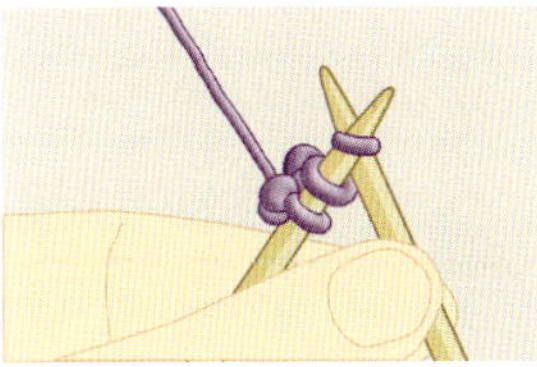

3 Knit across your stitches, pulling the yarn tight so it curls in on itself.

4 Continue knitting in this manner until you've knit your desired length of I-cord.

weaving in ends

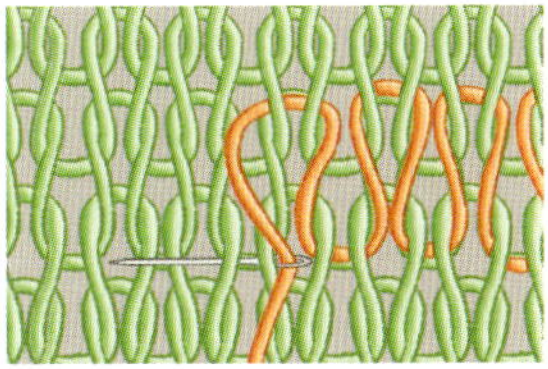

1 Thread the yarn through the loops along the edge of the work for around 4–5cm (1½–2 in), then sew back through a few of the last loops to secure.

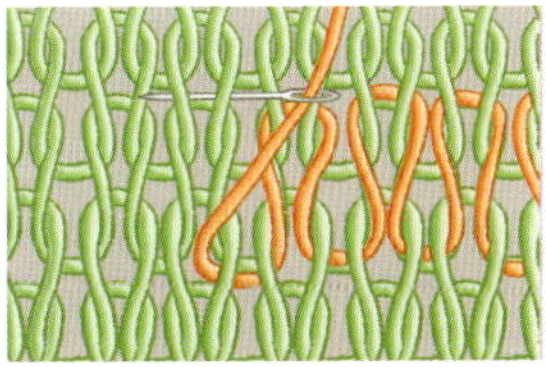

2 Pass the end through the stitches, inserting the needle from the top of the loop on the first, then the bottom on the next alternately for about 4–5cm (1½–2 in), then sew back through a few of the last loops to secure.

invisible seam (mattress stitch)

Sewing technique used to join two pieces of knitting. See sewing technique, page 30.

knitting in the round with double-pointed needles (dpns)

Divide the stitches evenly between three or four of the needles and, once the cast-on row has been made, use the fourth/fifth needle to knit. Once all the stitches from one needle have been knitted onto the fourth, use the free needle to work the stitches along from the next needle. Keep the tension of the stitches constant when transferring from one needle to another; always draw the yarn up firmly when knitting the first stitch at the change-over point to avoid a ladder or loopy stitch. Ensure the cast-on row is not twisted before you start knitting and use a stitch marker to identify the first stitch.

blocking

Blocking is a finishing technique that helps shape your knitted pieces and smooth out the stitches before sewing them together. Start by pinning your piece to a blocking board to the correct size. (I use my ironing board for small pieces in a pinch). You can use the steam from an iron to hover over and steam block your pieces, or you can pin and spritz your piece with a bit of water and let it air dry.

knitting abbreviations

CO: cast on
BO: cast off
k: knit
p: purl
st: stitch
sts: stitches
St st: stocking stitch
m1: make one stitch
k1f&b: knit one front and back
k2tog: knit two together
ssk: slip slip knit
dpn: double-pointed needle
con't: continue
rep: repeat
R: row

crochet

holding the hook and yarn

There are two methods for holding a crochet hook, the overhand knife hold and the pencil hold.

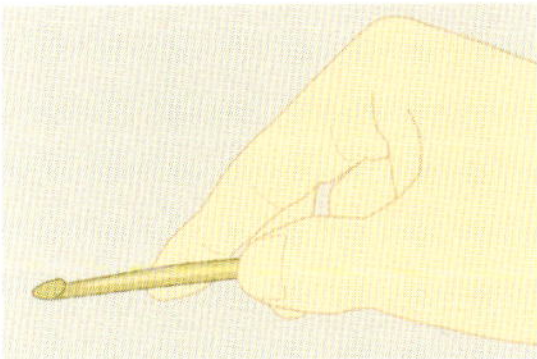

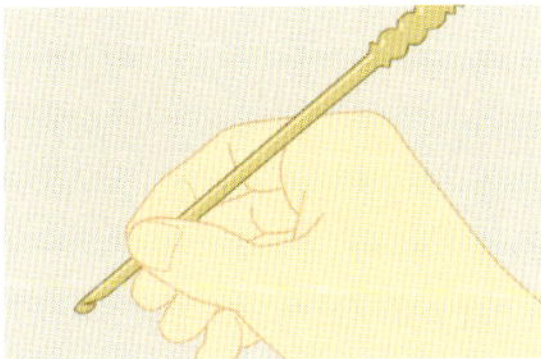

To hold the working yarn, weave it through your left hand as follows: over your index finger, under the middle finger, and over your ring finger. If this feels too loose for you, wrap the yarn around your little finger for tighter control. Another method is to simply wrap the yarn around your index finger twice.

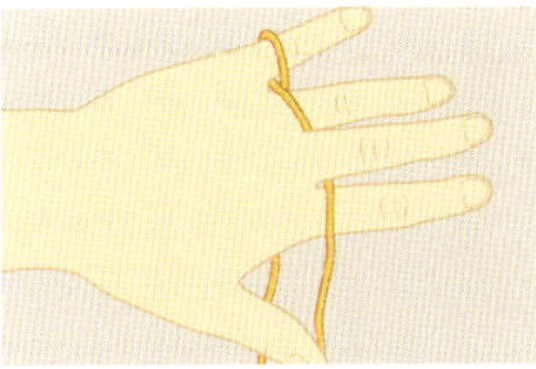

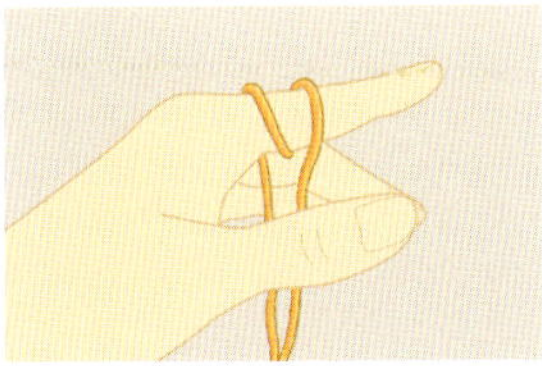

Choose whichever hook hold and yarn wrap are most comfortable and will give you the most control of your yarn tension.

chain stitch

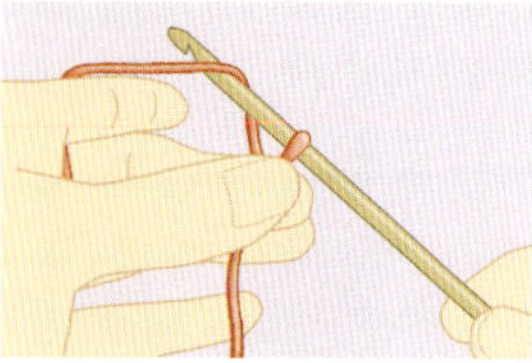

1 Begin with a slip-knot on your hook, holding the knot between the thumb and middle finger of your yarn hand.

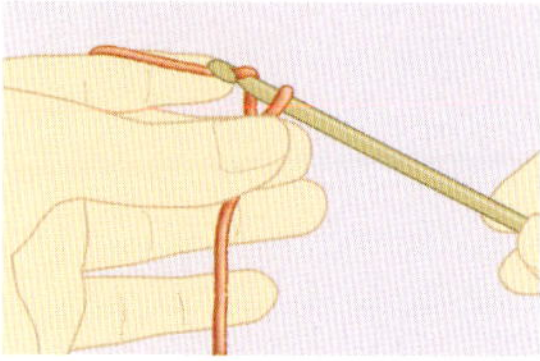

2 Bring the working yarn from behind and over the hook (this is called a yarn over).

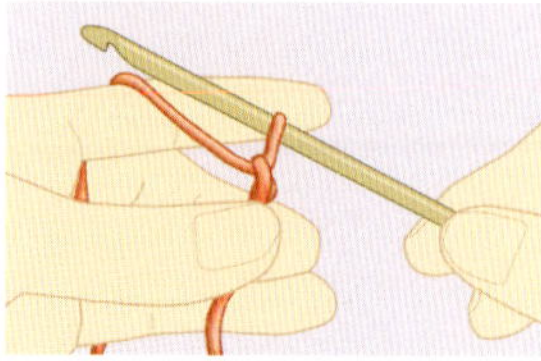

3 Slide your hook down, grasping the yarn and pulling it through the loop on your hook: 1 chain stitch made.

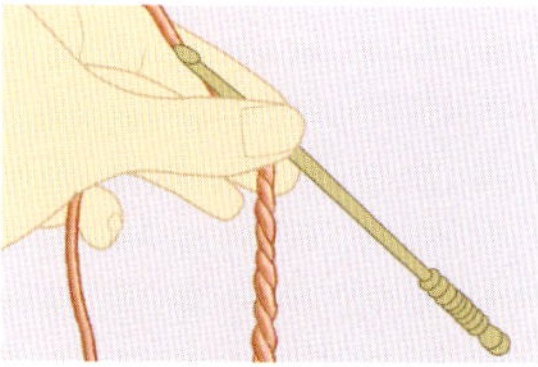

4 Keep moving your fingers up to hold each new chain as you make them to help you keep your tension even.

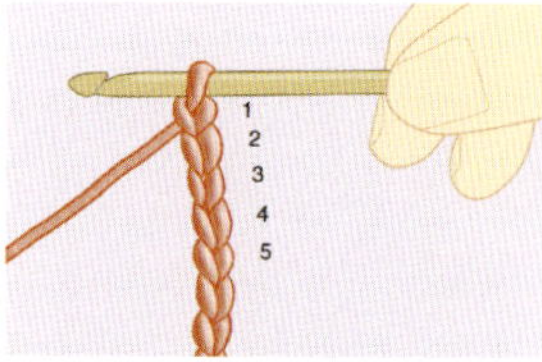

5 Notice the 'V' shape of the chains when viewed from the front. The number of stitches can be counted easily this way. Turn the chain over and you will see the back ridges, the 'spine' of the chain.

double crochet (dc)

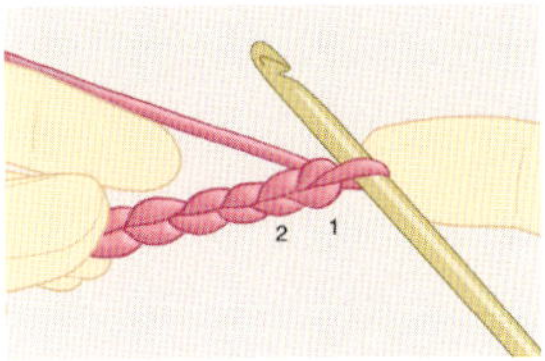

1 Insert your hook into the second v of the stitch.

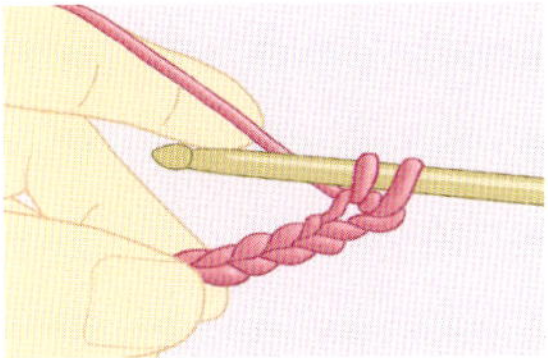

2 Yarn over and pull up a loop. You will have two loops on your hook.

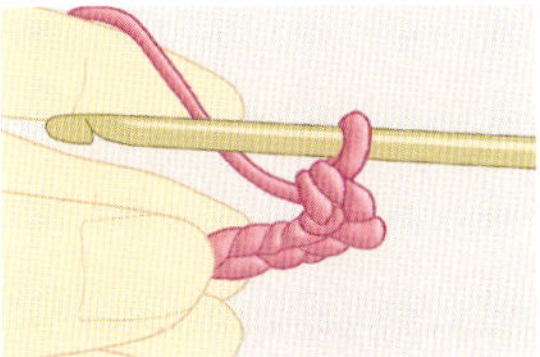

3 Yarn over and draw it through both loops on your hook to complete the stitch. Insert your hook into the next chain and complete steps 2 and 3. Repeat into each chain across.

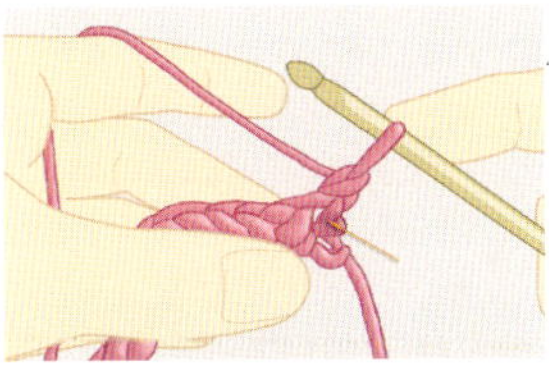

4 To work the next row, chain 1 and turn your work. Insert your hook into the first stitch under the top two loops and complete steps 2 and 3. Continue working single crochet stitches across the row.

half treble crochet (htr)

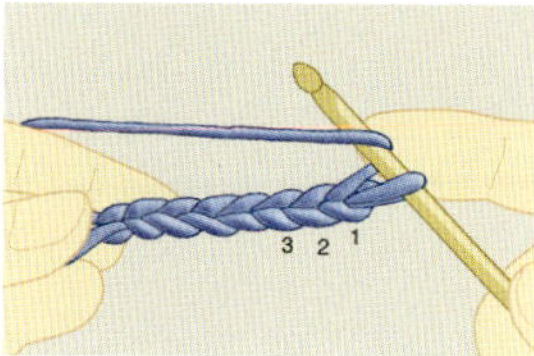

1 Yarn over and insert your hook into the third chain from your hook.

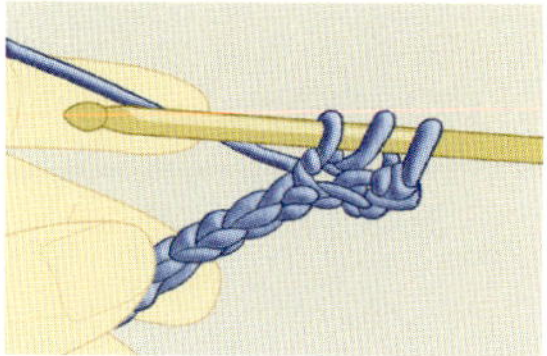

2 Yarn over and pull up a loop. You will have three loops on your hook.

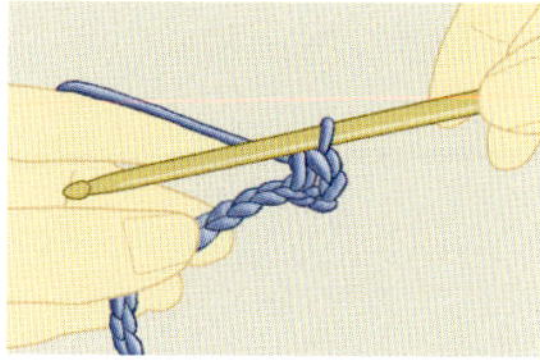

3 Yarn over and draw through all three loops on your hook to complete the stitch. Yarn over and insert your hook into the next chain and repeat steps 2 and 3. Repeat into each chain across.

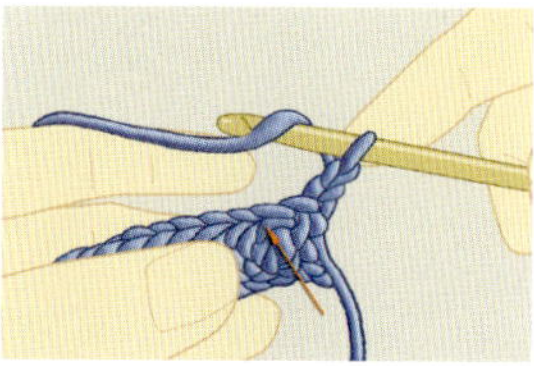

4 To work the next row, chain 2 and turn your work. Insert your hook into the second stitch (skipping the first stitch because the chain 2 counts as a stitch). Work under the top two loops and complete steps 2 and 3.

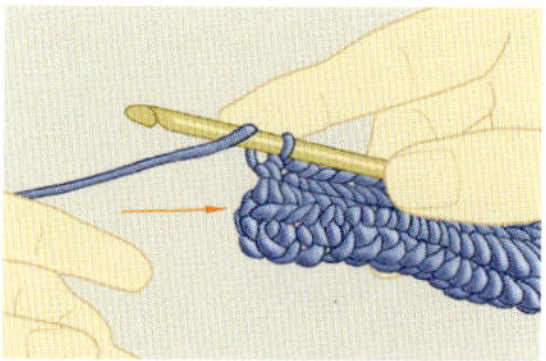

5 Continue working stitches into each stitch across the row. Your last stitch will be made into the top chain of the previous row turning chain.

Be aware that some patterns using this stitch do not count the chain 2 turning chains as a stitch because it tends to leave gaps in the row edges. If that is the case, then you would work the first stitch of your row into the first stitch and you would not work a stitch into the turning chain at the end of the row.

magic ring

For a really tight centre round that has a lot of stitches this is the method of choice. However, do not use this method when working with slippery yarns because the yarn end may work loose.

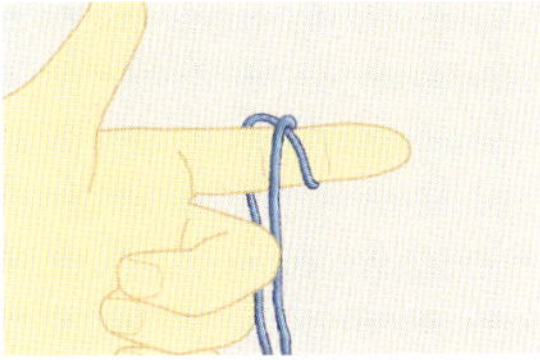

1 Encircle the yarn around your index finger counter clockwise and cross it over the working yarn. Make sure to leave at least a 15-cm (6-in) tail for weaving in later.

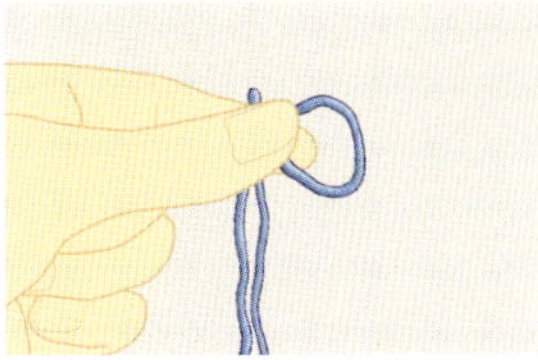

2 Slide the loop off your finger while pinching the 'X' overlap you just made.

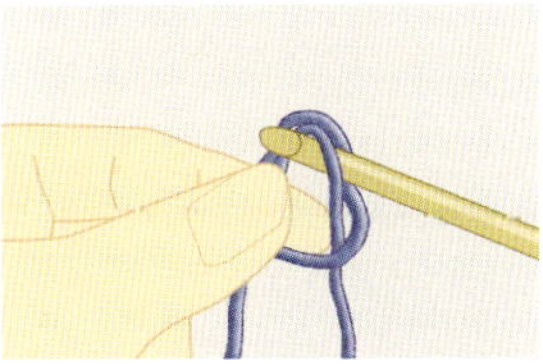

3 Insert your hook in front of the loop but behind your working yarn.

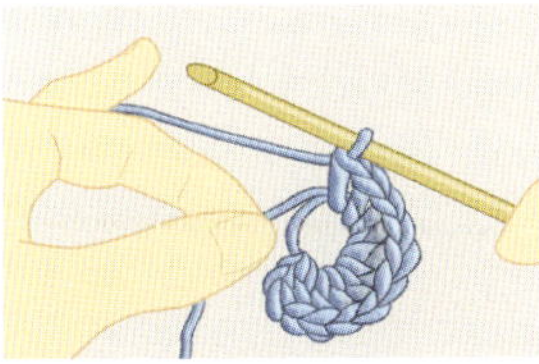

4 Pull up a loop with the working yarn and hold it on your hook with your index finger. Yarn over and ch 1 to secure. Crochet over both the loop and yarn tail as you complete the first round. Pull the yarn tail to tighten.

increasing

To increase the number of stitches within a row or round you simply place more than one stitch into a stitch of the previous row or round.

double crochet decrease

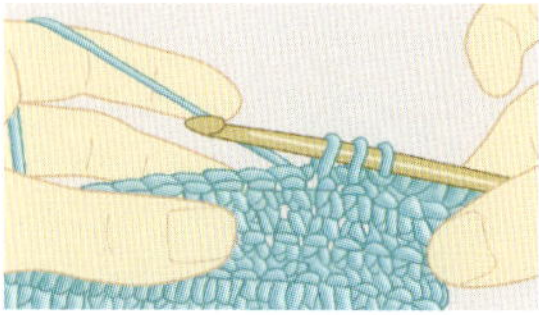

1 Insert the hook into the first stitch and pull up a loop. Insert the hook into the next stitch and pull up a loop.

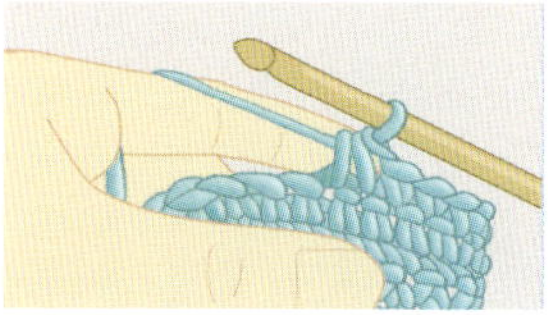

2 You will have three loops on your hook. Yarn over, and draw through all three loops.

joining in a new yarn or colour

Typically you'll want to change to a new ball of yarn at the end of a row, or colour changes may be indicated in the pattern you are crocheting. The technique for both is the same.

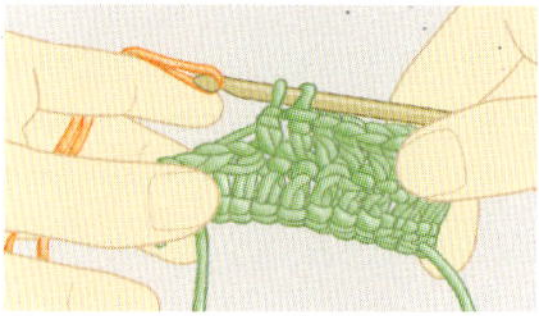

1 Work the last stitch but stop at the last step before drawing through the final yarn over. You will have two loops on your hook.

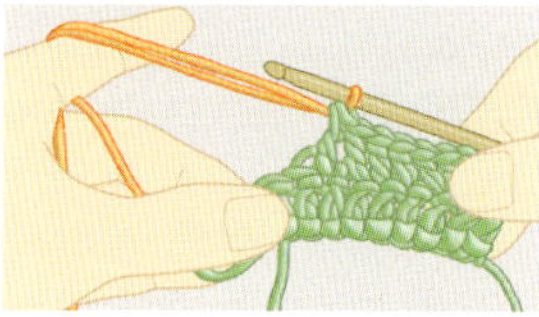

2 Drop the old yarn behind your work and draw the new yarn through to complete the stitch. Continue working with the new yarn.

weaving in ends

Weave in the yarn tail ends on the wrong side of your fabric with a blunt tapestry needle. Draw the yarn through at least 5 cm (2 in) of stitches and then weave back in the opposite direction for 2.5 cm (1 in) to prevent the end from working loose. Make sure to weave through the loops of stitches and not into the yarn itself.

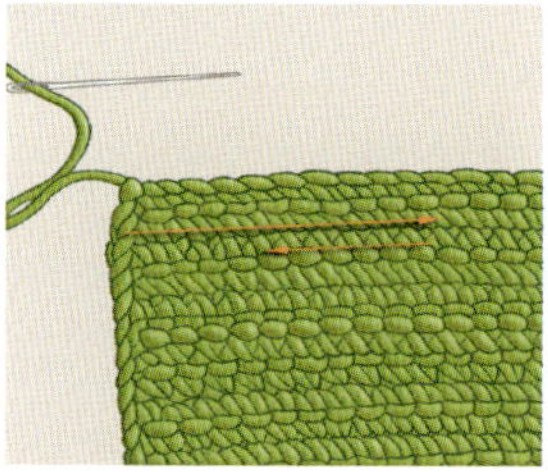

abbreviations

ch: chain
dc: double crochet
htr: half treble crochet
st: stitch
sts: stitches
dc2tog: double crochet two together
skp: skip
con't: continue
rep: repeat
rnd: round

needle felting

Needle felting requires at least one needle, wool roving, and a foam cushion. There are needle felting holders that can hold up to six needles at one time to felt a larger surface. Multiple needles make felting faster! I like to use two to three needles at a time to get my general shape, and then one needle to do more detailed shaping.

Needle felting is a process that uses a special felting needle to 'sculpt' wool into any shape. The needle has tiny barbs at the tip, which when pushed into wool, interlocks the fibres and forms a harder mass when jabbed repeatedly. You'll push the needle all around your wool and in whatever area you want to move inwards to shape your piece. Watch out for your fingers, as the needle is very sharp and hurts if you stab yourself with it, which most people do their first few times.

Always use a foam cushion underneath your work to protect your worktable and your needle, which is very fragile. When needle felting, try not to twist your needle in a different direction to your hand. This is an easy way to break your tip. Move the needle in the same motion as your arm and stab straight into the wool and don't twist. Remember to turn your wool and stab all around your piece. Sometimes the wool will stick to the cushion if you don't pick it up and turn it.

It's important to get a tight roll to your wool when you begin. The tighter you roll it, the less work you'll have to do, because in the end, you want a more solid piece. You'll see holes where you've felted, and you can rub those out with your fingernail, or by rolling your piece in between your hands as a finishing technique.

sewing

straight stitch

This is the most common stitch in sewing. All sewing machines make straight stitches. You can make straight stitches by hand with a sewing needle and thread as well. In this book, I refer to hand-sewing straight stitches as the embroidery backstitch. You can also make straight stitches using a running stitch.

running stitch

This is a hand-sewing stitch that can be sewn in a straight line or along a curve. Thread your needle with a length of thread and insert your needle into the fabric from back to front, but don't pull your needle all the way through yet. Weave your needle from the front of the fabric to the back in even short lengths until you've run out of room on your needle. End with your needle on the front side and pull the thread through. Repeat the running stitch for the length needed. Your stitches will look like dotted lines.

embroidered backstitch

This is a simple stitch that I love to use for handsewing straight stitches, or for embroidering line details such as mouths on faces. Thread your needle with a length of embroidery floss and insert into the fabric from back to front. Don't pull your needle all the way through yet. Weave your needle to the back and then front again in short even lengths. Pull your thread through and insert your needle back to through the second hole you made, from front to back, making a 'backstitch'. Insert your needle from back to front the same stitch distance from the stitch you just made, and pull the thread back through. Insert your needle back through the hole where the last stitch ended, from front to back, and repeat backstitching for as long as you need. The right side will look like a continuous line, as in machine sewing, but the wrong side will have longer overlapping stitches.

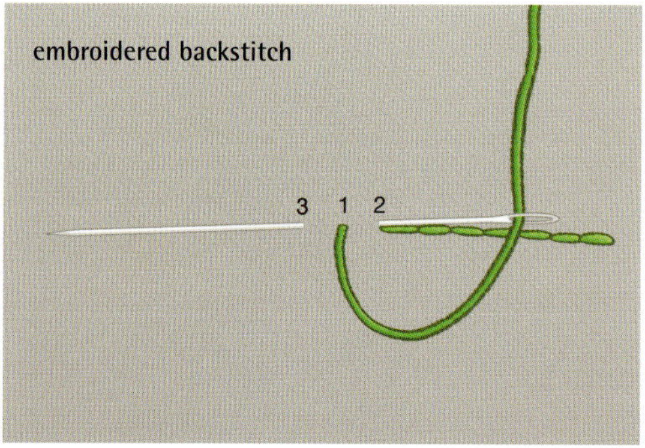

blanket stitch

The blanket stitch is another favourite stitch that I like to use to sew pieces together, and to create a finished-looking edge on felt projects. Thread your needle with a length of thread and knot one end of the thread. Insert your needle about 0.5 cm ($^{1}/_{4}$ in) below the fabric edge (or desired stitch height), from back to front. Insert your needle from back to front again through the same hole you made to anchor your stitch. Pull your needle from left to right through the top of your anchor stitch and insert your needle about 0.5 cm ($^{1}/_{4}$ in) to the left of your anchor, and 0.5 cm ($^{1}/_{4}$ in) below the fabric edge from front to back. Wrap the thread clockwise around the needle before pulling through. You've made one blanket stitch. Continue stitching as stated for your remaining stitches, keeping them as even as possible. Knot your thread in the back to secure at the end.

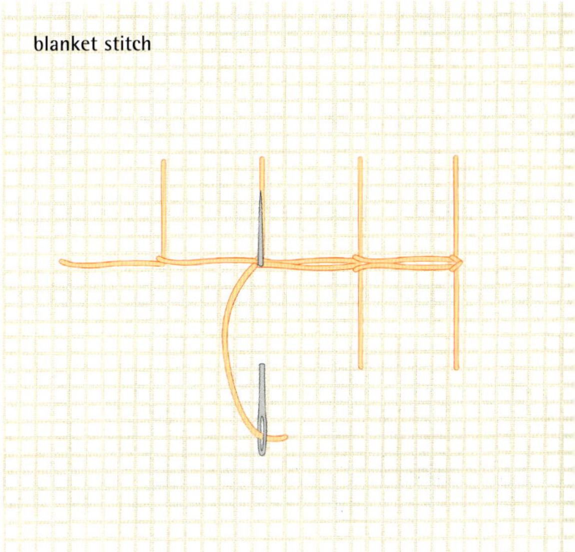

machine backstitch

Backstitching is also a term used when sewing with a sewing machine. It's an anchor at the beginning and end of your sewing to secure your stitches. Begin a few stitches ahead of where you want to begin and reverse stitch a few stitches, then stitch forwards as normal. When you get to the end, reverse stitch a few stitches along your stitch line to secure.

topstitch and edge stitch

Topstitch and edge stitch are very similar. They're straight stitches along an edge, but the difference is the distance between the two. Edge stitches are much closer to the edge – about 0.1 cm ($^{1}/_{16}$ in) to 0.25 cm ($^{1}/_{8}$ in) away, and topstitches are 0.5 cm ($^{1}/_{4}$ in) or more away the edge. Both are visible stitches on the right side of the fabric.

basting stitch

Basting stitches are straight stitches that are long and loose. They are not anchored, so they're easy to remove. Basting stitches are used to tack two pieces of fabric together (in place of pinning) before sewing, or used to gather fabric as in the ballerina project. When the instructions in this book call for basting pieces together, it's usually for thicker fabrics or felts that tend to pucker when pinned.

invisible stitch

A lot of the sewing patterns in this book call for an invisible stitch sewn by hand to close up the toys. This is done by turning (or pressing) the edge to the wrong side of the fabric and weaving the needle back and forth from one fabric edge to the other in even stitches. Once you pull the thread and fabric together, you won't see the stitches, thus making them invisible.

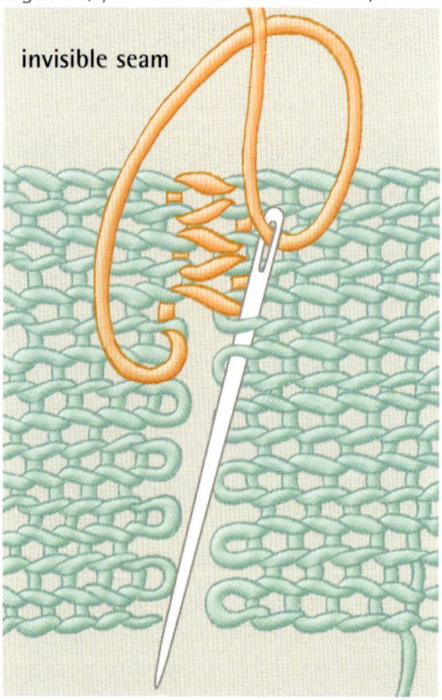

invisible seam (used to sew knitted pieces)

With right sides of both pieces of fabric towards you, secure the yarn at the bottom of one piece. Pass the needle to the other section and pick up one stitch, which you can see on the needle in this picture. Pull the yarn through and pull tightly. Insert the needle through one stitch of the first section, entering where the yarn exited previously. Continue in this way, from one side to the other, as if lacing a corset, until you reach the last stitch; secure tightly. If you have entered through the right section as shown, the seam will be virtually indistinguishable from the rest of the fabric.

rolled hem

A rolled hem is a good way to finish an edge. The fabric is folded over twice on itself and pressed flat, so the raw edge doesn't show. It makes a clean edge on the back of the fabric so there's no fraying. Top stitch on the right side of the fabric to secure your rolled hem.

how to read the patterns

It is important to read the pattern through before beginning any project to make sure you understand the instructions and abbreviations, and have all the materials and tools necessary. If you're unfamiliar with any knit or crochet abbreviations, refer to the appropriate abbreviation section.

The sewing patterns all include enough room for the seam allowance when enlarged to the correct size. The seam allowances are not drawn, but you can use the guidelines on your sewing machine to sew the correct-sized seam. Or, you can measure and mark the seam allowance on the fabric with chalk or a marker. Some of the sewing patterns have written measurements, which are always for straight-edge cuts such as squares or rectangles, or for perfect circles.

transferring patterns to fabric

There are a few ways to transfer patterns onto fabric. Use whichever you're most comfortable with and works best for your fabric.

Cut out the paper pattern, pin it to the fabric, and cut the fabric around the paper pattern. This method may not be completely true to size because the pinning may pucker the fabric a bit.

Cut out the paper pattern and place it on top of your fabric. Use fabric weights to hold the pattern to the fabric and cut around the paper pattern. This will give you a more accurate cut than pinning.

Transfer your pattern to a carbon-coated tracing paper and place the paper carbon side on your fabric. Use fabric weights to weigh down the paper, and use a tracing wheel to trace around the pattern and transfer onto the fabric. Remove the paper and weights and cut out the pattern along the lines.

Almost all of the patterns in this book need to be enlarged, and I tried to keep most of them within 20 x 28 cm (8½ in x 11 in) size for easy home printing. I like to use this method for cutting out felt projects and much smaller pieces: print out the pattern onto a thicker cardstock paper and cut it out. Place the pattern onto the fabric and weigh down with fabric weights. Use a fabric marker (or any marker, because you'll be cutting inside the lines and they won't show up on your pieces), and trace around the cardstock onto the fabric. Remove the weights and cardstock and cut along the lines.

stuffing

There are different types of stuffing that you can use for toys, such as cotton, wool or polyester. You can use whichever type you prefer. Rice and beans are another type of stuffing that is added at the base of some toys for weight in this book. For a few projects, only rice or beans are necessary for stuffing.

The amount of filling and how you stuff your toy is important for the overall look and feel of the toy. For the fibre filling, take a little stuffing and push it in gently. You want to avoid the lumpy and clumpy brothers, so keep gently adding stuffing so that the fibres mesh together and stay fluffy inside.
Most stuffing comes with a wooden stick to help reach hard-to-get corners, so use it gently to push your stuffing into place if necessary. Do not over stuff. You'll know when you've done it if you see the stuffing showing through your knit or crochet toy. Knitted toys are the stretchiest, so be extra careful when stuffing those. At the end, massage the toy to smooth out any clusters and to squish your toy into shape before closing up.

age suitability and safety

The toys in this book can be made for babies up to adults, although none of the toys in this book should be given to kids under 3 without parental supervision. The first chapter is geared towards babies and toddlers, but a lot of the animals, play food, doll, and everyday objects can be made for children up to about age 6. Some of the everyday objects, make believe, and fitness & games are suited for children ages 6–12. Teenagers and adults can enjoy the games as well.

Use your judgment when selecting a toy to make for a child, whether it be for safety or something you think they'll like. Each child is different. Be sure to swap out the plastic eyes for embroidered ones to prevent a choking hazard if you're going to make any of the animals or creatures for babies or toddlers. And, of course, small game pieces are not suitable for children under 3 years old.

time-saving tips

Keep your tools, fabric, yarn and notions organised. It helps you to quickly see what you have to work with, and it lets you focus on being creative instead of trying to search for a certain piece. For all materials, I suggest sorting by colour and type (yarn weight, fabric material, etc). Below are a few organisational tips.

1. Organise yarn by weight and then colour. It makes it easier to see and combine different yarns of the same weight for one project.

2. Tie fabric of similar colours into small bundles to help keep your fabric scraps neat and orderly.

3. Wind bits of ribbon or thread onto embroidery card holders to keep them from getting tangled.

how to store toys

There are a number of ways you can store your toys. Depending on the number of toys you have, and your space, you can store them in clear plastic tubs, or in baskets. Toy chests are wonderful for keeping most toys in one place. Favourite toys can be displayed on shelves so they can be played with everyday. Adding cedar blocks or lavender sachets to yarn or fabric toys helps to keep moths away, while adding a pleasant scent to your toys.

first toys

These toys will engage and delight children in the early stages of life. Simple, yet colourful, and from blocks to rattles, they're sure to add a soft touch to their little hands.

textured knitted block

see variations page 55

materials

- yarn: Brown Sheep Lamb's Pride Worsted (85% wool, 15% mohair, 100g (4oz), 175m (190 yds), 1 skein each of Limeade, Lotus Pink, Autumn Harvest, Aztec Turquoise, Charcoal Heather, Regal Purple
- 5 mm (US size 8) knitting needles
- cable needle
- tapestry needle

tension: 4½ sts: 2.5cm (1 in)
finished dimensions: 6-cm (2½-in) cube after stuffing

instructions

This knitted block is made using six different stitch patterns and a different colour for each side, creating different textures and colours that will stimulate any child.

seed stitch (Limeade)
CO 10 sts.
R1: *k1, p1* rep to end.
R2: *p1, k1* rep to end.
Continue working these two rows until piece is 5.5cm (2¼ in) wide. BO and weave in ends.

mini basketweave stitch
(Charcoal Heather)
CO 10 sts.
R1: *k2, p2* rep once more, k2.
R2: *p2, k2* rep once more, p2.
Continue working these two rows until piece is 5.5cm (2¼ in) wide. BO and weave in ends.

larger basketweave stitch
(Autumn Harvest)
CO 10 sts.
R1: k5, p5.
R2–6: rep R1.
R7: p5, k5.
R8–12: rep R7.
BO and weave in ends.

rib stitch (Regal Purple)
CO 10 sts.
R1: *k1, p1* rep to end.
Rep R1 until piece is 5.5cm (2¼ in) wide. Rib stitch is stretchy; pull the piece to 5cm (2 in) wide when measuring the height. BO and weave in ends.

cable stitch
(Aztec Turquoise)
CO 14 sts (wider than the other squares – the cabling will shorten the width).
R1: p4, k6, p4.
R2–4: k the knits, p the purls.
R5: p4, slip the next 3 sts onto a cable needle and hold in back, k3, k3 from cable needle, p4.
R6–9: k the knits, p the purls.
R10: rep R5.
R11–13: k the knits, p the purls.
BO and weave in ends.

duplicate stitch for lettering
(Lotus Pink base, Limeade)
CO 10 sts.
K 12 rows.
BO and weave in ends.
Use a contrasting yarn to make duplicate stitch alphabet letters on your square.

Block all squares so they're even and of matching sizes. Cut approx. 1m (40 in) yarn, and with edges facing out, stitch together with running stitch. Before closing last edge, stuff.

felt cow finger puppet

see variations page 56

materials

- wool felt in white, pink, yellow and black
- embroidery thread in black, white and pink
- tracing paper
- pencil
- dressmaking pins
- tailor's chalk
- embroidery needle
- fabric glue

finished dimensions:
5cm (2 in) wide, 6.5cm (2¾ in) high

instructions

With tracing paper and a pencil, trace the cow's body (white), nose (pink), belly (pink), cowbell (yellow) and eyes (black) and cut out. Pin the templates onto the felt, then trace around the shapes with tailor's chalk, and cut out two body pieces and one each of the other pattern pieces. Cut out a number of spots as well – not too symmetrical – and decorate your little cow as you see fit. Six spots were used in the pictured puppet.

Make two stitches on the face in black for each eye, and then two stitches on the pink nose in black for each nostril. Glue the nose, belly, cowbell and black spots onto the body. Wait for the glue to dry, embroider the cowbell chain, and, with white embroidery thread, blanket stitch the body together starting at the right bottom edge and ending at the left bottom edge.

Using pink embroidery thread, blanket stitch around the pink felt nose and belly.

Enlarge by 200% to make to actual size.

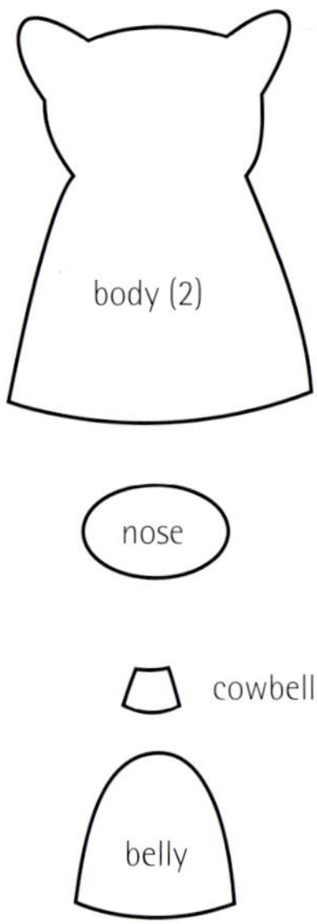

Enlarge by 250% to make to actual size.

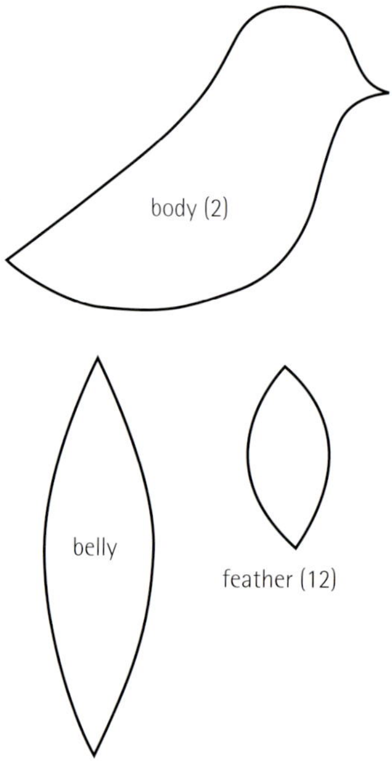

fabric birds mobile

see variations page 57

materials

- lightweight cotton fabric in varying shades of pink, 25cm (1/4 yd) each colour
- tracing paper
- dressmaking pins
- tailor's chalk
- sewing thread to match the fabric
- sewing needle
- stuffing
- embroidery thread in black
- 2 dowels, 30cm (12 in) and 23cm (9 in)
- tan-coloured yarn
- glue
- string for hanging
- screw hook

finished dimensions:
14cm (5½ in) long (including tail), 3cm (1¼ in.) wide

instructions

Transfer the bird pattern to your fabric. Cut out two main body pieces, one belly piece and six feathers – three for each wing. With a length of double-stranded black embroidery thread and needle, make a few stitches for the eyes on the right side of both body pieces on the head.

Pin one of the body pieces and the belly piece with the right sides together, and straight stitch, beginning at the tail end. Once you get to the other end of the belly piece, pin the second body piece so that it matches the other body. Continue stitching and leave a 2.5-cm (1-in) opening at the end. Turn inside out and use a point turner to push the beak and tail out, then stuff. Sew closed with an invisible stitch. When you finish the bird body, arrange three wing pieces so they fluff/fan out for the wing, and sew into place with a few stitches. Do the same for the other wing.

Make three more birds in varying colours. Wrap tan yarn around each dowel and secure with glue. Knot approximately 15cm (6 in) of string through the top of each bird's body, and tie 5cm (2 in) in from the dowel ends. Secure the knots with a dab of glue. Connect the dowels with yarn at the centre, with the 30-cm (12-in) dowel on the top tier, and leaving around 7.5cm (3 in) between sticks. Hang from a screw hook from the ceiling.

crochet maraca rattle

see variations page 58

materials

- yarn: Brown Sheep Nature Spun Worsted (100% wool, 100g (3½ oz), 224m (245 yds)), 1 skein each of (A) Peruvian Pink, (B) Lemon Grass, (C) Natural
- 4 mm (US size G/6) crochet hook
- stuffing
- jingle bell ball insert (one for each maraca)
- tapestry needle

tension: 5 sts over 6 rows = 2.5cm (1 in)

finished dimensions: 11.5cm (4½ in) high, 4cm (1½ in) wide

instructions

With B make 6 dc in a magic ring, sl st in first ch to join. [Ch 1, dc in next 6 sts, sl st] for 6cm (2½ in) and stuff as you crochet. Break yarn and change to A.

Rnd 1: ch 1, [dc in next st, 2 dc in next st] around, sl st in first dc to join – 9 dc.

Rnd 2: ch 1, [dc in next 2 sts, 2dc in next st] around, sl st in first dc to join – 12 dc.

Rnd 3: ch 1, [dc in next 3 sts, 2dc in next st] around, sl st in first dc to join – 15 dc.

Rnd 4: ch 1, [dc in next 4 sts, 2dc in next st] around, sl st in first dc to join. Fasten off A, join C – 18 dc.

Rnd 5: ch 1, [dc in next 5 sts, 2dc in next st] around, sl st in first dc to join – 21 dc.

Rnd 6: ch 1, [dc in next 6 sts, 2dc in next st] around, sl st in first dc to join – 24 dc.

Rnd 7: ch 1, dc in next 24 sts, sl st in first dc to join.

Rnd 8: ch 1, dc in each st across, sl st in first dc to join. Fasten off C, join A.

Rnd 9: ch 1, [dc in next 6 sts, dc2tog] around, sl st in first dc to join – 21 dc.

Rnd 10: ch 1, [dc in next 5 sts, dc2tog] around, sl st in first dc to join – 18 dc.

Begin to stuff and insert jingle bell, then continue stuffing until end.

Rnd 11: ch 1, [dc in next st, dc2tog] around, sl st in first dc to join – 12 dc.

Rnd 12: ch 1, [dc2tog] around, sl st in first dc to join – 6 dc.

Fasten off and weave in ends.

Make another maraca.

crochet triangle block

see variations page 59

materials

- yarn: Brown Sheep Cotton Fleece (80% cotton, 20% merino wool, 100g (3½ oz), 196m (215 yds)), 1 skein each of (A) Wild Orange, (B) Robin Egg Blue, (C) Celery Leaves
- 3.75 mm (US size F/5) crochet hook
- tapestry needle
- stuffing

tension: 5 sts over 6 rows = 2.5cm (1 in)
finished dimensions: 5cm (2 in) wide, 6.5cm (2¾ in) high

instructions

R1: dc in 2nd ch from the hook, dc in each st across, turn – 14 sts
R2: ch 1, dc2tog, dc in each dc to the last 2 dc, dc2tog, fasten off A, join B, turn – 12 sts
R3: ch 1, dc in each st across, turn – 12 sts
R4: ch 1, dc2tog, dc in next 10 dc, dc2tog, fasten off B, join C, turn – 10 sts
R5: ch 1, dc in each st across, turn – 10 sts
R6: ch 1, dc2tog, dc in next 8 dc, dc2tog, fasten off C, join A, turn – 8 sts
R7: ch 1, dc in each st across, turn – 8 sts
R8: ch 1, dc2tog, dc in next 6 dc, dc2tog, fasten off A, join B, turn – 6 sts
R9: ch 1, dc in each st across, turn – 6 sts
R10: ch1, dc2tog, dc in next 4 dc, dc2tog, fasten off B, join C, turn – 4 sts
R11: ch 1, dc in each st across, turn – 4 sts
R12: ch1, dc2tog, dc in next 2 dc, dc2tog, fasten off C, join A, turn – 2 sts
R13: ch 1, dc in each st across, turn – 2 sts
R14: ch 1, dc2tog – 1 st
Fasten off and weave in ends.

Repeat R1–14 to make a matching triangle.

With C, ch 5.
Ch 1, dc across each row until piece measures21.5cm (8½ in).

Line up your pieces and pin together. With B, crochet seams together by making a slip loop and begin at the bottom right corner of the triangle.
Dc through the turning chain or post, and make two dc in each post to keep the seam from puckering. Repeat for the back triangle, and stuff when you have 4cm (1½ in) left. Stuff and finish seaming. Mattress stitch the C strip edge closed.

knitted kitten hand puppet

see variations page 60

materials

- yarn: Brown Sheep Nature Spun Worsted (100% wool, 100g (3½ oz), 224m (245 yds)), 1 skein of Natural
- 4.5 mm (US size 7) dpns
- embroidery thread in black
- tapestry needle
- felt in black and pink for the eyes and nose
- sewing needle
- sewing thread in black and pink
- tracing paper
- dressmaking pins
- tailor's chalk
- light pink cotton fabric, 25cm (¼ yd)

tension: 5 sts over 7 rows = 2.5cm (1 in)
finished dimensions: 9cm (3½ in) wide, 18cm (7 in) high (sized for avg. ages 5-10)

instructions

CO 26 sts. Divide evenly between 3 dpns and join for working in the round, being careful not to twist your sts.
Rnd1: * k1, p1 * rep to end.
Rnd2: * p1, k1 * rep to end.
Rnd3: * k1, p1 * rep to end.
Rnds4–24: k.

Begin mouth and work flat from here.

top mouth

Knit 15 sts and place the remaining 10 sts onto one dpn for bottom of mouth.
R1–9: work in st st.
R10: k1, ssk, k to last 3 sts, k2tog, k1. 2 sts decreased.
R11: p.
R12–17: rep R10 and 11.
BO remaining 7 sts and weave in ends.

bottom mouth

Attach yarn (RS) and work 6 R in st st.
R7 (RS): k1, ssk, k to last 3 sts, k2tog, k1.
R8: p.
R9–10: rep R6 and 7.
BO remaining sts and weave in ends.

ears

At 5cm (2 in) from the base of the top mouth, and at the left edge, pick up 3 sts with the dpn. Attach yarn at the right edge of the sts you just picked up, and k 3 sts. K the next 2 rows, and k3tog. Break yarn and weave in ends. Repeat for the right ear.

face

Cut three 5-cm (2-in)-long strands of black embroidery thread for the whiskers and sew at the tip of the nose. Cut almond-shaped black eyes and a rounded triangle pink nose from felt. Sew in place.

inside mouth

Trace and cut out the mouth pattern. Pin this to the pink fabric, trace around it with tailor's chalk, and cut out.

Enlarge to 400%
to make to actual size.

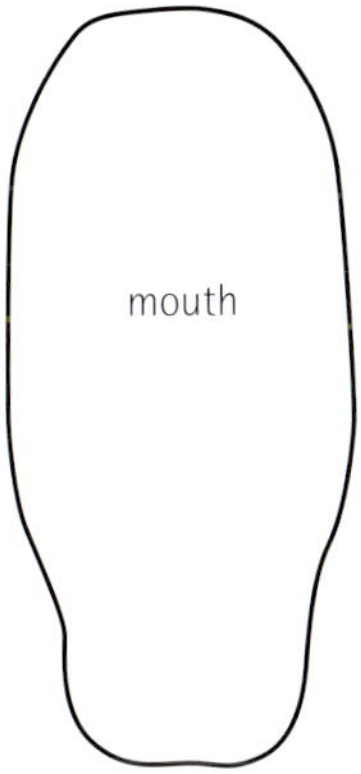

Turn the knit puppet inside out and pin the fabric into place with the wider end at the top of the mouth and the wrong side facing you. Blanket stitch together and turn the puppet right side out.

knitted ring rattle

see variations page 61

materials

- yarn: Brown Sheep Shepherd's Shades (100% wool, 100g (3½ oz), 120m (131 yds)), 1 skein each of (A) Pearl, (B) Wintergreen
- 6 mm (US size 10) straight knitting needles
- stuffing
- jingle bell ball insert
- tapestry needle

tension: 4½ sts over 6 rows = 2.5cm (1 in)
finished dimensions: 10.5cm (4¼-in) diameter

instructions

With A, CO 24 sts.
R1 and all odd rows: p.
R2: k1, *m1, k2*, rep to last st, m1, k1 – 36 sts.
R4: k1 *m1, k3*, rep to last 2 sts, m1, k2 – 48 sts.
R6: change to B and k.
R8: change to A and k.
R10: rep R6.
R12: rep R8.
R14: *k2, k2tog* rep to end – 36 sts.
R16: *k1, k2tog* rep to end – 24 sts.
R18: BO leaving a tail for sewing up.

Fold in half lengthwise and sew edges together to form a ring, stuffing as you sew. Insert jingle bell ball halfway through and sew closed. Weave in ends.

needle felt ball

see variations page 62

materials

- wool roving in orange, yellow, black, and white
- felting foam pad
- size 38 or 36 felting needle

finished dimensions:
9cm (3½-in) diameter

instructions

ball

Take enough roving to roll a (10–11.5cm (4–4½ in) ball, starting at one end and tucking in the sides as you go, so you end up with a tight ball. Keep in mind that it will shrink down a bit as you needle felt.

Place the ball on the foam pad and hold the ends in place with your finger. Take the felting needle in your other hand and jab the ends together. Watch your fingers and keep them clear of the area you're jabbing with the needle.

Stab all over the piece until you feel it firming up and holding together. Keep jabbing any protruding areas until you have a sphere.

bumblebee

Adding colour to a needle felt piece is very easy. Start with a bit of yellow roving for the belly of the bee and roll it into a small, flat ball between your fingers. Hold it in place on your orange ball with one finger and jab the felting needle through the yellow onto the orange. Keep jabbing until the yellow ball is held in place. You can use the needle tip to tuck the edges gently into place.

Now take a small length of black roving to make the bumblebee stripes. Give it a little twist so the fibres are tight together. This will help you to needle felt a clean straight line. Hold it in place on top of the yellow needle felt. Make two more stripes and then trim off the excess ends.

Now use the same method and the white roving to make the head, antennae, and wings as in the photograph.

materials

- yarn: Brown Sheep Lamb's Pride Worsted (85% wool, 15% mohair, 100g (4 oz), 175m (190 yds), 1 skein Aztec Turquoise; Brown Sheep Nature Spun Worsted (100% wool, 100g (3½ oz), 224m (245 yds)), 1 skein Natural; Caron Country Yarn (75% microdenier acrylic, 25% merino wool, 75g (3 oz), 170m (185 yds)), 1 skein Ocean Spray
- 4 mm (US size G/6) crochet hook
- stuffing
- tapestry needle
- tracing paper
- felt in white and blue for propellers
- cotton thread for hanging
- inside hoop of a 15-cm (6-in) embroidery hoop
- glue
- screw hook

tension: 4½ sts over 5 rows = 2.5cm (1 in)
finished dimensions: 9cm (3½ in) long, 6cm (2½ in) wide

crochet aeroplanes mobile see variations page 63

instructions

aeroplane body

Rnd 1: 6 dc in a magic ring, sl st in first ch to join.
Rnd 2: ch 1, [dc in next st, 2 dc in next st] 3 times, sl st in first dc to join – 9 dc.
Rnd 3: ch 1, dc in each st across, sl st – 9 dc.
Rnd 4: ch 1, [dc in next 2 sts, 2 dc in next st] 3 times, sl st in first dc to join – 12 dc.
Rnd 5: ch 1, [dc in next 3 sts, 2 dc in next st] 3 times, sl st in first dc to join – 15 dc.
Rnd 6: ch 1, dc in next 15 sts, sl st in first dc to join – 15 dc.
Rnd 7: ch 1, [dc in next 4 sts, 2 dc in next st] 3 times, sl st in first dc to join – 18 dc.
Rnd 8: ch 1, [dc in next 5 sts, 2 dc in next st] 3 times, sl st in first dc to join – 21 dc.
Rnds 9–15: ch 1, dc in each st across, sl st in first dc to join – 21 dc.
Rnd 16: ch 1, [dc in next 5 sts, dc2tog] 3 times, sl st in first dc to join – 18 dc.
Begin stuffing and continue stuffing as you go.
Rnd 17: ch 1, [dc in next st, dc2tog] 6 times, sl st in first dc to join – 12 dc.
Rnd 18: ch 1, [dc2tog] 6 times, sl st in first dc to join – 6 dc.
Fasten off and weave in ends.

wings

Ch 6, turn.
R1: dc 2nd ch from hook, dc in next 5 sts, ch1, turn.
R2: dc 2nd from hook, dc in next 3 sts, 2 dc in next 2 sts, dc in next 4 sts, ch 1, turn.
R3: dc 2nd from hook, dc in next 4 sts, 2 dc in next 2 sts, dc in next 5 sts, ch 1.
Fasten off and crochet another wing. With a tapestry needle, stitch wings in place and weave in ends.

tail wings

Ch 5, turn.
Dc 2nd from hook, dc in next 3 sts.
Fasten off and crochet two more tail wings. With tapestry needle, stitch wings in place at the smaller end of the plane, and weave in ends.

propellers

Trace and cut propellers out of blue and white felt and sew at the nose of the aeroplane. Make two more aeroplanes. Cut cotton thread to hang the planes at 30cm (12 in), 23cm (9 in), and 15cm (6 in) from the embroidery hoop. Secure knots with a dab of glue.

Cut four more strands of thread 20cm (8 in) long and tie onto the embroidery hoop with even spacing. Secure with dabs of glue.

Knot four strings together at top. Cut one more length of string to desired hanging length from the crib and attach at this knot. Secure to the ceiling with a screw hook.

Enlarge to 250% to make to actual size.

propeller (1 per plane)

fabric bear rattle

see variations page 64

materials

- fabric: Kokka Large Gingham (100% cotton), 25cm (1/4 yd) of Beige; Kokka Small Gingham (100% cotton), 25cm (1/4 yd) of Brown
- tracing paper
- dressmaking pins
- tailor's chalk
- cardstock
- sewing needle
- sewing thread
- felt in brown
- embroidery thread in black
- stuffing
- jingle bell ball insert

finished dimensions: 10cm (4 in) wide, 10cm (4 in) tall

instructions

Transfer the bear head pattern to your fabric – the bear head and ears on the brown gingham, and the muzzle on the beige gingham – and cut out. Cut a second muzzle out of cardstock, then trim it down so your cardstock fits inside the brown-fabric muzzle cutout, leaving about 0.25cm (1/8 in) of fabric visible all around.

To turn the muzzle edges in smoothly, make a basting stitch 0.25 cm (1/8 in) in from the edge, and around the whole muzzle. Centre your inside muzzle cardstock on the wrong side of the fabric and pull the thread tightly so it wraps around the cardstock. This creates a smooth edge around the oval. Iron flat and remove the cardstock. Pin the muzzle just below the centre of the face and back stitch into place with right side facing you.

Cut two small ovals for the eyes, and a rounded triangle for the nose. Sew these onto the face and stitch a smiling mouth onto your bear.

Pin the ears with the right sides together and sew with a 0.5-cm (1/4-in) seam allowance, leaving an opening at the straight edge. Turn inside out and lightly stuff.

Pin the finished ears in between the face fabrics with right sides together so they point down and are angled inwards towards the centre. Hand or machine sew these pieces together, leaving a 5-cm (2-in) opening at the bottom of the head, and turn inside out. Stuff the bear halfway and insert your jingle bell ball. Continue stuffing until the bear is nice and fluffy. Invisible stitch the bottom edge closed.

Enlarge patterns to 340%, so the head is 11.5cm (4½ in) in diameter

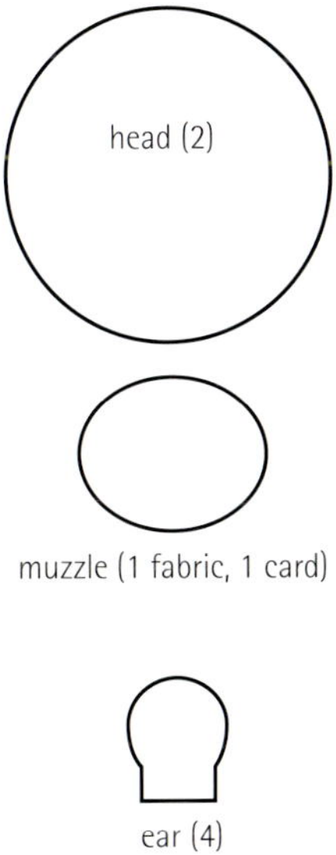

needle felt clouds mobile see variations page 65

instructions

clouds

Take a length of roving and roll it tightly into an oval shape, tucking in the sides as you roll. Follow the rolling and felting instructions from 'needle felt ball' (see page 48). Keep jabbing protruding areas until they blend into the oval.

materials

- white wool roving, approx. 75g (3 oz)
- size 38 or 36 felting needle
- felting foam pad
- string for hanging
- sewing needle with large eye
- screw eye

finished dimensions: 50cm (20 in) high from bottom cloud to top cloud; widest cloud 20cm (8 in)

Once you have your base, add more tufts of wool to form the 'bulbous' cloud. Simply repeat the same method, but use less wool and make smaller ovals.

To attach a new piece to your base oval, hold the smaller oval in place where you want it to go, and jab the felting needle through both pieces so that your needle 'barbs' make it through to the base piece. Keep felting until you feel it is anchored in place.

Don't worry about the 'seam' where your pieces connect. You can hide this by pulling a thin piece of wool and wrapping it over the seam and lightly felting it into place.

Keep adding balls of wool until you have a cloud shape you're happy with. If there are any imperfections, you can always cover up wrinkles and seams by adding more wool.

Make your clouds three different sizes – approximately 10cm (4 in), 15cm (6 in), and 20cm (8 in) wide.

stringing

Thread the sewing needle with a length of string and knot it into the top of the largest cloud, going right through the wool. Make sure the wool is dense enough to hold the string. If not, then needle felt the area you'll be attaching the string to so that it can hold the string. You can hide the knot and ends in the cloud by covering it with more wool and felting it until it blends in.

Leave about 10cm (4 in) between each cloud, and continue knotting the string from the top of the cloud to the bottom of the next cloud and covering up the knots. Hang your mobile from a screw eye in the ceiling.

variations

textured knitted block

see base design page 35

textured knitted book

Follow the different stitch patterns as for the blocks, and make 12.5-cm (5-in) squares. Block them, stack them together, and sew the texture squares using a backstitch along one edge into a book of textures and colours.

embossed letters & numbers

Emboss knit using moss stitch to make raised numbers or letters on the blocks. Use graph paper to chart out the letters and numbers before you begin.

appliqué letters & numbers

Print out letters to 3cm (1¼ in.) square to use as your pattern. Trace and cut them out of felt and pin to knit blocks. Use whip stitch to appliqué them.

colour memory fabric block game

Make a set of fabric blocks as a colour memory matching game by cutting out 6-cm (2½-in) squares of different colours – one for each block – and pinning and sewing all the edges together. Stuff and close.

crochet nesting box set

Make five flat squares for one box and whip stitch the edges together to form a box. Crochet each set of five squares 5cm (2 in) larger than the last set to ensure that each box fits together.

variations

felt cow finger puppet

see base design page 36

farm animal finger puppets

Use the base pattern to create a set of farm animal finger puppets. Follow the base body and snout pattern, and use pink wool to make a pig. Eliminate the ears on the base body pattern, and use yellow wool to create a little chick. Cut a 0.5cm (¼-in) triangle out of orange felt to make the beak.

mini animal plushies

Stuff puppets, cut a circle 5cm (2 in) in diameter, and sew to the bottom to create little felt animal friends that can stand on their own.

stick puppets

Create flat felt puppets and attach them to thin dowels to make stick puppets.

barn stage for puppet theater

Make a barn 'stage' for the puppets by cutting a piece of cardboard or matboard to 43cm (17 in) square, and cutting the top to a point. Cut out a rectangle in the centre of the board to make an opening for the puppets. Paint or glue red felt to the barn, and add white line details.

cow pencil toppers

Resize the pattern and cut in half horizontally to make pencil toppers for older children. Follow the stitching instructions as in the original pattern on page 36.

variations

fabric birds mobile

see base design page 39

bird beanbags

Add rice inside the birds to make them into tossable beanbags.

bird's nest

Crochet a nest, following the head/body pattern for the 'crochet octopus' on page 87, and stopping halfway through. Use a bulkier yarn and larger crochet hook to make the nest big enough to fit two or three birds.

bird rattle wristband

Make one bird and insert a rattle or bell. To make the wristband, cut a strip of fabric 5cm (2 in) wide by 12cm (5 in) long. Fold this piece in half lengthwise and sew. Turn right side out, turn in the two end edges, and topstitch closed. Sew two squares of hook-and-loop fastener at these ends so it closes into a wristband. Hand sew the bird rattle onto the centre of the wristband.

penguin mobile

Use the base pattern for the bird and use black fabric for the body and white for the belly to make a penguin. Cut one 'feather' for each wing, and little yellow feet and a beak out of felt. Stitch into place with matching thread. Make four penguins and follow the bird mobile instructions for stringing.

bat mobile

Cut two 6 x 4-cm (2½ x 1½-in) ovals for the body of the bat, and four 7.5 x 4-cm (3 x 1½-in) wings from black felt. Sew the ovals together and lightly stuff. Stitch the two layers of wings together and sew to each side of the body. Cut small triangular felt ears and stitch to the head.

variations

crochet maraca rattle

see base design page 40

egg shaker rattle

Follow the maraca pattern, omitting the green handle. Make 6 dc in a magic ring and begin at rnd 1. Crochet a solid colour, insert jingle bell ball or rattle insert, and shake away!

yellow long-necked pumpkin

With yellow yarn, follow the crochet maraca pattern and insert a pipe cleaner when you+re halfway through crocheting and stuffing. Continue to end. Bend the squash neck to the side slightly.

flower

Follow the maraca pattern, and use the pink yarn for the entire bulb. Cut eight 2.5-cm (1-in) flower petals out of pink felt and sew onto the bulb, staggering the petals and overlapping them as you sew.

microphone

Follow the maraca pattern and begin with black yarn. Crochet up until you begin to increase. Change to grey yarn and work to end. Cut a thin strip of white felt and sew to the centre of the mic head.

light bulb

Crochet the maraca pattern and [ch 1, dc in next 6 sts, sl st] for 2.5cm (1 in) with light grey yarn. Change to white yarn for the bulge. Embroider black light bulb wire lines from the base of the bulge to the centre.

variations

crochet triangle block

see base design page 43

stacking blocks

Crochet a few triangle and square stacking blocks to make a set. To make a square block, ch 15, turn, and dc in 2nd ch from hook, and dc in ea st across, ch 1. Continue dc across 14 sts each row until 14 rows, or your row length matches the foundation ch.

colour wheel

Make eight triangular fabric blocks in eight different colours to fit together. Cut your triangles to your desired width, including a 0.5-cm (¼-in) seam allowance, at 45-degree angles. Measure total of all three sides and add 1.25cm (½-in) Cut a strip of fabric to this length and the desired width to make the block. Pin and sew the triangle and side strip together with wrong sides facing, and repeat for the back triangle block. Leave an opening where your side strip ends meet. Stuff and sew closed with an invisible seam.

candy corn (pictured)

Crochet in stripes of white, yellow and orange to make candy corn, alternating the colours every 4 rows. Follow the same stripe pattern for the side strip to match the front and back. Whip stitch your pieces together.

slice of cherry pie

Follow the triange block pattern (R1-14 twice) in yellow yarn, omitting all directives to change yarn colours – you will end up with two matching yellow triangles.. With red yarn, ch 5. Ch 1, sc across each row until piece measures 21.5cm (8½ in). Then follow assembly instructions on page 43.

whole cherry pie

If you follow the above pattern 8 times, you will have a whole pie! Use a running stitch of a sparkly thread to add sugar on top if desired.

variations

knitted kitten hand puppet

see base design page 44

puppy hand puppet

Use the base kitten pattern to create a puppy using brown yarn, picking up two more stitches for each ear, and garter stitching until the ears are 5cm (2 in) long.

washcloth puppet

Knit the puppet with a cotton or terry cloth yarn and use it as a fun washcloth at bathtime.

kitten mittens

Knit two kitten hand puppets and use them as mittens in winter. Crochet 15cm (6 in) chain and tie to the end of each mitten and attach the other end to mitten clips to keep your kittens safe.

kitten snuggle blanket

Knit just the head section of the kitten, stuff, and sew closed. Cut a 1.2-m (4-ft) square (larger if it's for a larger person) out of fleece. Turn the edges in and hem, then stitch the head onto one of the corners.

lucky cat puppet

Turn your puppet into the classic Chinese 'lucky cat' by sewing a red felt collar and gold bell at the centre neck. Cut small triangles out of red felt and use fabric glue to attach to the inside of the ears.

variations

knitted ring rattle

see base design page 47

key ring

Cut out felt keys by tracing an exaggerated version of actual keys for reference. Cut two pieces of felt for each key and blanket stitch together. String the keys onto a piece of yarn and loop through your knit ring rattle.

duck rattle (pictured)

Knit a ring rattle in yellow and follow the knitting instructions for the knitted duck head (page 94) and add an increase row after row 5 (k4, m1, repeat). Add an extra decrease row after row 7 (k3, k2tog, repeat). Stuff and stitch the head to the top of the knit rattle.

life preserver

Use red and white yarn to knit a mini life preserver. CO with white yarn, and add red stripes evenly on the first row of knitting. Continue with the red and white stripes until the end.

chain of rings

Knit three rings in different colours and sizes using fingering and sportweight yarns and corresponding needles. Make one complete ring, and loop the next ring through its hole before closing off. Repeat for the next ring to form a chain.

hand mirror

Knit a handle to sew onto the ring rattle to make a hand mirror. Using the same weight yarn and needles, CO 14 sts and knit in st st for 10cm (4 in) K2tog across the last row to make the bottom of the handle. BO, seam up the long edge, stuff, and sew to the ring.

variations

needle felt ball

see base design page 48

needle felt caterpillar

Make five small needle felt balls, 4cm (1½ in) in diameter, and string them together with yarn. Needle felt wool over the yarn ends to hide them, and felt eyes and a smiley mouth onto the face of the first ball. Pull shorter pieces of yarn with a pointy yarn needle horizontally through the rest of the balls near the base to create legs. Knot these at the ends to keep them from coming out.

needle felt sports ball

Felt a football, baseball or a basketball by following the bumblebee instructions on page 48 for adding colour to your ball, shaping the lines according to the type of ball you're making.

mini ball pit

Needle felt enough balls to make a mini 'ball pit' in a basket for your little one. Use polystyrene as a centre base to wrap the wool roving around and needle felt to make the balls lighter and use less wool.

rattle ball

For extra charm, add a bell inside a ping pong ball – make a little slit with a craft knife and insert the bell. Wrap your wool around it thickly and needle felt the whole thing.

planet mobile

Crochet different coloured and sized ball 'planets' by (follow 'crochet octopus' on page 87 for the balls). Use different weights of yarn and appropriately sized needles to make the planets larger and smaller. Follow the 'crochet airplanes mobile' instructions on page 51 for stringing into a mobile.

variations

crochet aeroplanes mobile

see base design page 51

mobile with clouds

Needle felt small wool clouds to the mobile strings, following the 'needle felt clouds mobile' pattern on page 54.

helicopter mobile

Crochet a helicopter mobile by using the base pattern for the airplane body. Make helicopter blades by cutting two lengths of grey felt 10cm (4 in) long and 1.25cm (½-in) wide. Sew these to the upper side of the airplane body using grey thread. String the helicopters together following the instructions for the 'crochet airplanes mobile' on page 51.

space-age mobile

Print out images of spaceships and planets to use as outline patterns for cutting them out from felt. Double up the felt to make stiffer pieces and use fabric glue to attach wings and other details. String together as for the 'crochet airplanes mobile' on page 51.

airplane rattle

Make an airplane into a rattle by adding a jingle bell ball or rattle insert before closing up. Chain stitch a 30-cm (12-in) string, add a clip to one end, and knot the other end onto the airplane. Clip to the baby's shirt or stroller to keep it from 'flying' away!

fuller wings

Crochet twice as many wings as for the 'crochet airplanes mobile' on page 51, and sew them in pairs to make the wings fuller.

variations

fabric bear rattle

see base design page 52

dog head rattle

Follow the bear base pattern to make a dog head rattle by lengthening the ears by 7.5cm (3 in) to make them floppy. Add a 7.5-cm (3-in) pink felt tongue hanging out of the side of the mouth.

rabbit head rattle

Use the bear head base pattern to make a rabbit head rattle. Cut 12.5-cm (5-in)-long pointy ears and sew together. Sew the ears onto the head following the bear ear instructions. Add 9cm (3½-in) whiskers on either side of the nose.

frog head rattle (pictured)

Use green fabric to make a frog head and cut white circles from felt for the eyes and black felt for the irises. Sew the eyes where the bear's ears would be. Stitch two small black nostrils in the centre of the face and a smiling mouth below it.

monkey head rattle

Use brown and tan fabric to make a monkey head. Make ears 5cm (2 in) tall and 4cm (1½ in) wide and sew to either side of the head. Cut an oval about 2.5cm (1 in) smaller around than the head pattern from tan felt for the face. Embroider eyes, nose, and mouth on the face.

bear head ring rattle

Resize this pattern to 50 percent and follow the pattern as stated. Knit the ring rattle on page 47, and sew the bear head where the knit seam meets.

variations

needle felt clouds mobile

see base design page 54

raindrop chimes

Use ribbon to knot little bells to the felt clouds as 'raindrops'. They'll act as gentle wind chimes.

needle felt animal or object 'clouds'

When cloud watching, often we can spot things in the clouds. Try sculpting your white wool into a car, a tree, a rabbit... Keeping the shapes loose and fluffy, let your imagination guide you.

sun & stars

Cut two yellow circles out of felt and sew them together to make a sun. Repeat to make a few stars. String these along with the clouds on an embroidery hoop, following the instructions for the 'crochet airplanes mobile' on page 51.

cloud garland

Needle felt 10 mini clouds (5 x 7.5cm (2 x 3 in)) and string together to make a garland to decorate a child's room.

birds in the clouds

Sew a few birds from the 'fabric birds mobile' pattern on page 39 to tie and hang from the bottoms of the clouds.

animals & creatures

Step into the prehistoric age with dinosaurs, or frolic through the forest with woodland animals. The creatures in this chapter are sure to pull you into their world.

fabric rabbit

see variations page 95

materials

- fabric: Freespirit Fabrics Hope Valley, Fiesta Cactus Calico (100% cotton), 25cm (1/4 yd); Robert Kaufman Kona Cotton (100% cotton), 25cm (1/4 yd) of Bone
- tracing paper
- dressmaking pins
- sewing thread
- sewing needle
- sewing machine (optional)
- stuffing
- rice or dried beans
- embroidery thread in black
- wool roving in white
- size 38 felting needle

finished dimensions:
12cm (5 in) long, 4.5cm (1 3/4 in) wide, 4 in. high

instructions

Trace and cut two body pieces (turning the pattern to reflect the opposite sides), one face piece, and two ear pieces out of the Fiesta Cactus Calico. Cut the belly and two ear pieces out of Bone.

Pin one Calico and one Bone ear piece together and sew with a 0.5-cm (1/4-in) seam allowance and the wrong sides facing out. Turn inside out. Repeat for the second ear.

Pin the face strip to the face, and pin an ear so that the Bone fabric faces the body. Sew with a 0.5-cm (1/4-in) seam allowance, and do the same for the other side.

Pin the belly piece to the belly of the body, starting just below the neck, all the way to the tail. Sew together with a 0.5-cm (1/4-in) seam allowance, and leaving a 6-cm (2 1/2-in) opening on one side of the belly.

Turn inside out and stuff. Add rice or beans for weight just before you finish stuffing. Sew an invisible stitch to close. Embroider eyes, whiskers, and nose onto the face, and needle felt a small ball about 1.25cm (1/2-in) in diameter for the tail.

Enlarge to 550% to make actual size.

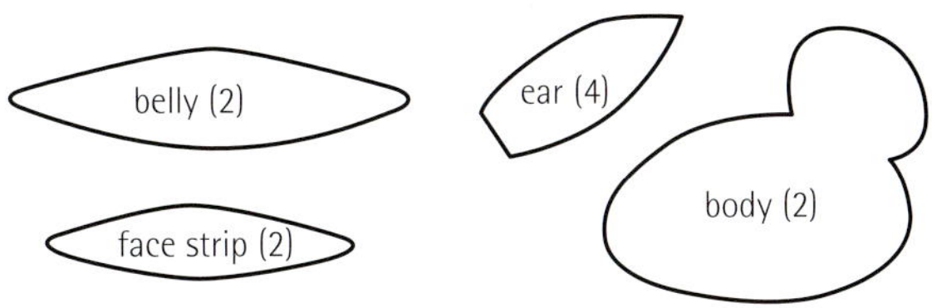

plushie t-rex

see variations page 96

materials

- fabric: Robert Kaufman Remix 2012 (100% cotton), 25cm (1/4 yd) Green Dotted Rows; Robert Kaufman Kona Cotton (100% cotton), 25cm (1/4 yd) Buttercup
- tracing paper
- tailor's chalk
- sewing machine (optional)
- sewing thread
- stuffing
- embroidery thread in black

finished dimensions: 18cm (7 in) long, 11cm (4 1/4 in) wide, 16.5cm (6 1/2 in) high

instructions

Trace and cut out two T-Rex bodies – both sides of the legs and one side of each arm – from the Green Dotted Rows fabric, making sure to flip the pattern for the opposite side of the body/leg/arm. Cut the belly piece and two inside arm pieces out of the Buttercup fabric.

Embroider some eyes onto the head using a length of double-stranded black embroidery thread.

Pin the two body pieces with the right sides together, and sew with a 0.5-cm (1/4-in) seam allowance, starting from the base of the head, going around the head, back, and tail, and stopping about 9cm (3 1/2 in) in from the bottom tail.

Pin one edge of the belly piece to the belly of the body with the right sides together and sew together with a 0.5-cm (1/4-in) seam allowance. Turn your dinosaur over and repeat

Enlarge to 250% to make to actual size.

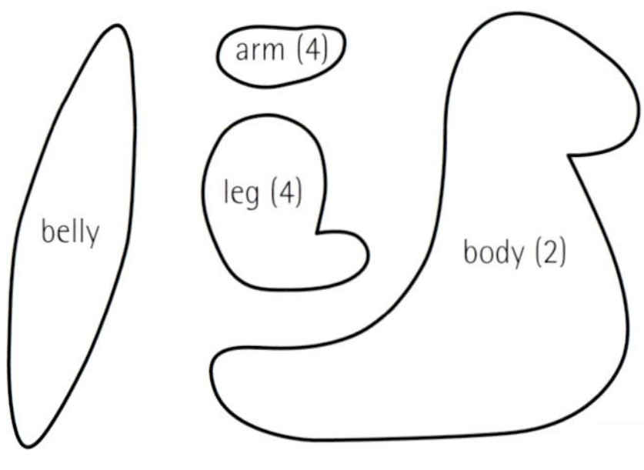

on the other belly edge, leaving a 6-cm ($2\frac{1}{2}$-in) opening. With scissors, snip little 'V' shapes around any curves, taking care not to snip the thread. This will help make your dinosaur smoother once you turn it inside out.

Turn your dinosaur inside out and stuff. Hand sew closed with an invisible stitch.

Sew the legs and arms with the right sides together and leave a 4-cm ($1\frac{1}{2}$-in) opening. Turn inside out and stuff. Hand sew closed with an invisible stitch.

Pin the legs and arms on either side of the body, and make two stitches for each appendage, to attach to the body.

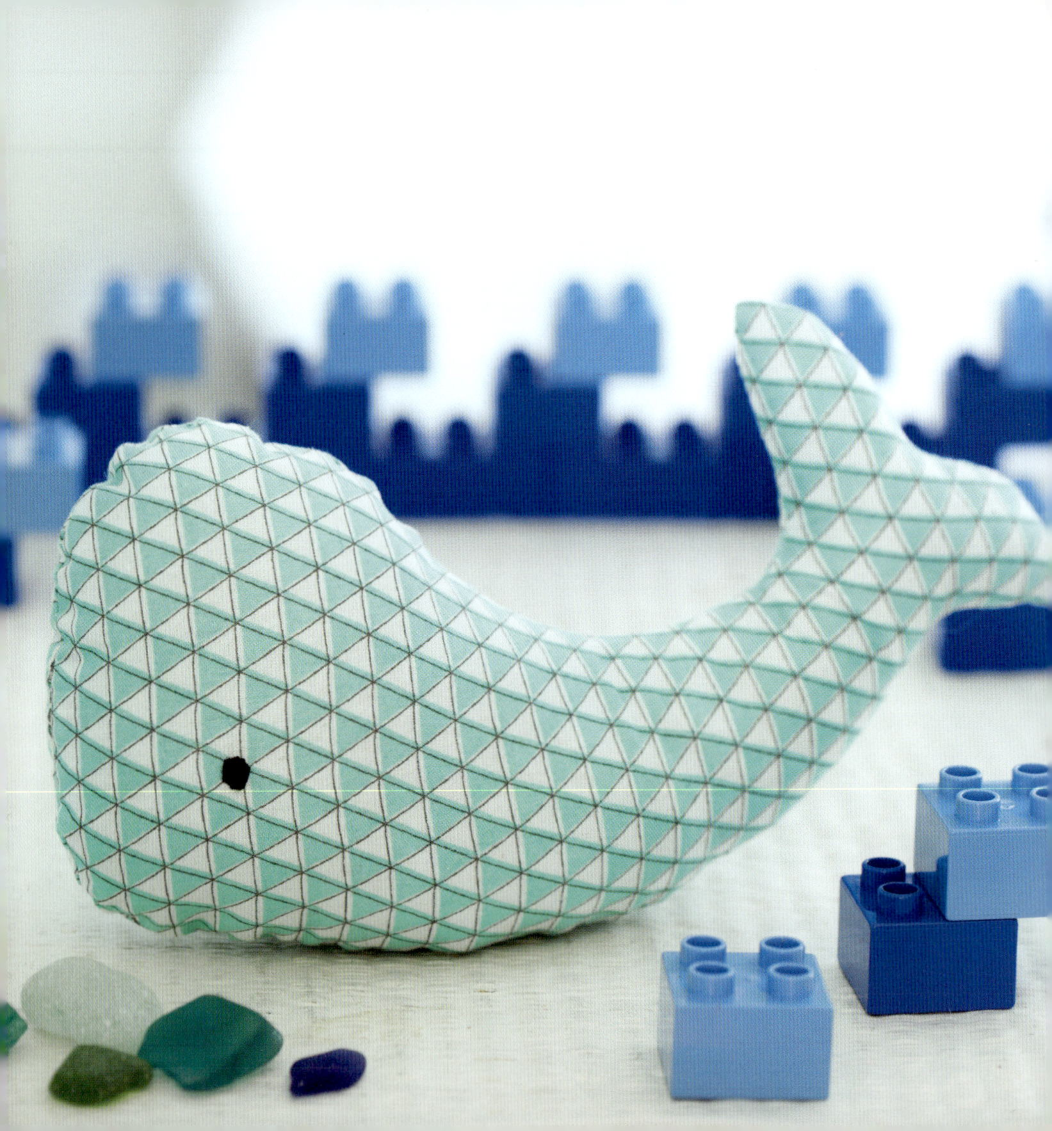

fabric whale

see variations page 97

materials

- fabric: Cloud9 Fabrics (100% organic cotton), 25cm (¼ yd) of Monsterz
- tracing paper
- dressmaking pins
- embroidery thread in black
- sewing thread in black
- sewing machine (optional)
- slim knitting needle
- stuffing

finished dimensions:
23.5cm (9¼ in) long, 10cm (4 in) high

instructions

Transfer the whale pattern to the fabric and cut, making sure to turn the pattern to reflect the opposite side of the body.

Embroider oval eyes with black thread – one on each right side of the whale.

With the right sides together, hand or machine sew beginning 12cm (5 in) from the tail at the belly. Continue sewing up the tail, over the back, around the face, and leaving a 7.5-cm (3-in) opening at the belly.

Turn the whale inside out and use a point turner to help push out the corners of the tail. Stuff the body bit by bit, using a slim knitting needle to help push stuffing into the tail.

Once you're finished stuffing, hand sew an invisible stitch to close up the belly.

Enlarge to 390% to make to actual size.

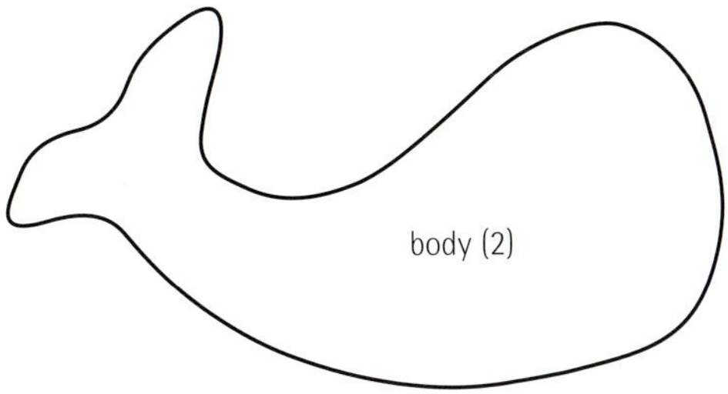

needle felt bear

see variations page 98

instructions

To make the belly, start with enough roving to roll a 10–11.5cm (4–4½-in) ball, starting at one end and tucking in the sides as you go to keep a tight ball. Keep in mind that the ball will shrink a little with felting. Hold the end in place.

Place on the felting foam pad and hold the ball with your fingers either side of it, so that the centre is clear for felting. Jab the ends in place, and keep stabbing the wool all around your ball until you feel it tightening up, but not so tight that it keeps you from felting.

Once you have your base piece, shape the belly by flattening out the top where the head will go. Narrow the shoulders by jabbing that area with your needle until you see it taper. For the head, take a smaller length of brown roving and roll and stab as you did for the body. Shape the muzzle by jabbing and tapering the front of the face into a muzzle shape.

Take a little wool and roll it into a tiny tube between your fingers to make the ears. Needle felt the wool a bit to hold it together and roll the tube into a 'U' shape. Hold it in place on the bear's head and stab through the ear into the head until the ear is firmly in place. Repeat for the other ear.
Roll tiny pieces of black wool between your fingers to make the eyes and nose. Hold in place on the head and stab through the eyes and nose into the head with your felting needle until they're secure. Felt the lines of a mouth just below the nose by stabbing repeatedly backwards and forwards in a line.

Roll a small piece of wool into a tube and needle felt into an arm. If you need more wool, simply wrap more wool around the tube and felt together. Leave one end of your tube with wispy ends to attach to the body. Do the same for the other arm and both legs, making the legs longer and slightly thicker than the arms. Trim off any excess wool.

To attach the arms and legs, hold them against the body and stab until secure. If you need to hide any seams, wrap a small bit of wool around that seam and felt right over it, smoothing it out and blending it in with the rest of the body.

materials

- wool roving, approx. 25g (1 oz) of light brown and a little black
- felting foam pad
- size 38 felting needle

finished dimensions:
4cm (1½ in) long, 3cm (1¼ in.) wide,
5cm (2 in) high

knitted fox

see variations page 99

materials

- yarn: Brown Sheep Nature Spun Worsted (100% wool, 100g (3½ oz), 224m (245 yds)), 1 skein each of (A) Pomegranate, (B) Natural
- 4.5 mm (US size 7) dpns
- stuffing
- tapestry needle
- stitch marker
- wool felt in white and black
- sewing thread in black and white
- 0.5cm (¼-in) black plastic eyes
- dried beans

tension: 5 sts over 7 rows = 2.5cm (1 in)

finished dimensions: 7.5cm (3 in) long, 9cm (3½ in) wide, 15cm (6 in) high

instructions

body

With A, CO 8 sts, divide between 3 dpns, place marker, and join in the round.

Rnd 1 and all odd rounds: k.

Rnd 2: [k1, m1] rep to end (16sts).

Rnd 4: [k2, m1] rep to end (24sts).

Rnd 6: [k3, m1] rep to end (32sts).

Rnd 8: [k4, m1] rep to end (40sts).

Rnds 9–19: k. Add beans for weight and stuffing as you knit.

Rnd 20: [k8, k2tog] rep to end (36 sts).

Rnd 22: [k7, k2tog] rep to end (32 sts).

Rnd 24: [k6, k2tog] rep to end (28 sts).

Rnd 26: [k5, k2tog] rep to end (24 sts).

Rnd 28: [k4, k2tog] rep to end (20 sts).

Rnd 30: [k3, k2tog] rep to end (16 sts).

Rnd 32: [k2, k2tog] rep to end (12 sts). Break yarn and run yarn end through al sts then close off end and weave in ends.

head

With A, CO 8 sts, divide between 3 dpns, place marker, join in the round.

Rnd 1 and all odd rounds: k.

Rnd 2: [k1, m1] rep to end (16sts).

Rnd 4: [k2, m1] rep to end (24sts).

Rnd 6: [k3, m1] rep to end (32sts).

Rnds 7–13: k.

Rnd 14: [k6, k2tog] rep to end (28 sts).

Rnd 16: [k5, k2tog] rep to end (24 sts).

Rnd 18: [k4, k2tog] rep to end (20 sts). Stuff.

Rnd 20: [k3, k2tog] rep to end (16 sts).

Rnd 22: [k2, k2tog] rep to end (12 sts). Break yarn and run yarn end through all 12 sts and close off end and weave in ends.

ears

Pick up 7 sts on the top left of the head and attach yarn on the right-hand side.

R1 & 3: k.

R2 & 4: p.
R5: k1, ssk, k1, k2tog, k1.
R6: p.
R7: ssk, k1, k2tog.
R8: p.
R9: k3tog.
Weave in ends. Make a second ear.

tail

With A, CO 8 sts, divide between 3 dpns, place marker, join in the round.
Rnd 1 and all odd rounds: k.
Rnd 2: [k1, m1] rep to end (16sts).
Rnd 4: [k2, m1] rep to end (24sts).
Rnds 5–21: k. Begin to stuff lightly and continue to end.
Rnd 22: change to B, [k3, k2tog] rep to end (16 sts).
Rnd 24: [k2, k2tog] rep to end (12 sts).
Rnd 26: [k1, k2tog] rep to end (8 sts).
Rnd 28: k2tog to end (4 sts).
Break yarn, run yarn end through all, close off end, and weave in ends.

details

Cut muzzle and belly out of white felt. Embroider mouth onto the muzzle Baste these pieces in place before stitching and sew onto the face and body. Attach the eyes. Cut out a small black felt triangular nose 1.25cm (1/2-in) wide and 1cm (3/8 in) tall and sew onto the face.

fabric crab

see variations page 100

materials

- fabric: Robert Kaufman Kona Cotton (100% cotton), 25cm (1/4 yd) each of Tomato and Buttercup
- tracing paper
- cardstock
- sewing thread in red and beige
- stuffing
- 1.25-cm (1/2-in) black plastic eyes

finished dimensions:
29cm (11 1/2 in) long, 20cm (10 in) wide

instructions

Cut the inner body pattern out of cardstock. Transfer and cut the rest of the crab pattern from fabric: cut half of the legs and body from Tomato fabric, and half from Buttercup fabric (top and bottom of crab). Cut 4 legs that curve to the left, and 4 to the right, for the front and back legs. Cut both sides of the claws from Tomato fabric.

Pin the legs and claws, right sides together, and sew each with a 0.5-cm (1/4-in) seam allowance, leaving the straight edge open. Turn inside out and iron out wrinkles. Stuff lightly. Baste about0.5-cm (1/4-in) in from the body edges. Place the inner body card cutout on the centre of the wrong side of the fabric and pull the basting stitches tight around it. Do the same for both body pieces, and iron flat to make a smooth turned-in edge for the body.

Place the eyes about 2.5cm (1 in) from the front edge on the top right side of the red body, and about 7.5cm (3 in) apart. Lay the bottom half of the body right side down, and place the claws and legs sticking out from either side of it. Space evenly on each side, with the front claws curved in towards each other. Each side will have two legs turning opposite ways. Baste the legs and claws to the bottom body piece. Lay the top body piece on top, wrong sides together, and pin everything together. Topstitch 1cm (3/8 in) from the edge with red thread. Begin sewing at one of the back legs, and sew around until you get to the other back leg. Leave an opening at the back (about 9cm (3 1/2 in)). Stuff and continue sewing till closed.

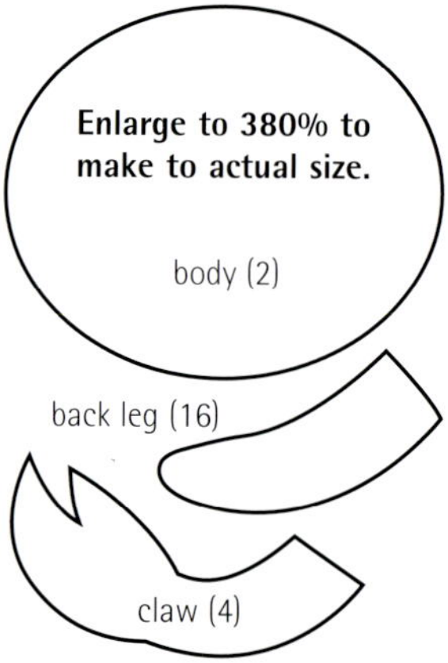

crochet owl

see variations page 101

materials

- worsted weight yarn in taupe, 1 skein
- size H crochet hook
- rice or dried beans
- stuffing
- fabric scraps in white and dark grey
- tracing paper
- embroidery thread in dark grey and yellow

tension: 4½ sts over 5 rows = 2.5cm (1 in)
finished dimensions: 6cm (2½ in) diameter, 10cm (4 in) high when stuffed

instructions

body

With the worsted weight yarn and crochet hook, make a slip knot and insert hook.
Rnd 1: Make 6 dc in a magic ring, sl st to join.
Rnd 2: 2 dc in each st across, sl st in first dc to join – 12 dc.
Rnd 3: ch 1, [dc in next st, 2 dc in next st] around, sl st in first dc to join – 18 dc.
Rnd 4: ch 1, [dc in next 2 sts, 2 dc in next st] around, sl st in first dc to join – 24 dc.
Rnd 5: ch 1, [dc in next 3 sts, 2 dc in next st] around, sl st in first dc to join – 30 dc.
Rnds 6–16: ch 1, dc in next 30 sts, sl st in first dc to join.
Rnd 17: ch 1, [dc in next 3 sts, skp 1, dc in next st] around, sl st in first dc to join – 24 dc.
Rnd 18: ch 1, [dc in next 2 sts, skp 1, dc in next st] around, sl st in first dc to join – 18 dc.
Begin to fill the owl with beans on the bottom, and either a stuffing or yarn and fabric scraps in a similar colour to your owl. Continue stuffing as you crochet the next couple rounds.
Rnd 19: ch 1, [dc in next st, skp 1, dc in next st] around, sl st in first dc to join – 12 dc.
Rnd 20: ch 1, [dc in next st, skp 1, dc in next st] around, sl st in first dc to join – 6 dc.
Fasten off and weave in ends.

face & wings

Trace the owl's face and wings. Cut out the shapes and pin to fabric scraps – there are three different sizes of wings. Cut a mix of five feathers for each wing. Embroider the owl's beak and eyes onto the face and blanket stitch the face in place. Pin the feathers and stitch in place with vertical stitches near the top of each feather. Finally, embroider small, random stitches on the belly.

Enlarge all template pieces to 400% to make to actual size.

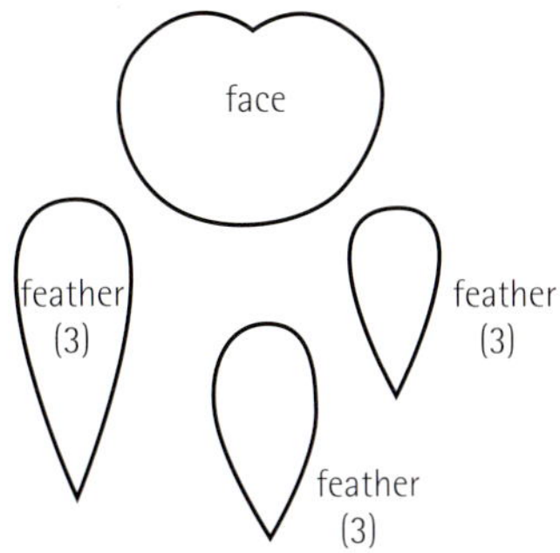

fabric grasshopper

see variations page 102

materials

- felt in sage green, cream, hunter green, black
- tracing paper
- dressmaking pins
- tailor's chalk
- sewing thread in colours to match felt
- sewing needle
- stuffing
- pipe cleaners or wire
- wire cutters

finished dimensions:
9cm (3½ in) wide, 14cm (5½ in) long, 9cm (3½ in) high

instructions

Transfer the grasshopper pattern to the following colours of felt and cut out: sage green – (2) bodies, (1) neck piece, (4) thighs; cream – (4) back legs, (4) front legs; hunter green – (2) wings; black – (2) antennae, (2) eyes.

Blanket stitch the two body pieces together and leave the belly section open. Do not break thread. Hold or pin the belly piece along one belly edge on the body, and continue blanket stitching together. Stuff the body, and continue stuffing as you stitch up the other side of the belly. Knot off and hide the ends on the inside.

Line up the wings along the grasshopper's back and stitch each wing to the body closest to the neck. Wrap the neck piece like a collar over the stitches you just made on the wings. Blanket stitch the collar onto the body and directly over the wings.

Adding wire inside the legs gives the grasshopper support to stand. To do this, cut a length of wire about 2.5cm (1 in) longer than the leg. Bend the tips inwards, so they won't poke out of the felt later. Bend the wire to match the leg shape and sandwich it inside two matching leg pieces. Blanket stitch together, and repeat for all legs.

Grasshoppers need strong hind legs for hopping, so we'll add thigh pieces on the back legs. Sandwich one back leg in between the two thigh pieces at a 45-degree angle at the thigh and leg join. Blanket stitch around the thigh and stuff lightly as you sew. Stitch to the body about 2.5cm (1 in) from the tail end. Repeat for the other leg. Sew the front legs onto the body, and the eyes and antennae to the head.

Enlarge all template pieces to 190% to make to actual size.

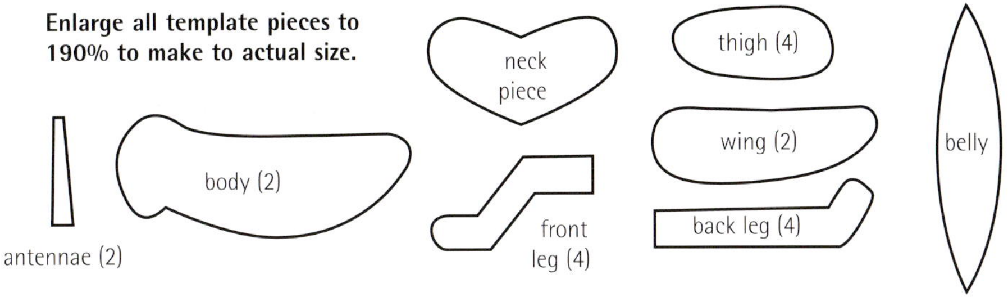

needle felt stegosaurus

see variations page 103

materials

- wool roving, approx. 12g (1/2 oz) of yellow ochre, and a bit of black for eyes
- wool felt in sage green
- felting foam pad
- size 38 felting needle
- sewing thread in yellow ochre
- sewing needle

finished dimensions: 14cm (5 1/2 in) long, 4.5cm (1 3/4 in) wide, 8.25cm (3 1/4 in) high

instructions

Take enough yellow roving to roll into a tight 11.5-cm (4 1/2-in)-long and 5.5-cm (2 1/4-in)-wide tube, with the middle section wider than the ends.

Place the rolled wool on the foam pad and hold the ends in place with your fingers. Take the felting needle in your other hand and jab the ends together. Stab all over the piece until you feel it firming up and holding together. Don't worry if your wool doesn't look smooth – you'll smooth it out at the end.

Shape the head and tail of the stegosaurus. If the head or tail needs to be longer, wrap a layer of wool around that end and continue. Do the same for the belly if it needs to be bigger.

Wrap another layer of wool around the whole piece to smooth it out, and gently tuck and felt the edges together so they all blend in.

Roll four smaller tubes for legs and leave one end wispy – this will make it easier to needle felt to the body. Hold the leg next to the body and needle felt them together.

With a bit of black wool, felt little black dots for eyes. Cut different-sized back scales out of green wool felt and sew onto the back.

crochet dragonfly

see variations page 104

materials

- yarn: Lion Brand Cotton Bamboo (52% cotton, 48% bamboo, 100g (3½ oz), 225m (245 yds)), 1 skein of (A) Persimmon; Brown Sheep Cotton Fleece (80% cotton 20% merino wool, 100g (3½ oz), 196m (215 yds)), 1 skein of (B) Cavern
- 4 mm (US size G/6) crochet hook
- tapestry needle

tension: 5 sts over 6 rows = 2.5cm (1 in)
finished dimensions: 11.5cm (4½ in) wide,14cm (5½ in) long

instructions

wings

With A, ch 11, turn.
R1: start 2nd ch from hook, 10 dc, turn.
R2: ch1, dc in next 9 sts, 2 dc in next 2 sts, 9 dc – 22 dc.
Break yarn and weave in ends.
Make three more wings.

body

With B, make 6 dc in a magic ring, sl st to join.
Ch 1, dc in next 6 sts, sl st for 7.5cm (3 in) and stuff with the same black yarn as you crochet.

Rnd 1: ch 1, [2 dc, 2 dc in next st] 2 times, sl st in first dc to join – 8 dc.
Rnd 2: ch 1, dc in next 8 sts, sl st in first dc to join.
Rnd 3: ch 1, [dc in next 3 sts, 2 dc in next st] rep once more, sl st – 10 dc.
Rnd 4: ch 1, dc in next 10 sts, sl st in first dc to join.
Rnd 5: ch 1, [dc in next 3 sts, dc2tog] rep once more, sl st – 8 dc.
Rnd 6: ch 1, dc in next 8 sts, sl st in first dc to join.
Rnd 7: ch 1, [dc in next 2 sts, dc2tog] 2 times, sl st in first dc to join – 6 dc.

head

Ch 1, [dc in next 6 sts, sl st] for 1.25cm (½-in) Fasten off and weave in ends. Block wings and pinch the flat ends together and sew onto either side of the bulge.

crochet octopus

see variations page 105

materials

- yarn: Brown Sheep Lamb's Pride Worsted (85% wool, 15% mohair, 100g (4 oz), 175m (190 yds), 1 skein each of (A) Limeade, (B) Pumpkin
- 5 mm (US size H/8) crochet hook
- 1.25-cm (½-in) black plastic eyes
- black embroidery thread

tension: 4½ sts over 5 rows = 2.5cm (1 in)
finished dimensions: 12cm (5 in) wide, 12cm (5 in) high

instructions

body

With A, make 6 dc in a magic ring, sl st in first dc to join.
Rnd 1: ch 1, 2 dc in each st across, sl st in first dc to join – 12 dc.
Rnd 2: ch 1, [dc in next 2 sts, 2 dc in next st] 4 times, sl st in first dc to join – 16 dc.
Rnd 3: ch 1, [dc in next 3 sts, 2 dc in next st] 4 times, sl st in first dc to join – 20 dc.
Rnd 4: ch 1, [dc in next 4 sts, 2 dc in next st] 4 times, sl st in first dc to join – 24 dc.
Rnd 5: ch 1, [dc in next 5 sts, 2 dc in next st] 4 times, sl st in first dc to join – 28 dc.
Rnd 6: ch 1, [dc in next 6 sts, 2 dc in next st] 4 times, sl st in first dc to join – 32 dc.
Rnds 7–10: ch 1, dc in next 32 sts, sl st in first dc to join.
Insert eyes 0.5cm (¼ in) from edge and 5cm (2 in) apart.
Rnd 11: ch 1, [dc in next 6 sts, dc2tog] 4 times, sl st in first dc to join – 28 dc.
Rnd 12: ch 1, [dc in next 5 sts, dc2tog] 4 times, sl st in first dc to join – 24 dc.
Rnd 13: ch 1, [dc in next 4 sts, dc2tog] 4 times, sl st in first dc to join – 20 dc.
Begin to stuff and continue stuffing to end.
Rnd 14: ch 1, [dc in next 3 sts, dc2tog] 4 times, sl st in first dc to join – 16 dc.
Rnd 15: ch 1, [dc in next 2 sts, dc2tog] 4 times, sl st in first dc to join – 12 dc.
Rnd 16: ch 1, [dc2tog] 6 times, sl st in first dc to join – 6 dc.
Stitch a small smiling mouth onto face. Break yarn, fasten off, and weave in ends.

tentacles

With B, make 6 dc in a magic ring, sl st to join.
Rnd 1: ch 1, [dc in next st, 2 dc in next st] 3 times, sl st in first dc to join – 9 dc.
Fasten off B, join A.
Rnds 2–10: ch 1, dc in next 9 sts, sl st in first dc to join.
Break yarn leaving enough to sew with, and stuff 2cm (¾ in) of tentacle. Make seven more tentacles. Flatten out the edge, then space out four legs evenly at the outside edge of the base of the body and sew into place. Space out the remaining four legs between and just under the first four and sew on. Weave in ends.

crochet pig

see variations page 106

materials

- yarn: Brown Sheep Shepherd's Shades (100% wool, 100g (3½ oz), 120m (131 yds)), 1 skein each of (A) Rose Petal and (B) Thistle
- 5.5 mm and 6 mm (US size J/10 and I/9) crochet hooks
- stuffing
- tapestry needle
- embroidery thread in black
- 0.5-cm (¼-in) back plastic eyes

tension: 4 sts over 4½ rows = 2.5cm (1 in)

finished dimensions: 14.5cm (5¾ in) long, 6.5cm (2¾ in) wide, 7.5cm (3 in) high

instructions

body (6 mm) hook

Rnd 1: with A, make 6 dc in a magic ring, sl st in first dc to join in the round.

Rnd 2: ch 1, 2 dc in ea ch across, sl st in first dc to join – 12 dc.

Rnd 3: ch 1, [dc in next st, 2 dc in next st] 6 times, sl st in first dc to join – 18 dc.

Rnd 4: ch 1, [dc in next 2 sts, 2 dc in next st] 6 times, sl st in first dc to join – 24 dc.

Rnds 5–9: ch 1, dc in ea st across, sl st in first dc to join.

Rnd 10: ch 1, [dc in next 3 sts, 2 dc in next st] 3 times, dc in next 12 sts, sl st in first dc to join – 27 dc.

Rnd 11: ch 1, [dc in next 4 sts, 2 dc in next st] 3 times, dc in next 12 sts, sl st in first dc to join – 30 dc.

Rnds 12–13: ch 1, dc in next 30 sts, sl st in first dc to join.

Rnd 14: ch 1, [dc in next 4 sts, dc2tog] 3 times, dc in next 12 sts, sl st in first dc to join – 27 dc.

Rnd 15: ch 1, [dc in next 3 sts, dc2tog] 3 times, dc in next 12 sts, sl st in first dc to join – 24 dc.

Rnds 16–20: ch 1, dc in next 24 sts, sl st in first dc to join – 24 dc.

Begin to stuff the body and continue stuffing to the end.

Rnd 21: ch 1, [dc in next 2 sts, dc2tog] 6 times, sl st in first dc to join – 18 dc.

Rnd 22: ch 1, [dc in next st, dc2tog] 6 times, sl st in first dc to join – 12 dc.

Rnd 23: ch 1, [dc2tog] 6 times, sl st in first dc to join – 6 dc.

Break the yarn and weave in the ends, closing the end off. The increased area is the belly.

snout (6 mm hook)

Rnd 1: with B make 6 dc in a magic ring sl st in first dc to join in the round.

Rnd 2: ch 1, 2 dc in each st across, sl st in first dc to join – 12 dc.

Rnd 3: ch 1, dc in next 12 sts, sl st in first dc to join.

Break yarn and leave enough yarn to sew snout to face.

<u>ears (6 mm hook)</u>

Ch 4 sts, ch 1, turn.

R1: dc in 2nd ch from hook, 2 dc, ch 1, turn.

R2: Dc in 2nd st from hook, 1 dc, 2 dc in next 2 sts, 2 dc. Break yarn, leaving enough to sew to head. It'll curl a little bit, which is fine. Make another ear.

<u>feet (6 mm hook)</u>

Rnd 1: with B, make 6 dc in a magic ring, sl st in first dc to join.

Rnd 2: ch 1, [dc in next st, 2 dc in next st] 3 times, sl st in first dc to join – 9 dc.

Rnd 3: ch 1, [dc in next 2 sts, 2 dc in next st] 3 times, sl st in first dc to join. Fasten off B, join A – 12 dc.

Rnds 4–7: ch 1, dc in next 12 sts, sl st in first dc to join. Break yarn and leave enough yarn to sew to body. Make three more feet.

<u>tail (5.5 mm hook with A)</u>

Ch 6, turn, and begin 2nd ch from hook, 3 dc in each st across. Leave enough sewing yarn and sew tail on.

Stuff feet and sew onto the body. Tuck ends into snout and stuff a little more if necessary, and sew to centre of the face. Add black plastic eyes and sew on ears and tail. Sew two black nostrils onto snout.

knitted caterpillar

see variations page 107

materials

- yarn: Brown Sheep Nature Spun Worsted (100% wool, 100g (3½ oz), 224m (245 yds)), 1 skein each of (A) Regal Purple, (B) French Clay, (C) Turquoise Wonder, (D) Impasse Yellow, (E) Peruvian Pink, (F) Lemon Grass, (G) Snow, (H) Pepper
- 4 mm (US size 6) straight knitting needles
- 3.75 mm (US size F/5) crochet hook
- stuffing
- tapestry needle
- 0.5-cm (¼-in) black plastic eyes

tension: 6 sts over 7½ rows = 2.5cm (1 in)

finished dimensions: 16cm (6¼ in) long, 3cm (1¼ in.) wide, 4cm (1½ in) high

instructions

With A, CO 8 sts.

R1: p.

R2: k1, m1, *k2, m1* three times, k1 – 12 sts.

R3: p.

R4: k1, m1, *k2, m1* five times, k1 – 18 sts.

R5–7: continue in st st.

R8: change to B and k.

R9–13: st st.

R14: change to C and k.

Continue knitting in this manner, changing to the next colour after six rows. Continue stuffing as you knit to the end. Once you get to colour G, work as follows:

R1–6: k.

R7: *k1, k2tog* rep to end – 12 sts.

R8: p.

R9: *k1, k2tog* rep to end – 8 sts.

R10: p.

BO and weave in ends, leaving enough sewing yarn. Attach plastic eyes and knot in black yarn (colour H) antennae on the head chain 4, and weave in. Mattress stitch down the length of the caterpillar, then stuff. Sew ends closed.

crochet brontosaurus

see variations page 108

materials

- yarn: Brown Sheep Lamb's Pride Worsted (85% wool, 15% mohair, 100g (4 oz), 175m (190 yds), 1 skein of Aztec Turquoise
- 5 mm (US size H/8) crochet hook
- tapestry needle
- stuffing
- pipe cleaner x 2
- black wool felt
- black embroidery thread

tension: 4 sts over 5 rows = 2.5cm (1 in)
finished dimensions: 32cm (12½ in) long, 11cm (4¼ in) wide,18cm (7 in) high

instructions

tail

Rnd 1: ch 2, 6 dc in 2nd ch from hook, sl st in first dc to join.
Rnd 2: ch 1, [dc in next st, 2 dc in next st] 3 times, sl st in first dc to join – 9 dc.
Rnds 3–10: ch 1, dc in next 9 sts, sl st in first dc to join.
Rnd 11: ch 1, [dc in next 2 sts, 2 dc in next st] 3 times, sl st in first dc to join – 12 dc.
Rnd 12: ch 1, dc in next 12 sts, sl st in first dc to join.
Rnd 13: ch 1, [dc in next 3 sts, 2 dc in nxt st] 3 times, sl st in first dc to join – 15 dc.
Rnd 14: ch 1, dc in next 15 sts, sl st in first dc to join.
Rnd 15: ch 1, [dc in next 4 sts, 2 dc in next st] 3 times, sl st in first dc to join – 18 dc.
Rnd 16: ch 1, dc in next 18 sts, sl st in first dc to join.
Rnd 17: ch 1, [dc in next 2 sts, 2 dc in next st] 6 times, sl st in first dc to join – 24 dc.
Rnd 18: ch 1, dc in next 24 sts, sl st in first dc to join.
Rnd 19: ch 1, [dc in next 3 sts, 2 dc in next st] 6 times, sl st in first dc to join.
Rnd 20: ch 1, dc in next 30 sts, sl st in first dc to join – 30 dc.
Rnd 21: ch 1, [dc in next 4 sts, 2 dc in next st] 6 times, sl st in first dc to join – 36 dc.
Roll the end of the pipe cleaner to a round tip and place inside the tail and begin to stuff. Continue stuffing as you crochet.
Rnds 22–30: ch 1, dc in next 36 sts, sl st in first dc to join.
Rnd 31: ch 1, [dc in next 4 sts, dc2tog] 6 times, sl st – 30 dc.
Rnd 32: ch 1, dc in next 30 sts, sl st in first dc to join.
Rnd 33: ch 1, [dc in next 3 sts, dc2tog] 6 times, sl st in first dc to join – 24 dc.
Rnd 34: ch 1, dc in next 24 sts, sl st in first dc to join.
Begin neck shaping across next 16 sts.
Row 35: ch 1, [dc in next 2 sts, dc2tog] 4 times, sl st in next dc to join, turn.
Row 36: ch 1, [dc in next st, dc2tog] 4 times, sl st in next dc to join, turn.
Rows 37–39: begin 2nd dc from

hook, dc in next 8 sts, sl st in next dc to join, turn.
Insert pipe cleaner into base of neck, pushing it at least 3-5cm (1-2 in) into the body, and stuff as you crochet.
Rnds 40–47: ch 1, dc in next 18 sts, sl st in first dc to join – 18 dc.
Rnd 48: ch 1, [dc in next 4 sts, dc2tog] 3 times, sl st in first dc to join – 15 dc.
Rnds 49–53: ch 1, dc in next 15 sts, sl st in first dc to join – 15 dc.

head shaping
Rnd 54: ch 1, [dc in next 2 sts, 2 dc into next st] 5 times, sl st in first dc to join – 20 dc.
Rnd 55: ch 1, [dc in next 3 sts, 2 dc into next st] 5 times, sl st in first dc to join – 25 dc.
Rnd 56: ch 1, [dc in next 2 sts, 2 dc into next st] 5 times, 10 dc, sl st in first dc to join – 30 dc.
Rnds 57–58: ch 1, dc in next 30 sts, sl st in first dc to join.
Rnd 59: ch 1, [dc in next 2 sts, dc2tog] 5 times, 10 dc, sl st in first dc to join – 25 dc.
Rnd 60: ch 1, [dc in next 3 sts, dc2tog] 5 times, sl st in first dc to join – 20 dc.
Rnd 61: ch 1, [dc in next 2 sts, dc2tog] 5 times, sl st in first dc to join – 15 dc.
Rnd 62: ch 1, [dc in next st, dc2tog] 5 times, sl st in first dc to join – 10 dc.
Rnd 63: ch 1, [dc2tog] 5 times, sl st in first dc to join – 5 dc.
Fasten off and weave in ends.

feet
Rnd 1: dc 6 in a magic ring sl st in first dc to join, ch 1.
Rnd 2: dc 2 into each st, sl st in first dc to join, ch 1 – 12 dc.
Rnd 3: [1 dc, 2 dc in next st] 6 times, sl st in first dc to join, ch 1 – 18 dc.
Rnds 4–9: 18 dc, sl st in first dc to join, ch 1.
Fasten off, leaving enough yarn to sew the foot to the body.
Make three more feet. Stuff and sew into place.

Cut two eyes out of black felt and stitch into place.

knitted duck

see variations page 109

materials

- yarn: Brown Sheep Co. Shepherd's Shades (100% wool, 100 g (3½ oz), 120m (131 yds)), 1 skein of Sunshine
- wool roving, a little orange for the beak
- 6 mm (US size 10) dpns
- stuffing
- tapestry needle
- 0.5-cm (¼-in) black plastic eyes
- felting foam pad
- size 38 felting needle

tension: 4½ sts over 6 rows = 2.5cm (1 in)

finished dimensions: 9cm (3½ in) long, 4.5cm (1¾ in) wide, 7.5cm (3 in) high

instructions

body

CO 8 sts, divide onto 3 dpns and join to knit in the round.

Rnd1: k.

Rnd2: * k2, m1* rep 3 times more to end – 12 sts.

Rnd3: k.

Rnd4: *k3, m1* rep 3 times more to end – 16 sts.

Rnd5: k.

Rnd6: *k4, m1* rep 3 times more to end – 20 sts.

Rnds7–14: k.

Rnd15: *k3, k2tog* rep 3 times more to end – 16 sts.

Rnd16: k. Begin to stuff body and continue stuffing to end.

Rnd17: *k2, k2tog* rep 3 times more to end – 12 sts.

Rnd18: *k1, k2tog* rep 3 times more to end – 8 sts. Break yarn and pull remaining sts tight to close. Weave in ends.

head

CO 8 sts onto 3 dpns and join to knit in the round.

Rnd1: k.

Rnd2: * k2, m1* rep 3 times more to end – 12 sts.

Rnd3: k.

Rnd4: *k3, m1* rep 3 times more to end – 16 sts.

Rnds5–7: k.

Rnd8: *k2, k2tog* rep 3 times more to end – 12 sts. Begin to stuff head and continue to end.

Rnd9: k.

Rnd10: *k1, k2tog* rep 3 times more to end – 8 sts. Insert plastic eyes, using the photo on page 109 as a guide.

Rnd11: k

Break yarn, pull remaining sts tight to close. Weave in ends.

beak

Fold some orange wool roving into a beak, about 4cm (1½ in) long and 2.5cm (1 in) wide (it will shrink with felting). Place on the felting foam pad and stab with the felting needle, rounding the beak and leaving the other end wispy. Hold the beak against the face and felt through, turning up the corners on the top and bottom beak. Felt until smoothly blended in. Sew the head in place with yellow yarn. Hide the ends inside the duck.

variations

fabric rabbit

see base design page 67

rabbit appliqué

Use the rabbit body and ear patterns to create a sweet appliqué for a baby blanket or framed artwork for a child's room. Follow the appliqué instructions from the superhero cape pattern (see page 159) to transfer and sew the rabbit appliqué.

chocolate easter bunny

Follow the rabbit pattern and use chocolate brown fabric to create a 'chocolate' bunny for Easter. Tie a yellow ribbon around its neck and include your little bunny in Easter baskets.

rabbit doorstop

Enlarge the rabbit pattern by 150 percent, and follow the same instructions for sewing. Fill the base of the body with dried rice or beans to make a sturdy doorstop.

angora rabbit

Needle felt a fluffy angora rabbit using white wool roving. Felt a 5 x 7.5-cm (2 x 3-in) oval and a 3cm (1¼-in) round head. Attach and cut 4-cm (1½-in)-long ears and needle felt to the head. Take small tufts of wool and needle felt one end to the rabbit and leave the outside loose and wispy. Felt these tufts all around the rabbit until you've covered the whole rabbit including the face, but leaving an area around the nose and mouth open. Stitch the eyes, nose, and mouth onto the face. Needle felt a 2-cm (¾-in) white ball for the tail.

rabbit family

Resize the rabbit pattern by 100 percent to make mummy and daddy rabbits, and follow the same instructions for sewing and stuffing. Make three more rabbits using the pattern as normal to make baby rabbits for a family.

variations

plushie t-rex

see base design page 68

velociraptor

Follow the T-Rex pattern and extend the arms to curve downward and inwards. Cut the stomach curve on the main body pattern about 4cm (1½ in) in at the widest point, and tapering from the neck to the tail, to make your velociraptor more slender than the T-Rex.

dragon

Follow the T-Rex instructions but use a solid green cotton fabric. Cut two 7.5-cm (3-in) pointed wings out of orange cotton fabric. Sew together and leave a 4cm (1½ in) opening to turn right side out, lightly stuff, and stitch closed. Repeat for the other wing, and hand sew the wings onto the dragon's back just behind its front legs.

godzilla

Use a textured scaly pattern and follow the T-Rex instructions to make a Godzilla doll. Cut and sew scales along the back and tail, as in the felt stegosaurus pattern on page 83. Stitch white pointy teeth on the mouth. Needle felt tiny skyscrapers for Godzilla to knock down.

giant plushie t-rex

Resize the T-Rex pattern by 100 percent and follow the same sewing and construction instructions to make a larger dino to cuddle.

kangaroo

Use a light brown fabric to turn the T-Rex into a kangaroo. Sew 2.5–4-cm (1–1½-in) ears to the head. Use a cream-coloured fabric for the belly and sew a pouch onto the belly. Resize the pattern to make a little joey to fit inside.

variations

fabric whale

see base design page 71

narwhal (pictured)

Add a pointy tooth to make a narwhal. Cut two 12.5-cm (5-in)-long and 2.5-cm (1-in)-wide strips of white felt. Taper the 2.5cm (1 in) to a point and sew together.

orca

Use black fabric in place of the patterned fabric to make an orca (killer whale). Cut a 5-cm (2-in) triangular back fin and sew onto the whale's back. Cut white ovals for the face and white spots for the stomach out of felt and appliqué to the whale.

dolphin

Taper the whale's head to a point to make a dolphin's head. Use grey fabric for the body. Cut a 5-cm (2-in) triangular back fin and sew onto the whale's back.

baby whales

Shrink the pattern to quarter-size and cut and sew three flat felt baby whales. Sew a pocket on one side of the mummy whale to hold the calves.

shark

Taper the head of the whale to a rounded point for the shark's mouth. Embroider pointy teeth and gills on the side of the head. Cut a 7.5-cm (3-in) triangular shark's fin and sew onto the back.

variations

needle felt bear

see base design page 72

needle felt elephant

Follow the bear instructions but use grey wool. Needle felt 1.25-cm (½-in) floppy ears and make the elephant's trunk as you would the arms. Attach the trunk to the face in place of the muzzle and smooth over the seam with a layer of wool.

goldilocks & the three bears

Needle felt three bears in three different sizes, and then needle felt Goldilocks. Start by rolling a ball of blue wool for her body, and wrapping more wool on one end and shaping it into a cone for the skirt of her dress. Keep adding wool until it fans out. Felt a beige ball for her head, and cut strips of yellow yarn and needle felt each strand directly onto her head until her hair is full. Roll small tubes of beige wool for her arms and legs and needle felt all appendages in place. Add face, apron, shoes, and sleeve details.

lion

Use yellow wool in place of the olive green and follow the bear pattern. Felt bits of orange wool in a ring around the face, leaving wisps of wool loose for the lion's mane. Knot a 1.25-cm (½-in) tail with yellow embroidery at the back and make another knot near the end of the thread.

panda

Follow the bear pattern but use black and white wool to make a panda. Felt the belly and head with white wool, and the ears, legs, arms, and around the eyes with black. Wrap black wool across the panda's shoulders and blend in with the arms.

koala

Follow the bear instructions and use grey wool to make a koala. Make the ears twice as big as the teddy bear's ears and needle felt to the top of the head. Felt a larger black nose in the centre of the face. Cut a few eucalyptus leaves out of wool felt and stitch to the koala's paw.

variations

knitted fox

see base design page 74

scented fox

Insert a lavender sachet into the fox's belly before closing it up to make a soothing scented friend for bedtime.

knitted wolf

Follow the knit fox pattern but use grey yarn for the head, ears, body, and tail. Skip rows 4 and 22 on the tail pattern to make the wolf's tail narrower, and use grey yarn for the whole tail. Follow the belly and muzzle felt pattern as for the fox. To make a big bad wolf to go with the three little pigs (see page 106), embroider a black circle for the mouth, to show the wolf blowing the houses down.

knitted raccoon

Use a dark grey yarn in place of the Pomegranate. Cut a 1.25-cm (½-in) strip of black felt to sew over the eye area and a 0.5-cm (¼-in) strip of white felt to sew above the eyes (like eyebrows). Use the white muzzle from the fox pattern for the raccoon. Add an extra white stripe to the tail by changing to B (Natural) for rnds 10-15.

knitted mouse

Use a light brown yarn and follow the knitted fox pattern to create a little mouse. Omit the felt muzzle and cut light brown rounded ears from felt to sew onto the head. Crochet a 10-cm (4-in) chainstitch tail from the same brown yarn and stitch in place of the fox's tail.

larger fox

Multiply all quantities and measurements by four to make a plushie fox big enough to cuddle.

variations

fabric crab

see base design page 76

stitch details

With a matching colour embroidery thread to the belly, embroider a bell-shaped belly 'flap', with the larger width of the bell towards the bottom of the crab. Embroider four lines horizontally from the belly flap towards the legs.

crayfish

Make the body according to the crab instructions, but using the crayfish template (right). Follow the crab instructions for sewing and stuffing as well as for the legs and claws.

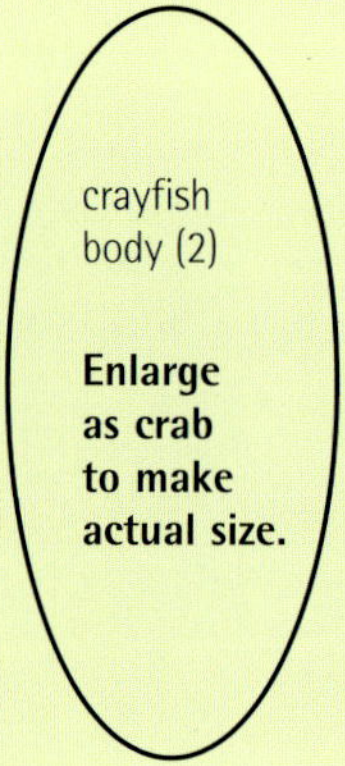

lobster

Follow the crab claw and leg patterns and make them out of fabric. Knit a tube for the lobster's body about 25cm (10 in) long and with a 23-cm (9-in) circumference. Stuff and gather the tail together at the closed end. Cut a fan-shaped tail out of red fabric, sew, and stuff lightly. Hand sew the tail on, along with the legs and claws. Add black eyes and 15-cm (6-in)-long antennae.

hand puppet

Use the same colour fabric as the belly and sew a pocket onto the belly big enough for your hand. Sew the pocket on before you sew the crab together.

marionette crab

Tie two dowels together in the centre to form an 'X'. Make two – one for each set of legs. Attach strings to each leg, claw, and body, and tie or glue the ends to the dowels. You're now ready to animate your crab!

variations

crochet owl

see base design page 79

felt baby owl (pictured)

Use a tuft of wool roving and lightly needle felt into an oval to make a baby owl. Needle felt little round black eyes and cut a yellow beak out of felt and needle felt to the body. Cut two wings from white felt and needle felt on either side of the body.

owl hand puppet

Follow the crochet owl instructions up to row 16. Break yarn, weave in the ends, but don't stuff the owl. This will fit a child's hand.

bowling owls

Crochet six owls to make a small bowling ball set. Make a needle felt ball for the jack following the instructions in the 'needle felt ball' pattern on page 48.

crochet nesting owls

Make three nesting owls by following the crochet owl pattern and, like the hand puppet variation, stop and weave in at row 16. Follow the face and wing details. Use a fingering-weight yarn and corresponding hook, and a bulky-weight yarn and corresponding hook to make a larger and smaller version of the owl so the three can nest together.

sleepytime sounds

Purchase a prerecorded lullaby or record soothing sounds onto a sound chip, and insert it in the centre of your owl. Stuff to the end and close off. Your owl will be a squeezable bedtime friend.

variations

fabric grasshopper

see base design page 80

cricket

Follow the grasshopper pattern and size it down by a quarter. Use chocolate brown and black felt to make your cricket and extend the antennae by 10cm (4 in).

habitat for grasshopper

You'll need a glass jar big enough to fit your grasshopper. Needle felt a round disk to fit into the bottom of the jar. Cut a number of green felt strips of varying lengths tapered to a point to make grass. Sew or needle felt these strips at the base onto the felt disk until it's nice and full. Place the grass into the jar and nestle your grasshopper in its new home. Substitute the glass jar with a paper or cardboard box for younger children.

stick puppet

Insert a bamboo skewer into the belly of the grasshopper to create a stick puppet. Make a window stage and include paper grass and trees along the bottom and sides.

grasshopper mobile

Follow the grasshopper pattern and make five grasshoppers using browns, tan, and brighter greens for different types. Follow the instructions for the 'fabric birds mobile' on page 39. Add felt leaves and grass to the dowels.

embroidered details

Embroider the vein details on the grasshopper's wings using a lighter shade of green to backstitch. Stitch even horizontal lines across the belly with a darker thread.

variations

needle felt stegosaurus

see base design page 83

dinosaur mobile

Needle felt a stegosaurus, brontosaurus, and T-Rex (see pages 92 and 68). Follow the stegosaurus instructions for the bodies. To create a brontosaurus, roll a 10-cm (4-in) tube and needle felt together to make the neck. Roll and felt a small head to attach to the neck. Cover up seams with a layer of wool and felt in the eyes with black wool. To create the T-Rex, lengthen the legs by another inch, and roll and felt little 2.5-cm (1-in) arms. Felt about 2.5cm (1 in) for the neck and 4cm (1½ in) for the head to attach on top.

needle felt triceratops

Follow the stegosaurus instructions but omit the back scales. Cut a curved 4cm (1½-in) flap for the head out of a matching colour of felt and stitch to the base of the neck. Cut 2.5-cm (1-in) pointy horns out of white felt and sew to the top of the head.

crochet stegosaurus

Follow the first section of the crochet brontosaurus pattern on page 92 to make a stegosaurus. When you get to the neck, continue to dc in each st around to make the stegosaurus's head for about 7.5cm (3 in) Loop yarn through the stitches on the last row, and pull together to close. Make a knot to secure and hide the ends on the inside.

giant stegosaurus

Multiply all quantities and measurements by 10 to create a giant stegosaurus.

dinosaur eggs

Needle felt seven 25-cm (10-in) dinosaur eggs. Make one end smaller and more pointed than the other. Add different-sized spots all over the eggs.

variations

crochet dragonfly

see base design page 84

shadowbox specimen

Make three dragonflies to place into a shadowbox or picture frame. Cut a sheet of corkboard or foamcore to fit inside your frame. Cover with a neutral fabric and secure with glue on the back. Once it's dry, insert it into the frame and use dressmaking pins to pin your dragonflies inside.

dragonfly mobile

Crochet five dragonflies with different wing colours, and string to dowels for a mobile (as for the 'fabric birds mobile' on page 39).

butterfly

Crochet the body following the dragonfly body, but stop after crocheting 7.5cm (3 in). Stuff and sew closed. For the wings dc two rows, each 10cm (4 in) long. Make three more wings, fold in half, and sew to the centre of the body. Make two antennae out of black felt and sew to the head.

dragonfly hairclip

Scale the dragonfly down by 50 percent to make it small enough for a hairclip. Sew to the hairclip, or use a strong adhesive to bond.

dragonfly magnets

Crochet a set of dragonflies with different-coloured wings, and use them to decorate magnets. Use 1.25-cm (1/2-in) round strong magnets and cut a circle of felt to sew over each onto the back of the body.

variations

crochet octopus

see base design page 87

sewn squid

Cut two sheets of felt 20cm (8 in) long and 10cm (4 in) wide and tapered to a point at the end. Sew these two pieces together and stuff before closing. Crochet eight 20-cm (8-in)-long tentacles and stitch to the base of the squid. Sew black eyes onto either side of the mid-section.

jellyfish

Crochet half of the octopus body to make a jellyfish body using pink yarn, so that you have a half-dome shell. Make a mix of straight chainstitch tentacles, and curled tentacles following the pattern for the crochet pig's tail (see page 88). Sew tentacles to the inside centre of the body dome.

coral

Follow the instructions for the tentacles to make a cluster of coral. Use red yarn and make multiple lengths of coral. Stitch together at the base and sew some pieces extending off longer pieces.

suction cups

Cut 0.5-cm (¼-in)-diameter circles in orange felt and stitch onto the inside of each tentacle to make suction cup details.

octopus rattle

Add a rattle inside the octopus's head before closing up. Add crinkly plastic inside the tentacles for a different sound effect.

variations

crochet pig

see base design page 88

kissing pigs

Insert a strong magnet inside the pig's snout before closing up. Knit another pig and add a magnet inside its snout too. You'll have a pair of kissing pigs!

crochet lamb (pictured)

Following the pig instructions, use white yarn for the body and change to black yarn at the end of row 17. Crochet the ears in black yarn and attach to the head with the ears pointed down. Crochet another black ear and stitch in the back for the tail. Crochet the feet with black yarn and sew to the body. With white wool roving, needle felt tufts of white wool all over the body, to give your lamb a fluffy fleece.

crochet cow

Use the pig pattern but crochet with white yarn for the body and legs. Use pink yarn for the nose, and black yarn for the ears. Cut black spots out of felt to sew randomly onto your cow.

three little pigs

Crochet three pigs following the base design, and make three houses out of stiff felt – yellow for the straw house, brown for the stick house, red for the brick house. Cut four 30-cm (12-in) squares for each house, and four 35.5-cm (14-in)-square roofs (these will be flat). Use fabric glue to add felt straw, stick, and brick details to each house along with windows and doors. Don't sew the straw or stick house together – they'll lean together and be 'blown' down. Sew the sides and roof of the brick house together to make it sturdy!

needle felt piglet

Use pink wool and follow the main body instructions for the stegosaurus pattern on page 83 to make a piglet. Roll and felt a 2.5-cm (1-in) round head and attach to the body. Felt the legs in the same way as the stegosaurus, and roll and felt a tiny 1.25-cm (½-in) tail. Roll a bit of wool between your fingers and shape with a felting needle to make the ears. Felt two black eyes and two small circles for the snout.

variations

knitted caterpillar

see base design page 91

bookworm

Embroider round black glasses around the eyes to turn your caterpillar into a smart little bookworm.

convertible butterfly

Sew a medium-sized button on the centre back of the caterpillar and cut two 3 x 10-cm (4-in) felt wings. Snip a buttonhole on each wing to button to the centre back of the caterpillar to convert it into a butterfly.

knitted earthworm

Follow the caterpillar pattern but use brown yarn. Work rows 1–7 in st st, rows 8–13 in reverse st st, and keep alternating every six rows between st st, and reverse st st to the end.

needle felt slug

Use green wool roving and follow the 'needle felt stegosaurus' instructions on page 83 to create the body. Wrap more wool around the tail and head ends and felt so that everything tapers smoothly. Cut two 2.5-cm (1-in) antennae out of felt and sew onto the head.

knitted snake

Begin by working rows 1–4 of the caterpillar pattern with green yarn and continue working in st st across 18 sts until you reach 63.5cm (25 in) Follow instructions to decrease rows 7–10. Cut a 7.5-cm (3-in) snake tongue out of red felt, cut a 'V' in the centre, and sew onto the mouth.

variations

crochet brontosaurus

see base design page 92

loch ness monster

Crochet the brontosaurus, but omit the legs. Cut four 10-cm (4-in) leaf-shaped fins out of felt and stitch on details. Sew onto the body.

wheelie brontosaurus

Push two 10-cm (4-in) wooden dowels through the body where the legs would normally be. Slide four wooden wheels onto the dowels and secure them in place to make your brontosaurus mobile.

roaring brontosaurus

Add a prerecorded sound chip, or record your best brontosaurus impersonation onto a sound chip, and insert it into the dinosaur's belly before stitching closed.

party brontosaurus

Stitch a mini felt bow tie on the neck just under the head, and make a cone-shaped party hat with felt and elastic cord for the head. Add polka dots or felt pom poms to the hat for embellishment. Your brontosaurus is ready to party!

dinosaur habitat

Make a 50 x 50-cm (20 x 20-in) dinosaur play mat habitat for your dinosaurs to live in, using felt. Cut an amorphous 20 x 25-cm (8 x10-in) blue watering hole, and an 20 x 20cm (8 x 8-in) volcano. Add strips of felt grass sticking up, and felt palm trees supported with dowels on the inside.

variations

knitted duck

see base design page 94

duck on wheels

Push two 7.5-cm (3-in) wooden dowels through the bottom front and back of the duck. Attach wooden wheels. Tie a string to the duck's neck so it can be pulled along.

ducklings

Knit three little ducks and string them together with yarn to make a line of little ducklings to pull along with your duck on wheels.

knitted goose

To make a goose, follow the knit duck instructions. For the body, use light brown yarn, and use black yarn for the head, and black wool for the beak. To make the neck CO 8 sts with black yarn and work in st st for 4cm (1½ in) Stitch the sides closed to form a tube for the neck. Sew onto the body, stuff, and sew the head on top.

duckie washcloth

Follow the duck pattern for the head and use a cotton yarn. Knit a beak by casting on 3 sts with orange yarn and knitting 8 rows in st st. Fold the beak in half lengthwise, stitch the sides together, and stitch onto the face. Knit a 12.5-cm (5-in)-square washcloth in garter st, and sew the duck's head to a corner.

beanbag ducks

Knit five ducks and fill the bodies with dried beans before closing up. They'll make a great set of beanbags for a tossing game.

play food

The food in this chapter are the exception to the rule when playing with your food! It includes the essential fruits and vegetables, along with savoury and sweet treats. Great additions to tea parties or teddy bear's picnics.

knitted apple

see variations page 127

materials

- yarn: Brown Sheep Shepherd's Shades (100% wool, 100g (3½ oz), 120m (131 yds)), 1 skein of Fire
- wool felt in chocolate brown and olive green
- 6 mm (US size 10) dpns
- stitch marker
- stuffing
- dried beans
- tapestry needle
- sewing needle
- embroidery thread in brown and green

tension: 4½ sts over 6 rows = 2.5cm (1 in)
finished dimensions: 6.5cm (2¾ in) diameter, 9cm (3½ in) high

instructions

apple

CO 8 sts, place marker, and join in the round.
Rnd 1 and all odd rows: k.
Rnd 2: [k1, m1] rep to end – 16 sts.
Rnd 4: [k2, m1] rep to end – 24 sts.
Rnd 6: [k3, m1] rep to end – 32 sts.
Rnds 7–11: k.
Rnd 12: [k6, k2tog] rep to end – 28 sts.
Rnd 14: [k5, k2tog] rep to end – 24 sts.
Rnd 16: [k4, k2tog] rep to end – 20 sts. Begin to stuff and continue stuffing to end.
Rnd 18: [k3, k2tog] rep to end – 16 sts.
Rnd 20: [k2, k2tog] rep to end – 12 sts.
Rnd 21: [k1, k2tog] rep to end – 8 sts.
Add beans for weight just before closing off. Break yarn, leaving enough to pull through from the bottom to the top of the apple. Thread yarn onto tapestry needle and pull so the bottom cinches in a little and then loop through the top, and back to the bottom, so that both ends cinch. Secure at the bottom of the apple.

stem

Cut a strip of brown wool felt 4cm (1½ in) long and 1.5 cm (⅝ in) wide. Fold in half lengthways and stitch together and onto the top of the apple.

leaves

Trace and cut two leaves out of green felt. Make a running stitch down the middle of each leaf with a darker green thread. Sew to the stem base.

Enlarge to 200% to make to actual size.

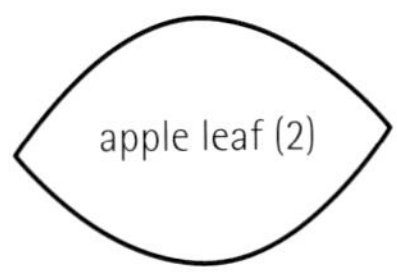

sewn banana

see variations page 128

materials

- yarn: Brown Sheep Cotton Fleece (80% cotton, 20% merino wool, 100g (3½ oz), 196m (215 yds)), 1 skein Truffle
- fabric: Robert Kaufman Kona Cotton (100% cotton), 25cm (¼ yd) of Buttercup
- tracing paper
- dressmaking pins
- sewing needle
- sewing thread in yellow and brown
- sewing machine (optional)
- stuffing
- 4 mm (US size G/6) crochet hook

finished dimensions:
21.5cm (8½ in) long, 4.5cm (1¾ in) wide, 5cm (2 in) high

instructions

banana

Trace all the pattern pieces onto cotton fabric and cut out. Pin one edge at a time with the right sides together and sew. It helps to pin both ends of the banana together first, then the middle, to line up the curved edges evenly.

Once you have finished sewing all the edges, cut little 'V's along the seam edge, being careful not to cut too close to your sewing. This will help to smooth out the curves and keep the seams from bunching up once you turn the banana inside out. Turn the shape inside out and stuff, beginning at the bottom opening.

banana ends

Top: With Truffle yarn, make 6 dc in a magic ring, sl st to join, ch 1, and dc in next 6 sts. Break yarn, fasten off, and sew onto the tip of the banana.

Bottom: With Truffle yarn, make 6 dc in a magic ring, sl st.
Rnd 1: ch 1 [2 dc in next st] rep 5 more times, sl st, turn – 12 sts.
Rnds 2–4: ch 1, dc in next 12 sts, sl st.
Break yarn, fasten off, and weave in ends. Sew with sewing thread onto the end of the banana.

Enlarge to 480% to make to actual size.

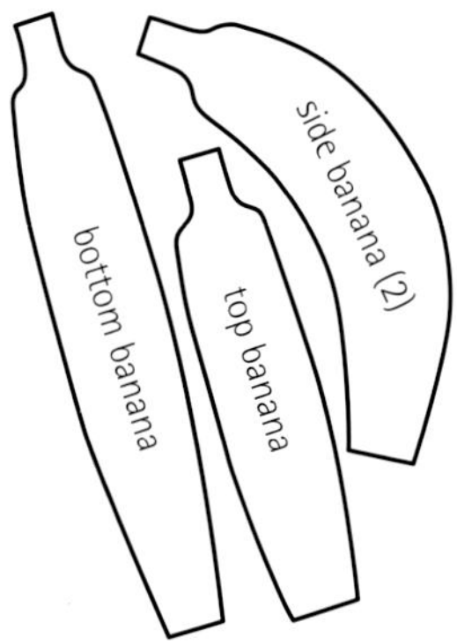

crochet carrot

see variations page 129

materials

- yarn: Brown Sheep Lamb's Pride Worsted (85% wool, 15% mohair, 100g (4 oz), 175m (190 yds), 1 skein Autumn Harvest
- wool felt, olive green
- 5 mm (US size H/8) crochet hook
- stuffing
- tapestry needle
- tracing paper
- sewing needle
- embroidery thread in olive green

tension: 4½ sts over 5 rows = 2.5cm (1 in)
finished dimensions: 16.5cm (6½ in) tall, 4.5cm (1¾ in) wide

Enlarge to 120% to make to actual size.

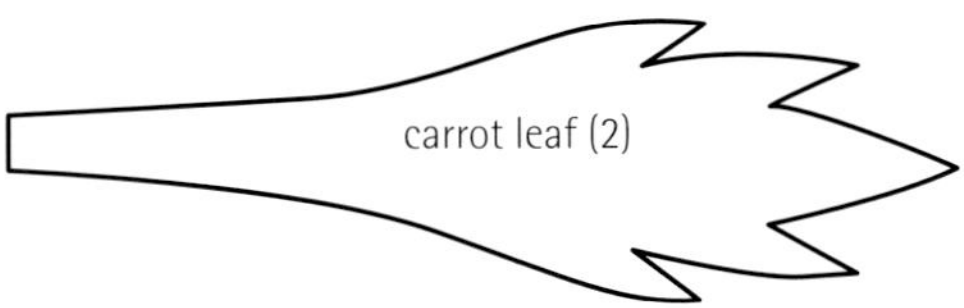

instructions

Ch 6 and sl st in first dc to join in a ring. For this pattern, dc in the front loop only.
Rnd 1: dc in next 6 ch, sl st in first dc to join.
Rnd 2: ch 1, 2 dc in ea st across, sl st in first dc to join – 12 dc.
Rnd 3: [1 dc, 2 dc in next st] 6 times, sl st in first dc to join – 18 dc.
Rnd 4: [2 dc, 2 dc in next st] 6 times, sl st in first dc to join – 24 dc.
Rnds 5–20: ch 1, dc in next 24 sts, sl st in first dc to join. Begin to stuff and continue stuffing to end.
Rnd 21: dc in next 11 sts, sk 1, dc in next 11 sts, sk 1, sl st – 22 dc.
Rnd 22: dc in next 10 sts, sk 1, dc in next 10 sts, sk 1, sl st – 20 dc.
Rnd 23: dc in next 9 sts, sk 1, dc in next 9 sts, sk 1, sl st – 18 dc.
Rnd 24: dc in next 8 sts, sk 1, dc in next 8 sts, sk 1, sl st – 16 dc.
Rnd 25: dc in next 7 sts, sk 1, dc in next 7 sts, sk 1, sl st – 14 dc.
Rnd 26: dc in next 6 sts, sk 1, dc in next 6 sts, sk 1, sl st – 12 dc.
Rnd 27: dc in next 5 sts, sk 1, dc in next 5 sts, sk 1, sl st – 10 dc.
Rnd 28: dc in next 4 sts, sk 1, dc in next 4 sts, sk 1, sl st – 8 dc.
Rnd 29: dc in next 3 sts, sk 1, dc in next 3 sts, sk 1, sl st – 6 dc.

<u>leaves</u>
Trace and cut two leaves out of green felt and sew to the top of the carrot.

needle felt cauliflower

see variations page 130

materials

- wool roving, 15g (½ oz) in white
- size 38 felting needle
- felting foam pad
- felt in olive green

finished dimensions:
5-cm (2-in) diameter, 3cm (1¼ in) high

Enlarge to 130% to make to actual size.

instructions

Take enough white roving to roll into a 5–6-cm (2–2½-in) ball, tucking in the sides as you roll to keep a round shape. Make a fairly tight roll, and hold the ends together.

Place on the felting foam pad and hold the piece with your forefinger and thumb on either side, making sure they're clear of the felting area. Jab the middle of the ball, and continue jabbing all over the piece, turning it over and over. Felt the piece until it holds together, but is not super-tight. To make the florets, needle felt a small, imperfect circle on the cauliflower. Keep felting around the floret outline, moving your needle over the same outline until you see a definite 'line' or indent. Continue until you have made florets for the whole cauliflower.

Trace and cut the leaves out of felt. Turn the cauliflower upside down and lay the smaller piece on the base, then larger leaves on top. Needle felt all three pieces together around the base then, turning it right side up, felt the leaves in tighter to the cauliflower. Turn the leaves slightly to give an organic feel.

knitted cupcake

see variations page 131

materials

- yarn: Brown Sheep Nature Spun Worsted (100% wool, 100g (3½ oz), 224m (245 yds)), 1 skein each of (A) Impasse Yellow, (B) Natural; scrap lengths of sprinkle-coloured yarn
- 4 and 4.5 mm (US size 6 and 7) dpns
- stitch marker
- dried beans
- stuffing
- tapestry needle
- wool roving in red
- size 30 felting needle
- felting foam pad

tension (4.5 mm): 5 sts over 7 rows = 2.5cm (1 in)
tension (4 mm): 6 sts over 8 rows = 2.5cm (1 in) (slightly stretched)
finished dimensions: 6.5-cm (2¾-in) diameter, 6cm (2½ in) high

instructions

base

With A and 4.5 mm dpns, CO 8 sts, divide onto 3 dpns, place marker, and join in the round.
Rnd 1: k.
Rnd 2: k1f&b in each st to end – 16 sts.
Rnds 3–5: k.
Rnd 6: rep row 2 – 32 sts.
Rnds 7–16: change to 4 mm dpns and [k1, p1] rep to end.
Rnd 17: change to 4.5 mm dpns, and B and [k4, m1] rep 8 times – 40 sts.
Rnds 18–19: k.
Rnd 20: [k8, k2tog] rep to end – 36 sts.
Rnd 21: [k7, k2tog] rep to end – 32 sts.
Rnd 22: [k6, k2tog] rep to end – 28 sts.
Rnd 23: [k5, k2tog] rep to end – 24 sts.

Place beans in the base for weight, and begin to stuff. Continue stuffing to end.
Rnd 24: [k4, k2tog] rep to end – 20 sts.
Rnd 25: [k3, k2tog] rep to end – 16 sts.
Rnd 26: [k2, k2tog] rep to end – 12 sts.
Rnd 27: [k1, k2tog] rep to end – 8 sts.

Break yarn and pull through remaining 8 sts tight to close off. Make knots in lengths of sprinkle-coloured yarn, one at a time at the top where you just closed off, and make short stitches for sprinkles around the white icing. Hide the ends inside. Needle felt a red ball for the cherry and sew on the top, covering the sprinkle knots. Squish the cupcake into shape with the bottom tapering in and the junction of the yellow and white jutting out a bit.

sewn eggs & bacon

see variations page 132

materials

- yarn: Brown Sheep Nature Spun Worsted (100% wool, 100g (3½ oz), 224m (245 yds)), 1 skein each of (A) Natural, (B) Impasse Yellow
- felt in red and white
- tracing paper
- dressmaking pins
- 4 mm (US size G/6) crochet hook
- sewing thread in white
- sewing needle
- stuffing

finished dimensions
(bacon): 19cm (7½ in) long, 5cm (2 in) wide, 1.25cm (½-in) high
(egg): 10cm (4 in) long, 6.5cm (2¾ in) wide, 2cm (¾ in) high

instructions

bacon

Trace and cut the bacon out of red felt. With yarn A, ch about 21.5cm (8½ in), make two of these for the white bacon fat. Pin onto one of the felt bacon pieces, following the wavy pattern of the bacon fat. Sew down the middle of the chain to attach to the felt.

Pin the felt pieces with the right sides out, and sew together, leaving the bottom edge open. Lightly stuff, and sew closed. Repeat to make another piece of bacon.

eggs

Trace and cut the egg out of white felt.
With yarn B, make 6 dc in a magic ring.
Rnd 1: Sl st, ch 1, 2 dc in each st around – 12 dc.
Rnd 2: Sl st, ch 1, [1 dc, 2 dc in next st] 5 more times – 18 dc. Break yarn, fasten off, and weave in ends.

Pin yolk onto one of the white pieces and sew together. Pin both white felt pieces together with the right sides out, and sew together, leaving about 4cm (1½ in) open. Lightly stuff and sew closed. Repeat to make another sunny-side-up egg.

Enlarge to 450% to make to actual size.

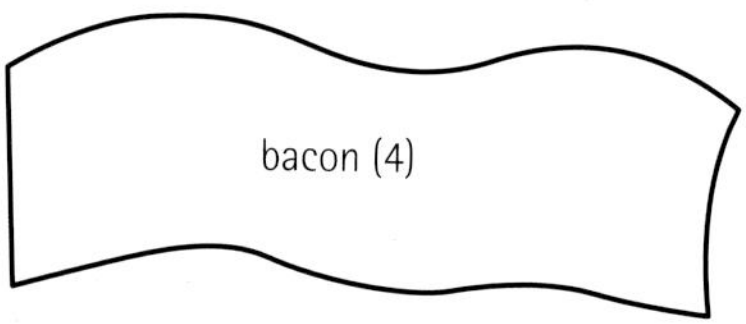

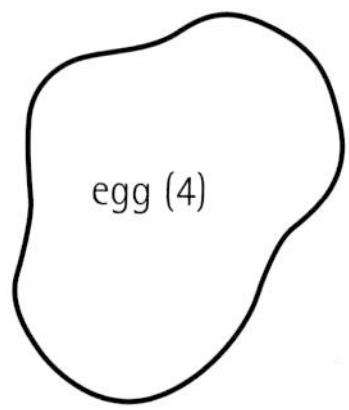

knitted sushi

see variations page 133

materials

- yarn: Brown Sheep Nature Spun Worsted (100% wool, 100g (3½ oz), 224m (245 yds)), 1 skein each in (A) Pepper, (B) Natural, (C) French Clay; Brown Sheep Shepherd's Shades (100% wool, 100g (3½ oz), 120m (131 yds)), 1 skein of (D) Sunshine
- wool felt in black
- 4.5 mm (US size 7) dpns
- stuffing
- tapestry needle
- 6.5 mm (US size 10.5) knitting needles
- sewing thread in black

tension (4.5 mm needles):
5 sts over 6 rows = 2.5cm (1 in)
tension (6.5 mm needles):
4 sts over 5 rows = 2.5cm (1 in)
finished dimensions
(salmon maki roll): 5-cm (2-in) diameter, 4cm (1½ in) high
(tamago nigiri): 9cm (3½ in) long, 5.5cm (2¼ in) wide, 4cm (1½ in) high

instructions

salmon maki roll

With 4.5 mm dpns and C, CO 6 sts, place marker, and join in the round.
Rnd 1: k.
Rnd 2: k1f&tb in each st to end – 12 sts.
Rnd 3: k.
Change to B.
Rnds 4–5: k.
Rnd 6: k1f&tb in each st to end – 24 sts. Change to A.
Rnds 7–18: k.
Rnds 19–20: change to B and k.
Rnd 21: k2tog to end – 12 sts. Begin to stuff and continue stuffing to end.
Rnd 22: change to C and k.
Rnd 23: k2tog to end – 6 sts.
Rnd 24: k. Break yarn and pull through all 6 sts closed. If the other salmon end is puffing out, pull yarn through the middle to that end, make a small loop, and pull back to the original end. Fasten off and hide ends inside.

tamago nigiri

With 4.5 mm needles and B, CO 12 sts and knit in st st for 18cm (7 in) BO and fold in half so that you have a 9 x 5-cm (3½ x 2-in) rectangle. Mattress stitch edges and stuff just before closing. Weave in ends. With 6.5 mm needles and D, CO 8 sts and knit in garter st for 7.5cm (3 in) BO, leaving a long enough tail to sew onto the rice. Cut a 2.5-cm (1-in) strip of black felt and wrap and sew around the centre of the sashimi.

crochet pizza

see variations page 134

materials

- yarn: Brown Sheep Nature Spun Worsted (100% wool, 100g (3½ oz), 224m (245 yds)), 1 skein each of (A) Saddle Tan, (B) Red Fox
- 4 mm (US size G/6) crochet hook
- tapestry needle
- felt in white and green
- embroidery thread in green
- sewing needle
- fabric glue

tension: 5 sts over 6 rows = 2.5cm (1 in)
finished dimensions: 18cm (7 in) crust length, 19.5cm (7 ¾ in) high, 1.25cm (½ in) wide

instructions

<u>pizza dough</u>

With A, ch 41.
R1–7: dc in second ch from the hook, dc in each st across, ch 1, turn – 40 dc.
R8–47: dc2tog, st in each dc across, ch 1, turn.
R48: dc2tog.
Break yarn, fasten off, and weave in ends.

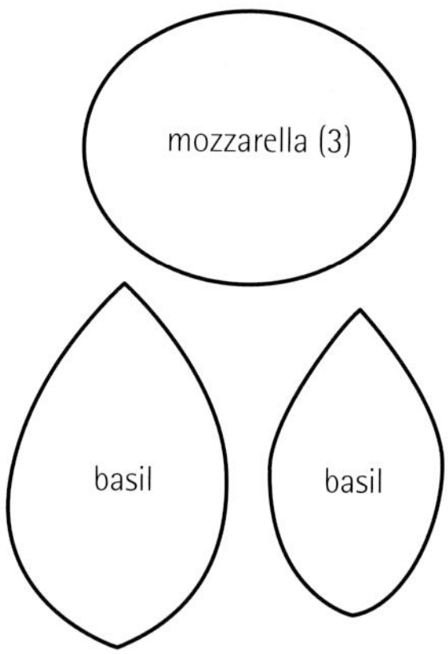

Enlarge to 200% to make to actual size.

<u>red sauce</u>

With B, ch 41.
R1: dc in second ch from the hook, dc in each st across, ch 1, turn – 40 dc.
R2–40: dc2tog, dc in each st across, ch 1, turn.
Break yarn and fasten off, leaving enough length to sew.
Block dough and sauce to lie flat.

<u>toppings</u>

Trace and cut out three slices of white oval mozzarella, and two basil leaves. Stitch leaf veins onto each basil leaf with matching thread.

<u>assembly</u>

Lay the sauce on top of the dough and baste around the triangles. Whip stitch together along the side edges with the red yarn. Fold the top tan section over the red sauce to make the pizza crust and stitch closed along the sides and straight along the crust with the tan yarn. Weave in ends. Finish by using fabric glue to attach the toppings to the red sauce piece.

crochet doughnut

see variations page 135

materials

- yarn: Brown Sheep Shepherd's Shades (100% wool, 100g (3½ oz), 120m (131 yds)), 1 skein each of (A) Chestnut, (B) Rose Petal
- 6 mm (US size J/10) hook
- tapestry needle
- pink and white yarn for sprinkles
- stuffing

tension: 4 sts over 4½ rows = 2.5cm (1 in)
finished dimensions: 9.5cm (3¾-in) diameter, 4cm (1½ in) high

instructions

With A, ch 21 and sl st in first dc to join, ch 1.

Rnd 1: begin 2nd from hook, dc in next 20 ch, sl st in first dc to join.

Rnd 2: ch 1, [dc in next st, 2 dc in next st] 10 times, sl st in first dc to join – 30 dc.

Rnd 3: ch 1, [dc in next 2 sts, 2 dc in next st] 10 times, sl st in first dc to join – 40 dc.

Rnds 4–8: ch 1, dc in next 40 sts, sl st in first dc to join.

Rnd 9: ch 1, dc in next 40 sts, sl st in first dc to join. Fasten off A, join B.

Rnds 10–13: ch 1, dc in next 40 sts, sl st in first dc to join.

Rnd 14: ch 1, [dc in next 2 sts, dc2tog] 10 times, sl st in first dc to join – 30 dc.

Rnd 15: ch 1 [dc in next st, dc2tog] 10 times, sl st in first dc to join – 20 dc.

Break yarn, leaving enough length to sew. With the tapestry needle, stitch pink and white sprinkles onto the pink icing and weave in ends. Sew edges together to form the doughnut ring, and stuff as you go. Continue stuffing until you close off.

variations

knitted apple

see base design page 111

needle felt orange (pictured)

Follow the instructions for the basic ball instructions for 'needle felt ball' on page 48. Use the apple's stem and leaf patterns and sew onto your orange.

knit pear

Use green yarn and follow the apple pattern up to and including row 15. Work 4 rows, then continue working rows 16–21. Cut and sew the stem and leaves onto the pear.

needle felt peach

Follow the 'needle felt ball' instructions on page 48 but use light to dark gradations of orange around the peach. Create the crease by needle felting backwards and forwards in a line. Taper the bottom in to a rounded point. Cut and sew the stem and leaves onto the peach.

scented apple

Insert some apple-scented potpourri in a small sachet into the centre of the fruit to make a wonderfully scented apple.

knit tomato

Use the knit apple pattern to make a tomato. Cut five thin 2.5-cm (1-in) green leaves out of felt and place them around and coming out of the stem (also made of green felt).

variations

sewn banana

see base design page 112

peeled banana

Resize the banana pattern so that it is 1.25cm (½-in) smaller all around. Trace the banana pattern and round out the top and bottom ends. Use a cream-coloured fabric and sew the banana fruit together, stuffing it before you close off. Trace and cut two of each of the banana pattern pieces to make the banana peel in yellow fabric. Sew each peel pair together and sew the four corners together halfway up the peel. Insert the banana.

banana split

Round out the top and bottom ends of the banana to make the inner fruit, and cut out two of each side panel. Sew and stuff these two sides separately to make a banana split. Crochet three scoops of ice cream – chocolate, strawberry, and vanilla – following the 'crochet octopus' body pattern on page 87. Cut blobs of 'hot chocolate' out of brown felt, and needle felt a red cherry on top.

banana zipped pouch

Sew a zipper to one of the top edges before sewing the other seams to make a banana zipped pouch. Cut out a few 4cm (1½-in) felt monkey outlines and embroider face details on each monkey. Make enough to fill the pouch.

bunch of bananas

Make five bananas with a strong magnet inserted into the top of each crocheted stem. They'll all hold together in a bunch at the top. Make sure the magnets are facing the right way so that the bananas connect together correctly.

alphabet wall chart

Use the curved side of the banana to make a 2-D appliqué for the letter B, for an alphabet wall chart. Make an apple for A, a carrot for C, and so on.

variations

crochet carrot

see base design page 115

crochet daikon (pictured)

With white yarn, follow the carrot pattern to make a daikon. Cut the leaf pattern out of felt and sew to the top of the daikon.

needle felt radish

With red wool roving, follow the 'needle felt ball' instructions on page 48 and felt a small 5-cm (2-in)-diameter radish. Shape the bottom into a point and wrap and felt white wool around the point. Cut a 7.5-cm (3-in) strand of white yarn and felt one end to the point to make the root of the radish. Use the carrot leaf pattern for the stalk.

crochet turnip

Follow the carrot pattern but omit rnds 7–20. Begin with a violet yarn, and change to white halfway through to create a turnip. Cut and sew a few felt leaves on top.

carrot for rabbit

Shorten the carrot by half its width and length to make a carrot for the sewn rabbit on page 67. Resize the leaves by 50 percent, and cut and sew to the carrot.

needle felt baby carrots

Use orange wool roving to make 5-cm (2-in) baby carrots. Roll the wool into a tube a little larger than the intended size and felt all around, rounding out the top and bottom. Felt one end smaller than the other, tapering it smoothly. Needle felt a bunch of baby carrots for a full bag.

variations

needle felt cauliflower

see base design page 116

needle felt broccoli

Follow the cauliflower pattern and use dark green wool to make the broccoli head. With a similar colour thread, make little French knots all around the broccoli for texture. Roll a 2.5-cm (1-in) tube of a lighter green wool and felt it into a stalk. Attach to the base of the broccoli head.

larger cauliflower

Increase all quantities and measures by four to make an actual-size cauliflower to add to your toy fruit and vegetable collection.

brussel sprouts

Needle felt an actual-size brussel sprout by making a felt ball the same size as the cauliflower, using bright green wool. Felt the leaf veins with a lighter green or yellow around the ball. Make a few sprouts for a bunch.

purple sprouting broccoli

Needle felt a more exotic purple sprouting broccoli. Add more texture detail by making little French knots sprinkled around the head using a matching purple thread.

bouquet of flowers

Make 8–10 little cauliflower heads and add wire or a pipe cleaner to the base to make a bouquet of flowers. Wrap the wire with olive green felt and use a dab of fabric glue at the ends to secure.

variations

knitted cupcake

see base design page 119

cheesecake cupcake

Follow the cupcake pattern up to the end of the ribbing and BO. Cut a matching yellow felt circle the diameter of the top of the cupcake and stuff and sew together. Needle felt three red cherries and sew to the cheesecake top.

blueberry muffin

Follow the cupcake pattern but use light brown yarn. Cut 0.5-cm (¼-in) circles out of dark blue felt and sew blueberries randomly around the muffin. Add some white stitches over the top of the muffin to represent sugar sprinkles.

cream puff

Use beige and white wool roving to needle felt a fluffy cream puff. Form a ball and shape the top into a tip. Wrap white wool around the middle for the cream and needle felt in. Make small white stitches with thread around the top of the puff for sugar.

kiwi tart

Follow the cheesecake variation and use a light yellow yarn and felt. Cut four 4cm (1½-in) green kiwi slices of felt. With black thread, stitch the seed details around the centre of each kiwi slice. Lay the slices around the top of the tart and needle felt together.

chocolate cake

Cut two 15-cm (6-in)-diameter circles for the top and bottom, and a 10 x 50cm (4 x 20-in) piece for the middle section, out of brown felt. Sew these pieces together to form your cake. Needle felt frosting around the top edge of the cake. Cut 4cm (1½-in) flower petals out of pink felt; use about eight petals per flower and make three flowers. Cut 5-cm (2-in) green leaves to go with the flowers and sew together in a cluster on your cake.

variations

sewn eggs & bacon

see base design page 120

toast

Cut four 15-cm (6-in) squares out of beige felt and cut little divots near the top to indicate the loaf shape. Cut two 5-cm (2-in) square slices of butter out of yellow felt. Sew onto one side of each piece of toast. Sew and stuff two pieces of beige felt together to make two slices of toast with butter.

felt sausage

Cut four 1 x 10-cm (4-in) sausage links with rounded ends out of medium brown felt. Sew and stuff two pieces of felt together and make two breakfast sausage links.

knit orange juice

Using orange yarn, follow rows 1–6 of the 'knit cupcake' pattern on page 119. Work 10cm (4 in) in orange then change to white and continue for 2.5cm (1 in) Next rnd, k2tog to end. Work 3 rnds, next rnd k2tog to end, knit one rnd, BO, and weave in. Insert beans and stuffing before closing off.

crochet plate

With any colour yarn you'd like to use for your plate, ch 2. Rnd 1: make 6 dc in 2nd ch from hook, sl st to join. Rnd 2: ch 1, 2 dc in ea st around, sl st – 12 sts. Rnd 3: ch 1, [dc in next st, 2 dc in next st] around, sl st – 18 sts. Rnd 4: ch 1, [dc in next 2 sts, 2 dc in next st] around, sl st – 24 sts. Continue as stated – dc in next 3 sts, 4 sts, 5 sts, etc. for each row before making 2 dc in the next st. You'll increase by 6 sts each row to make a circle. Continue until you have a 30-cm (12-in)-diameter plate.

utensils

Cut two 4 x 18-cm (1½ x 7-in) pieces of grey felt to make a butter knife. Round off the tips and stitch a horizontal line midway to show the handle. Cut two 5 x 18-cm (2 x 7-in) pieces of grey felt to make a fork. Taper the fork head down to 4cm (1½ in) for the handle. Sew and stuff these pieces together to make utensils. Stitch the fork head details with white thread.

variations

knitted sushi

see base design page 123

hand rolls

Knit a cucumber maki roll by replacing the salmon yarn with light green. Create an inside-out California roll by following the salmon roll pattern but using white yarn the whole way through. Cut two each of 1.25-cm (½-in) squares in pink, light green, medium green, and yellow felt. Line one of each colour up to form a square and sew to the centre top and bottom of the California roll. Make small stitches around the outside of the roll to mimic black sesame seeds.

salmon nigiri sushi (pictured)

Follow the tamago pattern and use pink yarn in place of the yellow to create a salmon nigiri. Embroider lines diagonally across the salmon with white thread. Knit up a slice of tuna with a dark pink yarn and follow the tamago pattern to make a tuna nigiri.

temaki sushi

Cut a 15-cm (6-in) square out of black felt. Roll into a cone shape with one corner of the square pointing straight up at the back opening of the cone. Sew along the edge to hold the cone together. Cut two layers each of slices of cucumber, avocado, carrots and tamago out of felt. Sew both layers of each ingredient together and place in the nori cone. Fill up the cone and make a few stitches with black thread to hold everything in place.

felt chopsticks

Cut four 1.25 x 25-cm (½ x10-in) chopstick pieces out of felt. Topstitch two pieces together and make a pair of chopsticks. Insert wire and wrap ends before closing off.

wasabi & pickled ginger

To make a dollop of wasabi, use green yarn and ch 10. Turn and begin 2nd from hook, and 2 dc in each st across. You'll have curly green wasabi. For the pickled ginger, cut 4cm (1½-in) ovals out of pink felt. Pile five or more together, bunch up a little, and make a few small stitches to hold them.

variations

crochet pizza

see base design page 124

pizza pie

Crochet eight slices of pizza to make a whole pizza. Use stiff white felt to make an 46-cm (18-in)-wide by 5-cm (2-in)-high pizza box. Hand stitch the edges together. Cut the word 'pizza' out of red felt and glue onto the lid.

felt toppings

Cut 5-cm (2-in)-diameter circles out of red felt to make pepperoni and glue onto the pizza. Cut 5-cm (2-in)-diameter mushrooms out of off-white felt and glue onto the pizza. Trace the oval mozzarella template on pink felt and cut out to make ham; yellow felt triangles can be added as pineapple to make a Hawaiian pizza.

cheese

Follow the pizza dough pattern and the red sauce pattern both using yellow yarn to create a triangular wedge of cheese. Cut black circles of varying sizes and glue them to the cheese – they are the holes. Pair with the knitted mouse from page 99 to make his day!

key lime pie

Follow the pizza dough pattern to make the pie crust, and use lime green yarn in place of the red sauce pattern to make the filling. Crochet two 5 x 40-cm (2 x 16-in.) rectangular side strips in lime green to create the height of the pie. Turn the crust up and sew the green triangle top and side strip together and stuff before closing off. Needle felt a dollop of white whipped cream to sew on top. Make a slice of lime garnish by cutting a a 5-cm (2-in)-diameter circle out of mint green felt. Embroider a dark green edge around the circle for the lime skin, and use white thread to make the lime texture.

variations

crochet doughnut

see base design page 126

powdered doughnut

Follow the doughnut pattern but use white yarn for the entire pattern. Make small stitches with white thread all around the doughnut for the powdered sugar texture.

chocolate long john doughnut

Cut two 7.5 x 18-cm (3 x 7-in) pieces out of felt; make the bottom one beige and the top one brown. Sew and stuff these two pieces together to make a chocolate long john doughnut.

brownie

Knit two 10 x 7.5-cm (4 x 3-in) rectangles, and a 4 x 35.5-cm (1½ x 14-in) strip using brown yarn. Sew these pieces together to make a brownie. Stitch caramel drizzle on the brownie top with a light brown yarn and tapestry needle.

chocolate chip cookie

Using beige felt, cut two 7.5-cm (3-in)-diameter circles. Cut 1.25-cm (½-in) chocolate chip circles out of dark brown felt. Needle felt the chocolate chips onto one beige circle. Sew and stuff the two beige circles together to make a chocolate chip cookie. Make a few more cookies to make a set.

macaroon

Needle felt 6-cm (2½-in)-diameter x 4cm (1½-in)-high macaroons out of pink wool roving. Wrap white wool around the centre to create the filling. Make multiple macaroons in green, brown, yellow, lavender, and blue.

poppy seed bagel (pictured)

Follow the doughnut pattern and use beige yarn for the entire pattern. Make small stitches with black thread all around the doughnut to create the poppy seeds.

dolls

Dolls make wonderful companions and great heroes or heroines. Whether you want to be a ballerina, or a pirate who sails the deep blue sea, these dolls will welcome you into their world of imagination.

felt face

see variations page 151

materials

- felt in dark tan, white, baby blue, black, red, brown, orange
- starched felt in dark tan
- tracing paper
- dressmaking pins
- sewing thread in colours to match dark tan felt
- sewing machine (optional)
- fabric glue

finished dimensions:
23.5cm (9¼ in) high,
18.5cm (7¼ in) wide

instructions

Transfer and cut the pattern pieces from the following colours of felt:
Tan: (2) heads, (1) starched felt, (1) nose
White: (2) woman's eyes, (2) man's eyes
Blue: (2) woman's irises, (2) man's irises
Black: (4) pupils (same for both sets of eyes), (1) mouth
Red: (1) woman's lips
Brown: (1) moustache, (1) man's hair
Orange: (1) woman's hair

pocket

Cut a 12 x 18-cm (5 x 7-in) pocket from tan felt and centre on a tan head piece. Topstitch 0.5cm (¼ in) from the edge, leaving the top 12-cm (5-in) edge open.

head

Sandwich the stiff felt in between the tan head pieces with the pocket on the outside, and topstitch together 0.5cm (¼ in) along the edge. If you don't have a sewing machine, you can hand-sew or use fabric glue to attach these pieces.

eyes

There are two sets of eyes – the rounder man's eyes, and the almond-shaped woman's eyes. Use a dab of fabric glue to stick the corresponding pupils and irises on top of each other. Use the back pocket to store all the pieces, and fold the hair to fit.

This project is a great way for toddlers to learn about facial features.

Enlarge to 900% to make to actual size.

sewn ballerina

see variations page 152

materials

- Fabric: Robert Kaufman Kona Cotton (100% cotton), 25cm ($\frac{1}{4}$ yd) of Bone; Cloud9 Fabrics Nursery Basic Speckles (100% organic cotton), 25cm ($\frac{1}{4}$ yd) of Sky
- tracing paper
- dressmaking pins
- tailor's chalk
- sewing thread to match fabrics
- sewing needle
- sewing machine (optional)
- embroidery thread in black, pink, cream, blue
- stuffing

finished dimensions:

19.5cm ($7\frac{3}{4}$ in) long,
5cm (2 in) wide,
29cm ($11\frac{1}{2}$ in) high

Enlarge to 430% to make to actual size.

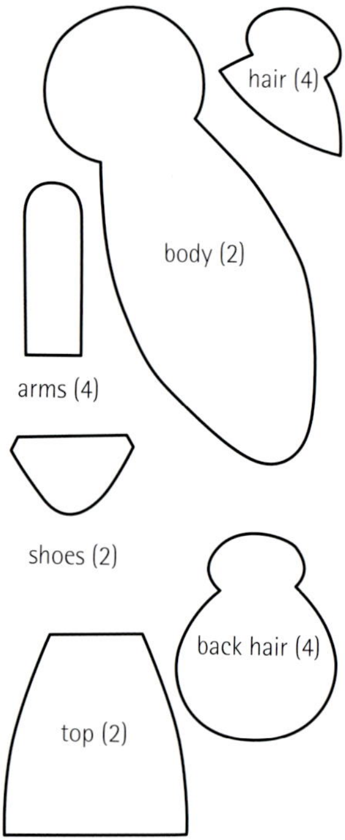

instructions

body

Trace and cut out ballerina pattern. Fold top and bottom edges of polka dot dress 1cm ($\frac{3}{8}$ in) to wrong side and press. Align and pin to body. Topstitch 0.5cm ($\frac{1}{4}$ in) from top and bottom. Align hair on the right side on front and back of the head. Pin and sew the hair only at the base of the head on back piece, and along the bangs on front piece. Fold top edge 1cm ($\frac{3}{8}$ in) to wrong side and press. Align ballet slippers with feet and pin. Topstitch top, 0.5cm ($\frac{1}{4}$ in) from edge.

Embroider eyes and mouth with double strands of black and pink embroidery thread. Backstitch line of the legs with cream embroidery thread from feet up to skirt line. Backstitch 'ribbon' ties of the ballet slippers in darker blue. Fold the arm in half with the right sides facing and sew along its length, leaving bottom edge open. Turn inside out and lightly stuff.

With ballerina right side up, angle arms slightly down. Place front of ballerina on top, right sides facing, and pin together. Machine or hand-sew around whole body, leaving a 7.5-cm (3-in) opening along the leg just under where the skirt will go. Turn inside out, stuff, then close off with invisible stitch. Tie and knot blue embroidery thread around base of hair bun and hide ends behind head.

tutu

Cut a 9.5 x 60-cm ($3\frac{3}{4}$ x 24-in) strip of polka dot fabric for tutu. Turn the top 60-cm (24-in) edge 0.5cm ($\frac{1}{4}$ in) to the wrong side and press. To hem, turn bottom 60-cm (24-in) edge 0.5cm ($\frac{1}{4}$ in) to the wrong side and press. Turn the edge again 1cm ($\frac{3}{8}$ in) to the wrong side and press. Turn skirt right side out and edge stitch the double folded hem with white thread. To make it ruffle, machine or hand baste 0.5cm ($\frac{1}{4}$ in) from the edge with white thread. Take one strand of thread (if machine basting) – the only thread (if hand basting) – and carefully pull and gather the fabric. Wrap around the waist and pull shorter or longer to fit. Pin and sew short edges together with seams inside to close tutu. The skirt will narrow, so squeeze the doll to pull skirt up. Pin and use running stitch with white thread around the waist and skirt over the seam to hide it.

crochet pirate

see variations page 153

materials

- yarn: Brown Sheep Nature Spun Worsted (100% wool, 100g (3½ oz), 224m (245 yds)), 1 skein each of (A) Pepper, (B) Natural, (C) Red Fox; Knit Picks Swish Superwash (100% Superwash wool, 100g (3½ oz), 100m (110 yds)), 1 skein of (D) Sand Dune; Brown Sheep Cotton Fleece (80% cotton, 20% merino wool, 100g (3½ oz), 196m (215 yds)), 1 skein of (E) Truffle
- 4 mm (US size G/6) crochet hook
- stuffing
- wool felt in black
- embroidery thread in black and light brown
- tapestry needle

tension: 5 sts over 6 rows = 2.5cm (1 in)

finished dimensions:
10cm (4 in) long, 5.5cm (2¼ in) wide, 23cm (9 in) high

instructions

body

With A, ch 2, 6 dc in 2nd ch from hook, sl st in first dc to join.

Rnd 1: ch 1, [2 dc in next st] x 6, sl st in first dc to join – 12 dc.

Rnd 2: ch 1, [1 dc, 2 dc in next st] x 6, sl st in first dc to join – 18 dc.

Rnd 3: ch 1, [2 dc, 2 dc in next st] x 6, sl st in first dc to join – 24 dc.

Rnd 4: ch 1, [3 dc, 2 dc in next st] x 6, sl st in first dc to join – 30 dc.

Rnds 5–9: ch 1, dc in next 30 sts, sl st in first dc to join.

Rnd 10: rep Rnd 9. Fasten off A, join B.

Rnd 11: ch 1, dc in next 30 sts, sl st in first dc to join.

Rnd 12: rep Rnd 11. Fasten off B, join C.

Rnd 13: ch 1, dc in next 30 sts, sl st in first dc to join.

Alternate between white and red every two rows until end of rnd 25.

Rnds 14–22: ch 1, dc in next 30 sts, sl st in first dc to join.

Rnd 23: ch 1, [3 dc, dc2tog] x 6, sl st in first dc to join – 24 dc. Stuff.

Rnd 24: ch 1, [2 dc, dc2tog] x 6, sl st in first dc to join – 18 dc.

Rnd 25: ch 1, [1 dc, dc2tog] x 6, sl st in first dc to join. Fasten off C, join D – 12 dc.

Rnd 26: ch 1, dc in next 12 sts, sl st in first dc to join.

Rnd 27: ch 1, [1 dc, 2 dc in next st] x 6, sl st in first dc to join – 18 dc.

Rnd 28: ch 1, [2 dc, 2 dc in next st] x 6, sl st in first dc to join – 24 dc.

Rnd 29: ch 1, [3 dc, 2 dc in next st] x 6, sl st in first dc to join – 30 dc.

Rnds 30–34: ch 1, dc in next 30 sts, sl st in first dc to join. Fasten off D, join C.

Rnd 35: ch 1, [3 dc, dc2tog] x 6, sl st in first dc to join – 24 dc.

Rnd 36: ch 1, [2 dc, dc2tog] x 6, sl st in first dc to join – 18 dc.

Sew an eye, cut out an eye patch 1.25-cm (½-in) square, and sew a moustache and mouth. Ch 15 in red yarn and tie to right side of bandana.

Rnd 37: ch 1, [1 dc, dc2tog] x 6, sl st in first dc to join – 12 dc.

Rnd 38: ch 1, dc2tog across next 12 sts, sl st in first dc to join – 6 dc.

Rnd 39: rep row 38 – 3 dc. Break yarn, fasten off, and close.

arms

With D, ch 2, 6 dc in 2nd ch from hook, sl st in first dc to join.

Rnd 1: ch 1, [1 dc, 2 dc in next st] x 3, sl st in first dc to join – 9 dc.

Rnd 2: ch 1, [2 dc, 2 dc in next st] x 3, sl st in first dc to join – 12 dc.

Rnd 3: ch 1, dc in next 12 dc, sl st in first dc to join.

Rnd 4: rep Rnd 3. Fasten off D, join C.

Rnd 5: ch 1, dc in next 12 dc, sl st in first dc to join.

Rnd 6: rep Rnd 5. Fasten off C, join B.

Rnd 7: rep Rnd 5.

Alternate white and red every two rows until end of R16.

Rnds 8–16: ch 1, dc in next 12 dc, sl st in first dc to join. Break yarn leaving enough to sew. Stuff. Sew arm flat to shoulder at the red stripe. Repeat for other arm.

legs

With A, ch 2, 6 dc in 2nd ch from hook, sl st in first dc to join.

Rnd 1: ch 1, [1 dc, 2 dc in next st] x 3, sl st in first dc to join – 9 dc.

Rnd 2: ch 1, [2 dc, 2 dc in next st] x 3, sl st in first dc to join – 12 dc.

Dc in next 12 sts for 9cm (3½ in) Break yarn, leaving a tail long enough to sew with. Stuff, and make another leg, starting with colour E for the peg, and work for 4cm (1½ in) Make a few 'wood splint' stitches on the peg with a lighter brown thread. Change to A until you reach 9.5cm (3¾ in) Flatten top edge and line legs up with arms. Whip stitch together, weave in ends.

sewn robot

see variations page 154

materials

- fabric: Robert Kaufman Kona Cotton (100% cotton), 25cm (¼ yd) of Medium Grey
- wool felt in red, 4cm (1½ in) square
- ruler
- tailor's chalk
- sewing needle
- embroidery thread in yellow and black
- dressmaking pins
- sewing thread in grey
- stuffing
- 2 x 1.25-cm (½-in) black plastic eyes
- fabric glue

finished dimensions:

28cm (11 in) long, 4cm (1½ in) wide, 30cm (12 in) high

instructions

Using a ruler and tailor's chalk, draw and cut out the following pieces out of fabric: head (2), 12cm (5 in) square; body (2), 15cm (6 in) square; arms and legs (8) 6 x 9.5cm (2½ x 3¾ in)

Fold and cut a heart shape out of the red felt, approximately 4cm (1½ in) square.

With yellow embroidery thread, backstitch 3cm (1¼ in) from the arm edge and chainstitch starting 4cm (1½ in) from the arm edge, as shown. Do this for both arms.

Pin two arm pieces together with the wrong side facing you, and sew three sides of the arm with a 0.5-cm (¼-in) inseam, leaving one 6-cm (2½-in) edge open. Repeat for the other arm and both legs. Turn inside out and use the needle to push the corners out. Stuff lightly.

Pin and sew three sides of the head together with a 0.5-cm (¼-in) inseam and turn inside out. To mark the eyes, measure 6cm (2½ in) down from the top of the head, and draw a line with fabric chalk 2.5–3cm (1–1¼ in) from the left and right edges. Insert the eyes. Draw a mouth 5cm (2 in) from the sides and 5cm (2 in) up from the bottom edge with tailor's chalk and backstitch a smile with black embroidery thread. Stuff the head.

The appendages are added inside the body and then turned right side out. Lay the head on one of the body pieces with the face down and line up the open edge with the top of the body, centreing it with 1.25-cm (½-in) on either side of the head. Pin in place, lay the other body piece on top, pin all the pieces together, and sew with a 0.5-cm (¼-in) inseam.

Lay the right arm on the inside of the body with the embroidery close to the body edge, and at the top corner right next to the head. Pin and sew with a 0.5-cm ($^1/_4$-in) inseam down the right side of the body. Line up the legs on the inside bottom corners of the body. Pin the left leg 0.5cm ($^1/_4$ in) from the left corner. Sew the bottom edge with a 0.5-cm ($^1/_4$-in) inseam. Pin and sew the left arm at the top left corner by the head with a 0.5-cm ($^1/_4$-in) seam, and leave a 6-cm ($2^1/_2$-in) opening on the left side of the body.

Turn right side out, stuff the body, and sew closed with an invisible seam. Use fabric glue to glue the heart at the top right-hand corner.

materials

- yarn: Brown Sheep Nature Spun Worsted (100% wool, 100g (3½ oz), 224m (245 yds)), 1 skein each of (A) Elf Green, (B) Saddle Tan; Lion Brand Cotton Bamboo (52% cotton, 48% bamboo, 100g (3½ oz), 224m (245 yds)) 1 skein of (C) Persimmon; Brown Sheep Shepherd's Shades (100% wool, 100g (3½ oz), 120m (131 yds)), 1 skein of (D) Chestnut
- 4 mm and 4.5 mm (US size 6 and 7) dpns
- stitch marker
- tapestry needle
- 4 mm (US size G/6) crochet hook
- stuffing
- embroidery thread in black and pink
- size 38 felting needle
- fabric glue

tension: 6 sts over 7½ rows = 2.5cm (1 in)

finished dimensions: 5cm (2 in) long, 3cm (1¼ in) wide, 19cm (7½ in) high

knitted mermaid

see variations page 155

instructions

body

With 4.5 mm dpns and A, CO 8 sts divide onto 3 dpns, place marker, and join in the round.

Rnd 1 and all odd rows until row 11: k.

Rnd 2: k4, m1, k4, m1 – 10 sts.

Rnd 4: k5, m1, k5, m1 – 12 sts.

Rnd 6: k6, m1, k6, m1 – 14 sts.

Rnd 8: k7, m1, k7, m1 – 16 sts.

Rnd 10: k8, m1, k8, m1 – 18 sts.

Rnd 12: k9, m1, k9, m1 – 20 sts.

Rnds 13–24: k.

Rnds 25–26: p.

Change to B.

Rnds 27–39: k.

Begin to stuff and continue stuffing to end.

Rnd 40: [k2, k2tog] 5 times – 15 sts.

Rnd 41 and all odd rows until row 45: k.

Rnd 42: [k1, k2tog] 5 times – 10 sts.

Rnd 44: [k2, m1] 5 times – 15 sts.

Rnd 46: [k3, m1] 5 times – 20 sts.

Rnds 47–52: k.

Rnd 53: [k2, k2tog] 5 times – 15 sts.

Rnd 54: [k1, k2tog] 5 times – 10 sts.

Rnd 55: k2tog to end – 5 sts.

Break yarn and pull through all 5 sts. Weave in ends.

fins

With A and crochet hook, ch 10, begin 2nd ch from hook.

Rnd 1: dc in next 9 sts, ch 1, turn.

Rnd 2: begin 2nd st from hook. 2 dc, [ch 2, 1 htr] three times, 3 dc, sl st.

Break yarn and fasten off.

arms

With B and 4.5 mm dpns, CO 6 sts. Knit in I-cord for 7.5cm (3 in) Break yarn with enough to sew. Make another arm and sew to the shoulders of the body. Weave in ends.

shells

With C and 4 mm needles, CO 5 sts and knit for 4.5cm (1¾ in)

face

Stitch on eyes and mouth as shown with black and pink embroidery thread.

hair

Cut 7 yds of D for the hair. Fold the hair over and over until it measures approximately 23cm (9 in) Bunch it up and make a knot with the same yarn 10cm (4 in) down the length. This will be the side-part hairline. Tie the hair to the head with yarn and hide the ends in the head. Spread the hair out over the head and hold together around the neck. Needle felt the knotted 'hairline' to hold the hair in place. Use fabric glue to secure the hair.

alice in wonderland & white rabbit doll

see variations page 156

materials

- fabric: Robert Kaufman Kona Cotton (100% cotton), 25cm (1/4 yd) each of Tomato, Buttercup, White, Bone; P&B Textiles Spectrum Solids (100% cotton), 25cm (1/4 yd) of Blueberry
- felt in white and black
- tracing paper
- dressmaking pins
- tailor's chalk
- sewing thread to match all fabrics
- sewing needle
- sewing machine (optional)
- embroidery thread in light pink, black, and bright yellow
- blue ribbon
- 2 white/pearl buttons
- fabric glue
- stuffing

finished dimensions:
6cm (2½ in) wide, 28cm (11 in) high

instructions

Trace and cut out the pattern from the following fabrics.
Alice: head – one side Buttercup, one side Bone; hair – Buttercup; dress (top and two skirt pieces) – Blueberry; apron – White.
White Rabbit: both head pieces and both sides of two ears – White; clothes – Tomato; pocketwatch – 2.5-cm (1-in) circle of white felt; eyes – black felt.

alice

Hair: Press all inner three edges of front hair cutout 0.5cm (1/4 in) to the wrong side. Snip the corners of the fringe a bit to help press in, and sew along the edge. Align with the head cutout, and sew together along inner hairline 1.25-cm (1/2-in) from the edge.
Face: Use tailor's chalk to draw U-shaped eyes, eyelashes, and a mouth onto the face. Embroider the mouth in pink thread, and the eyes in black thread. Tie a small bow with the blue ribbon and sew it to the left corner of Alice's hair. Top dress: Press the top blueberry dress edge 0.5cm (1/4 in) to the wrong side and align this piece with the bottom edge of the head, overlapping the bottom edge of the hair. Sew a straight line on the top edge only. Sew two white buttons on the dress, lining them up below the mouth.
Apron: Press both sides and bottom edges of the apron 0.5cm (1/4 in) to the wrong side and sew along the edge. Set aside for Alice's skirt assembly.

white rabbit

Ears: Sew each set of ears with the right sides together, leaving the bottom edge open. Turn inside out.
Top shirt: Press the top tomato shirt edge 0.5cm (1/4 in) to the

wrong side and align this piece with the bottom edge of the head. Sew a straight line at the top of the shirt only. Repeat for the back.

Face: Glue the eyes onto the face, embroider a triangular pink nose, knot some whiskers, and embroider the mouth.

Pocket watch: Embroider clock hands onto the felt circle with black thread. Pin the watch on the middle right of the tomato skirt, and make a running stitch along the outer edge with yellow thread. Stitch a small square on the top left of the watch, and daisy chain stitch a curved chain to the top of the skirt.

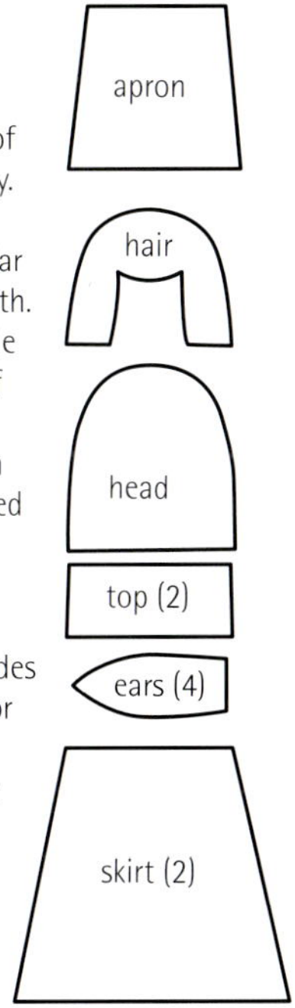

Enlarge to 760% to make to actual size.

assembly

Lay Alice and the White Rabbit's faces with the right sides together. Sew only the bottom straight edge. Repeat for the back head pieces. Flatten out these pieces. Place these pieces with the right sides together – Alice's face and head together, Rabbit's face and head together. Pin Rabbit's ears in between the Rabbit's head, aligned with the eyes, turned straight down, and pointing at the waist. Pin and sew around this oval, leaving a 7.5-cm (3-in) opening along one side. Turn inside out, stuff, and sew an invisible seam. Baste the white apron onto the top centre of the blueberry skirt. Sew the blueberry skirt sides with the right sides together, and do the same for the tomato skirt. Do not turn the skirts inside out yet. Pull the skirt on upside down over Alice's head with the narrower end and apron at her waist. Make a running stitch along the waist to sew the skirt and apron onto the body. Repeat on the other side for the Rabbit's red skirt. Pull the blue skirt down to line up with the red skirt. Press and pin both skirt edges together and sew along the bottom edge, so when you pull the skirt around for each doll, it will be one skirt and not two separate skirts. Enjoy two dolls in one!

fabric dollhouse

see variations page 157

materials

- medium-weight cotton, 25cm (1/4 yd) of teal
- 1 1/2 sheets of 30 x 46-cm (12 x 18-in) stiff felt
- dark brown tweed, 25cm (1/4 yd)
- felt in yellow, white, brown, black, orange
- tracing paper
- dressmaking pins
- tailor's chalk
- sewing machine (optional)
- sewing needle
- sewing thread in teal
- fabric glue
- 2 white buttons
- point turner

finished dimensions:

15cm (6 in) long,
15cm (6 in) wide,
24cm (9 1/2 in) high

instructions

Cut the following from stiff felt: Two each of the side house panels, two each of the chimney panels, two 12-cm (5-in) squares for the house, two 10 x 15-cm (4 x 6-in) rectangles for the roof, and one each of 9.5 x 2.5-cm (3 3/4 x 1-in) and 6.5 x 2.5-cm (2 3/4 x 1-in) pieces for the chimney.

house

Arrange the side house panels and house squares on top of two layers of the teal fabric as shown. Leave 0.25cm (1/8 in) between each edge surrounding the floor piece. Cut 1.25-cm (1/2-in) around the border. With the right sides together, lay the stiff felt in between the fabric. Pin and sew around the outside edges as close to the felt as possible. Leave an 20-cm (8-in) opening at the bottom centre edge. Remove the felt pieces, turn inside out, and reinsert the felt. Sew around the floor square and sew the open edge closed using invisible stitch. Fold and hand-sew the 12-cm (5-in) front and side panel edges of the house together.

roof

Lay the two felt roof pieces on two layers of the tweed with 0.25cm (1/8 in) between the 15-cm (6-in) edges. Cut 1.25-cm (1/2-in) around the border. Place the felt in between the fabric with the right sides together. Pin and sew around the border close to the felt, leaving one 6-in. opening. Remove the felt and turn the fabric inside out. Reinsert the felt, leaving 0.25cm (1/8 in) between the centre edges. Sew down the middle to make the crease of the roof, and invisible stitch the bottom opening closed. Hand-sew the roof onto the house with a 1.25-cm (1/2-in) overhang on all sides.

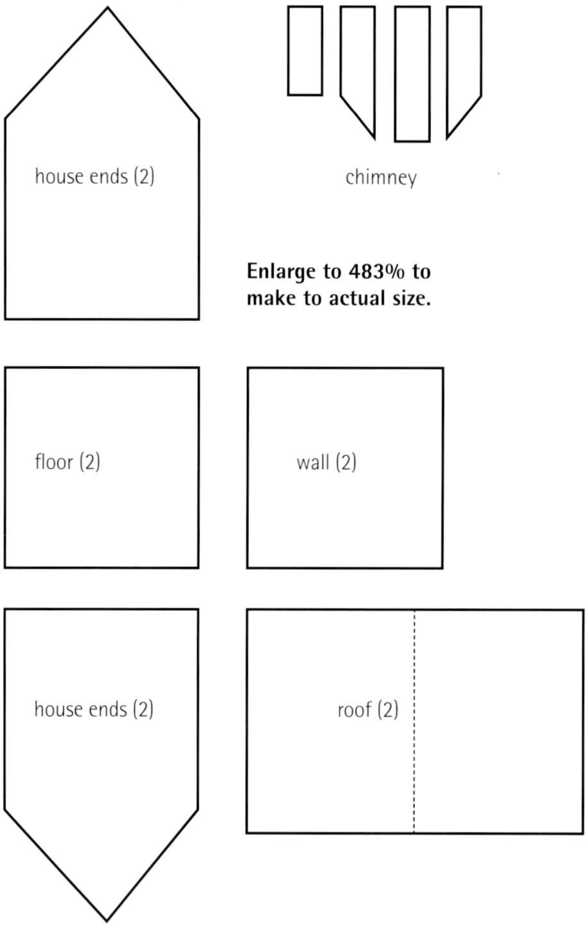

Enlarge to 483% to make to actual size.

chimney

Lay the chimney felt pieces on two layers of tweed fabric, leaving 0.25cm (1/8 in) between each felt piece. Cut 1.25-cm (1/2-in) around the border. Place the felt in between the fabric with the right sides together. Pin and sew close to the felt, leaving the right edge of the diagram open.

Remove the felt and turn the fabric inside out. Reinsert the felt and leave 0.25cm (1/8 in) between each piece. Sew down each 0.25-cm (1/8-in) space and hand-sew the open edge closed. Hand-sew the chimney closed and onto the roof.

details

Add felt door, window, and fireplace details to your house with fabric glue, and enjoy!

variations

felt face

see base design page 137

hook-and-loop fastener features

Cut two of each facial feature, stuff lightly, and sew together. Attach hook-and-loop fastener to the back of each piece and to where the eyes, nose, mouth, and hair will sit on the face.

additional features

Make bushy eyebrows with wool roving and needle felt to a small rectangle of felt. Cut ears out of beige felt and hand stitch the inner ear details with a slightly darker thread. Needle felt two small white balls to make 'pearl' earrings. Cut two 2.5-cm (1-in) pink circles out of felt for rosy cheeks.

puzzle shapes

Make a series of flat shapes to fit into a house puzzle. Cut two of each shape to sew together. Make a 10-cm (4-in) square for the main house, a 10-cm (4-in)-wide triangle for the roof, a 5 x 2.5-cm (2 x 1-in) door, two 2.5-cm (1-in) square windows, and a 5 x 2.5-cm (2 x 1-in) chimney.

memory game

Measure and cut 7.5-cm (3-in) felt squares – two for each card. Cut and sew triangles, squares, circles, and rectangles in different colours onto one side of each felt 'card+. Once you have your shapes all sewn, sew the matching square back onto each card along the edges.

bowler hat (pictured)

Cut a black bowler hat from felt that is the same width of the head and with a brim protruding 4cm (1½ in) from either side. Cut the hat 16cm (6¼ in) tall and round the top corners and brim. Needle felt a 4cm (1½-in)-tall strip of black felt at the base of the hat, and as wide as the hat.

felt ears

Cut two ears out of beige felt and hand stitch the inner ear details with a slightly darker thread. Needle felt two small white balls to make 'pearl' earrings.

variations

sewn ballerina

see base design page 138

paper doll

Make a flat ballerina doll (like a paper doll) out of felt, following the ballerina pattern. Sew the pieces to stiff felt. Make different-coloured felt dresses and tutus, shoes, and hair to interchange and lay over.

ballerina cat

Follow the ballerina pattern but omit the hair section. Cut 4cm (1½-in) triangles out of cream felt, and 2.5-cm (1-in) triangles out of light pink felt for the ears. Embroider a small triangular pink nose and white whiskers onto the face. Add a tail, and make the hands rounder, for paws.

spinning ballerina puppet

Resize the ballerina pattern to half size, and follow the instructions to make a smaller ballerina. Cut a 25-cm (10-in) length of yarn and attach to the top of the head, and the other end to a 7.5-cm (3-in) wooden dowel or ring. You can now make your ballerina spin and dance.

princess

Use yellow or orange felt for the hair, and make the tutu into a longer skirt that stops at the toes. Cut a 5-cm (2-in) tiara out of felt and sew onto the head. Embroider 'jewels' onto the crown using pink and red thread.

girl scout

Replace the felt hair with yarn. Cut a 40-cm (16-in) length of a bunch of yarn for the hair. Measure out 20cm (8 in), and sew at the 20-cm (8-in) mark to the top of the head at the centre hairline at the top front and back of the head. Pull the hair into pigtails on either side and tie together. Use green fabric for the skirt and white fabric for the blouse. Make white shoes and green knee-highs on the legs. Cut a 4 x 30-cm (1½ x 12-in) strip of green felt for the sash, and make little felt patches for badges. Sew the short edges together and sling over the girl scout's shoulder.

variations

crochet pirate

see base design page 140

hook hand

Cut a double layer of a 2.5-cm (1-in) long hook out of grey felt. Sew together with grey thread. Shorten one hand by omitting rows 3 and 4 of the arm pattern and change to C at the end of row 2. Sew the hook to the end of that hand.

treasure map (pictured)

Cut a 50 x 40-cm (20 x 15-in) piece of beige felt to make a treasure map. Stitch the outline of land and islands. Add cutout felt palm trees and pirate ships. Stitch dotted lines around the map for the search, and stitch a little treasure chest where X marks the spot!

superhero doll

Using the pirate pattern, swap out the shirt and pant colours for your superhero's outfit. Cut a 10-cm (4-in) square of felt to make the cape. Make a running stitch 1.25-cm (½-in) below the top edge and gather together. Sew the gathered edge to the back of the neck. Cut and sew a mask over the eyes and embroider two dots for the eyes.

mime doll

Use black yarn in place of the red to create a mime doll. Cut a 3-cm (1¼-in) white felt circle and sew to the face to make the white painted face. Stitch red lips and black vertical lines above and below the centre of the eyes. Use white yarn for the hands instead of the tan, and crochet both legs with black yarn.

ninja

Crochet the entire doll using black yarn. Cut a 2.5 x 1.25-cm (1 x ½-in) strip of beige felt for the eyes. Embroider eyes using black thread and sew onto the face. Chainstitch a 23 x 25-cm (9–10-in) black belt and tie to the waist.

variations

sewn robot

see base design page 142

3-D robot

To make your robot more boxy and 3-D, cut four 12.5-cm (5-in) squares for the head, four 15-cm (6-in) squares for the body, eight 6 x 9.5cm ($2^1/_2$ x $3^3/_4$-in) rectangles for the arms and legs, and four 6-cm ($2^1/_2$-in) squares for the ends of the arms and legs. Sew the squares and rectangles with their corresponding body parts to make them into 'blocks+. Stuff and hand-sew the appendages to the body.

astronaut (pictured)

Follow the robot pattern and use white felt in place of the grey fabric. Cut a 4-cm ($1^1/_2$-in)-high x 6-cm ($2^1/_2$-in)-wide rectangle using black felt for the helmet shade and needle felt onto the helmet. Cut four 1.25cm x 6-cm ($^1/_2$ x $2^1/_2$-in) red felt strips and needle felt to the cuffs and knees of the astronaut.

cyclops alien

Use green fabric and round out the corners of the robot pattern to make an alien. Cut out one 4 x 5-cm ($1^1/_2$ x 2-in) eye out of white felt, and an iris, out of black felt, to fit inside. Sew onto the centre of the face. Cut and sew 7.5 x 2cm (3 x $^3/_4$-in) antennae onto the head.

robot dog

With the same grey fabric as the robot, cut two 10 x 15-cm (4 x 6-in) rectangles for the body. Cut two 7.5 x 10-cm (3 x 4-in) rectangles for the head. Sew and stuff these pieces together and sew the head to the top right-hand corner of the body. Follow the robot's arms pattern to make four legs for your dog. Add a tail and eyes to the face.

female robot

Follow the robot pattern and cut the bottom half of the body to fan out into an 20-cm (8-in)-wide triangle skirt. Embroider eyelashes to the eyes and 1.25-cm ($^1/_2$-in)-diameter rosy circles on the cheeks.

variations

knitted mermaid

see base design page 145

merman

Follow the mermaid pattern but omit the shells. Cut the hair shorter and embroider chest muscle details with a slightly darker thread than the body yarn colour.

hawaiian hula dancer

Follow the mermaid pattern and begin at row 19 with yarn B. CO 20 sts and join in the round. Work the pattern from rnds 19–55, and work rnds 25 and 26. Knit two legs following the arm pattern. Flatten out your CO row and place the leg ends in between the edges and sew together. Make the hula skirt out of strands of the green yarn you used for the mermaid. Cut the grass skirt 5-7.5-cm (2–3 in) long and line up a thick layer of yarn for the skirt. Cut a 1.25-cm (½-in)-strip of green felt for the waistband. Wrap around the dancer and stitch to the waist. Follow the rest of the mermaid pattern, and make a lei for her neck out of felt flowers strung together, and a felt flower for her hair.

fairy

Follow the hula dancer variation to create a fairy doll. Knit the body in pink yarn up to the neck to make a pink dress. Use two shades of mixed pink yarn in place of the green grass skirt. Cut two 5-cm (2-in) wings out of white felt and sew to the back under the shoulder blades.

neptune

Create the Roman god of water and sea by adding a white beard, hair, and a trident. Cut the trident from two layers of yellow felt, and make it 15cm (6 in) long. Stitch the layers of felt together and embroider the line details with matching thread. Cut out a crown from felt and stitch to the top of the head.

seashell throne

Needle felt a clamshell throne for Neptune or the mermaid princess. Make each shell 10cm (4 in) wide and tall. Stitch the lines of the clamshell coming from the centre bottom, and fanning out to the edges. Felt the shells together so they sit open, as a seat.

variations

alice in wonderland & white rabbit doll

see base design page 146

goldilocks & the three bears

Follow the pattern for Alice to make Goldilocks and crochet curly hair by making a 10 chain and making 3 dc in ea st across for each lock of hair, and sew to the top of the head. Use brown fabric for the bear's face and cut rounded ears and sew in place of the rabbit ears. Embroider facial features. Cut two smaller ovals out of brown felt and make the faces and ears of two more bears and sew below the main face. Follow the rest of the doll instructions to assemble.

princess and prince

Follow the pattern for Alice for both sides of the doll. Use pink fabric for the princess's dress, and blue fabric for the prince's jacket (to rabbit pattern, but sew a row of buttons down the front). Give the prince shorter hair. Sew felt crowns to their heads.

little red riding hood & the wolf

Follow the instructions for Alice and the Rabbit, and use red fabric for Little Red. Use orange yarn in place of the yellow for the hair, and cut a triangle for her hood and sew to the back of her neck. Use grey fabric for the wolf. Shorten the rabbit ears to 4cm (1½ in) and sew on. Embroider the eyes, nose, and sharp teeth for the wolf, and use gingham for the wolf's skirt.

awake and asleep doll

Use the pattern for Alice for both ends of the doll. Embroider open eyes on one side, and closed eyes on the other. Use a small floral fabric on the sleeping doll to make a nightgown, and cinch and sew a matching nightcap for her head.

tortoise and hare

Cut an oval out of green felt for the tortoise's shell. Embroider the line details, lightly stuff, and sew to back. Use a lighter green for the front belly of the shell, medium green for the head, and solid green for the skirt. Follow the white rabbit pattern to make the hare, with brown fabric replacing white, and the red.

variations

fabric dollhouse

see base design page 148

cigar box doll bed

Measure the inside of a reclaimed cigar box or shoebox and cut two layers of fabric for a blanket to fit inside. Sew the blanket, right sides together, leaving the top end open. Turn right side out, turn the open edge in, and topstitch closed. Cut two layers of fabric the same width as the box and one-quarter of its length. Sew the pillow in the same manner as the blanket and stuff before sewing closed.

birdhouse

Follow the dollhouse instructions using a floral calico. Add another wall on the open side of the house and cut a 4cm (1½-in) hole in the centre of it. This wall will be a flap that swings open and closed. Hand-stitch the fabric edges around the hole and the left edge of the new wall to the left edge of the house. Sew a button to the middle right edge of the house, and make a loop on the right side of the new wall that it lines up with the button. Make a few birds from page 39 to live in your new birdhouse.

travel dollhouse case

To make the dollhouse a portable carrying case, add another wall flap the same size as the front of the house. Hand-sew the bottom edge of the wall flap to the bottom edge of the house. Sew a button at the top left- and right-hand corners of the house and make loops on the wall flap that line up and loop around the buttons. Make a handle on top of the house by cutting two 2.5 x 15-cm (1 x 6-in) brown felt strips and sewing them together around the edges. Pin the strip lengthwise 2.5cm (1 in) from the edges of the roof, and sew along the short edges to make the handle.

fairy dollhouse

Follow the dollhouse instructions and use a woodgrain fabric for the walls of the house. Add brown felt 1.25 x 2.5-cm (½ x 1-in) tiles to cover the roof, using fabric glue. Embroider vines and flowers organically around the outside walls of the house to make it more 'woodsy'.

costumes

Dress up in disguises and fool people with your new look, or don a crown to become a noble ruler in a faraway land. The costumes in this chapter will help you to become the character you are inside.

superhero cape

see variations page 178

materials

- fabric: P&B Spectrum Solids (100% cotton), 1m (1 yd) of Blueberry; Robert Kautman Kona Cotton (100% cotton), 25cm (1/4 yd) of Honey Dew
- sewing thread to match fabrics
- large safety pin
- neon-yellow 2-cm (3/4-in)-wide ribbon, 2 yds
- lightweight double-sided fusible interfacing
- tearaway stabiliser

finished dimensions:
67 x 74cm (26 1/4 x 29 in)

instructions

Cut the Blueberry fabric to a 112 x 76cm (44 x 30-in) rectangle. Hem both short edges with a 0.5-cm (1/4-in) hem. Hem the top long edge with a 3-cm (1 1/4-in) hem, leaving the sides open for the ribbon to pull through. Hem the bottom edge with a 4-cm (1 1/2-in) hem. Fasten the safety pin to the end of the ribbon and thread through the top edge. Cut the ribbon ends at an angle.

Trace the lightning bolt onto the liner paper that stays with the web of the fusible interfacing. Cut out the interfacing. Iron onto the wrong side of the Honey Dew fabric for just a few seconds. Cut the interfacing and fabric together along the traced line. Peel off the paper backing.

Lay the lightning bolt about 18cm (7 in) down from the neckline and centred at 56cm (22 in) from the sides, onto the back of the cape. Press for 10–20 seconds. Cut a piece of stabiliser bigger than the lightning bolt and iron onto the back of the bolt. Use yellow thread to sew a zigzag stitch about 0.25cm (1/8 in) wide, making the stitch length as short as possible. Sew along the edge of the lightning bolt. Tie the thread ends on the back of the cape and tear away the stabiliser.

Enlarge to 360% to make to actual size.

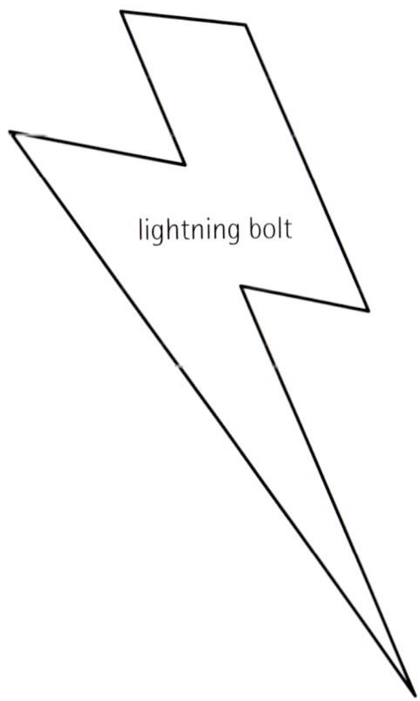

felt crown

see variations page 179

materials

- wool and rayon blend felt, 25cm (¼ yd) of yellow; 5-cm (2-in) square of turquoise
- 25cm (¼ yd) of interfacing
- tracing paper
- sewing thread to match felt
- 5-cm (2-in)-wide hook-and-loop fastener strip

finished dimensions:
9cm (3½ in) high, 58cm (23 in) wide (adjustable); fits 50–55-cm (20–22-in) head

instructions

The crown pattern shown is half of the full piece. Fold the yellow felt in half and place the crown pattern on top, lining up the right edge of the pattern with the folded crease of the felt. The fold will be the centre front of the crown. Cut two crown pieces and one crown piece from the sewn interfacing 0.5cm (¼ in) smaller all around. The interfacing will sit on the inside of the topstitched edge.

Trace and cut the oval jewel out of the turquoise felt. Baste to the centre front of the crown and blanket stitch together using turquoise thread.

Lay the cut interfacing between the two layers of the felt crown and baste around the edges. Topstitch 0.5cm (¼ in) all around the edge of the crown.

Cut a 5-cm (2-in)-square strip of hook-and-loop fastener and sew one side to the back right-hand end of the crown. Flip the crown over, and sew the other side of the hook-and-loop fastener to the other end. Sew an 'X' from corner to corner of both pieces of fastener to fix them firmly to the felt.

Enlarge to 720% to make to actual size.

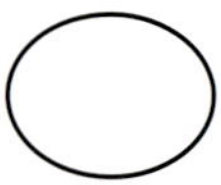

jewel

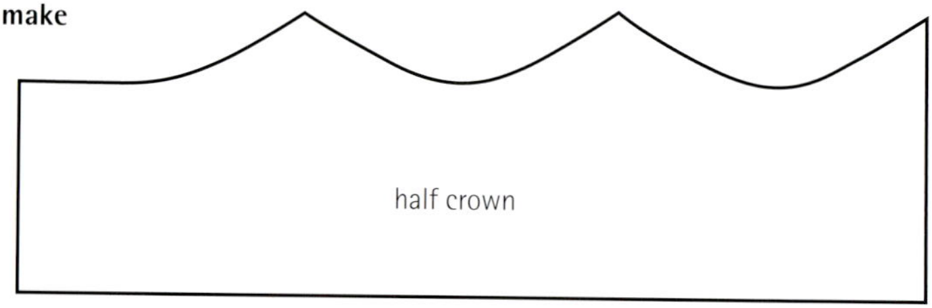

crochet sceptre

see variations page 180

materials

- Yarn: Brown Sheep Nature Spun Worsted (100% wool, 100g (3½ oz), 224m (245 yds)), 1 skein each of (A) Impasse Yellow, (B) Red Fox
- 4 mm (US size G/6) crochet hook
- size 38 felting needle
- wool roving in yellow

tension: 5 sts over 6 rows = 2.5cm (1 in)

finished dimensions: 34cm (13½ in) high, 6cm (2½ in) wide

instructions

With A, ch 2.

Rnd 1: make 6 dc in 2nd ch from hook. Sl st in first dc to join.

Rnd 2: ch 1, 2 dc in each st across, sl st in first dc to join – 12 sts.

Rnd 3: ch 1, [dc in next st, 2 dc in next st] across, sl st in first dc to join – 18 sts.

Ch 1, dc in each st across, sl st for each round until your work is 25cm (10 in) long, and stuff as you crochet until the end. Fasten off A, join B, and continue as follows.

Rnd 1: ch 1, [dc in next 2 sts, 2 dc in next st] across, sl st – 24 sts.

Rnd 2: ch 1, [dc in next 3 sts, 2 dc in next st] across, sl st – 30 sts.

Rnd 3: ch 1, [dc in next 4 sts, 2 dc in next st] across, sl st – 36 sts.

Rnds 4–10: ch 1, dc in ea st across, sl st.

Rnd 11: ch 1, [dc in next 4 sts, dc2tog] across, sl st – 30 sts.

Rnd 12: ch 1, [dc in next 3 sts, dc2tog] across, sl st – 24 sts.

Rnd 13: ch 1, [dc in next 2 sts, dc2tog] across, sl st – 18 sts.

Rnd 14: ch 1, [dc in next st, dc2tog] across, sl st – 12 sts.

Rnd 15: ch 1, dc2tog across, sl st – 6 sts.

Break yarn, fasten off, and weave in ends.

Crochet a 7.5-cm (3-in) chain with yellow yarn from the base of the red sceptre bulb to the tip. Make four of these chains and space evenly around the bulb. Knot in place at the bottom and top of each chain and hide ends in the bulb. Needle felt a 2-cm (¾-in) yellow ball and sew to the tip of the sceptre.

bandit mask

see variations page 181

materials

- fabric: Robert Kaufman Kona Cotton (100% cotton), 25cm ($^1/_4$ yd) of black
- tracing paper
- tailor's chalk
- ruler
- sewing thread in black

finished dimensions:
5.5cm ($2^1/_4$ in) high,
110cm ($43^1/_2$ in) wide

instructions

Fold the fabric in half so you have 55cm (22 in) from the centre fold. Fold the to scale mask pattern in half at the bridge of the nose. Fold this over the centre fold of the fabric. Trace around the top, bottom, and both sides of the eyes with tailor's chalk. With a ruler, extend the mask ties to the end of the fabric from the straight 6-cm ($2^1/_2$-in) edge.

Cut along the lines, fold the eye in half, and snip horizontally from end to end. Flatten and cut around the tracing. Repeat for the other eye. Once you're done, snip about 0.5cm ($^1/_4$ in) all around each eye so you can turn the edges in. Press. Repeat these steps to make the other side of the mask.

Pin the mask together with the right sides together, and the pressed eye snippets facing you. Sew together with a 0.5-cm ($^1/_4$-in) seam allowance and leave one 5-cm (2-in) edge open. Sew together with a 0.5-cm ($^1/_4$-in) seam, leaving one 5-cm (2-in) edge open. Turn right side out and press. Turn the 5-cm (2-in) edge in and invisible stitch closed. Pin above and below each eye. Backstitch 0.25cm ($^1/_8$ in) from the edge all around the eye with black thread, tucking in the snipped edges as you sew. Hide the thread on the inside.

Enlarge to 460% to make to actual size.

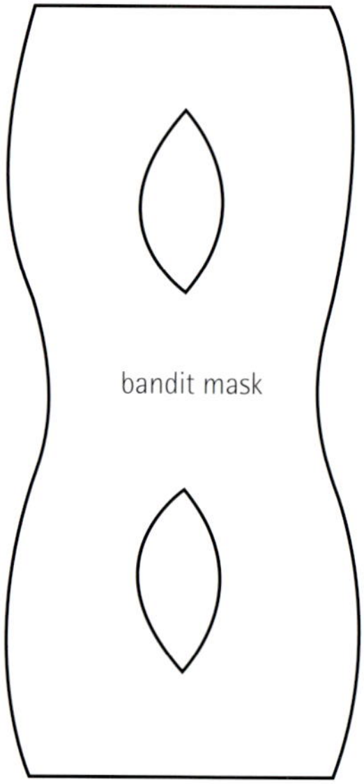

needle felt moustache

see variations page 182

materials

- wool roving, 7g (¼ oz) in chocolate brown
- felting foam pad
- size 38 felting needle
- sewing needle with large eye
- elastic cord or string

finished dimensions:
10cm (4 in) long, 0.5cm (¼ in) wide, 2.5cm (1 in) high

instructions

Pull a length of wool roving about 15cm (6 in) long, roll lengthwise, and tuck in side ends. Place on the foam pad and hold the ends together. Jab the felting needle through the ends to hold everything together. Continue stabbing your needle all over the wool until it is about 11.5cm (4½ in) long by 3–4cm (1¼–1½ in) wide and lightly felted.

Find the centre of the moustache, hold the wool upright, and felt repeatedly down the centre to form an indentation. Turn the piece over and felt on the other side of the centre indentation.

Lay the moustache flat again and felt the bottom edge to a point by stabbing in at the sides, moving the needle horizontally. Turn the piece over and shape the top curve of the moustache, beginning about two-thirds down from the centre point and curling the end up a little. Repeat for the other side. If there are areas of the moustache that are still very fluffy, lay it flat and felt vertically into those areas until they firm up. If you have wrinkles or creases, wrap a thin layer of wool over them and felt it smoothly in place.

Thread the needle with elastic cord or string and pull through the centre back point of the moustache. Cut and knot the cord to the desired size or leave enough string to tie around the back of the head.

felt magician's hat

see variations page 183

materials

- yarn: Brown Sheep Nature Spun Worsted (100% wool, 100g (3½ oz), 224m (245 yds)), 1 skein of Snow
- black felt, 45cm (½ yd)
- sew-in interfacing, 45cm (45cm (½ yd))
- pencil
- string
- fabric marker
- tailor's chalk
- tape measure
- dressmaking pins
- embroidery needle
- embroidery thread
- 4.5 mm (US size 7) knitting needles

tension: 5 sts over 7 rows = 2.5cm (1 in)

finished dimensions:18cm (7 in) high, 25-cm (10-in)-diameter brim, 18-cm (7-in) diameter top, 55-cm (22-in) head circumference

instructions

hat

Mark and cut two 25-cm (10-in) circles out of felt and one out of interfacing. Mark and cut two 18-cm (7-in) circles out of felt and one out of interfacing. Centre the small circle on top of the large circle and trace around the small circle with tailor's chalk. Cut out and discard the inner circle. Repeat for the other 25-cm (10-in) felt circle and the 25-cm (10-in) interfacing circle. This will be the brim of the hat.

Using measuring tape and chalk, measure, mark, and cut a 58 x 18-cm (23 x 7-in) rectangle, and a 57.5 x 18-cm (22⅜ x 7-in) rectangle on the black felt and the interfacing. When the felt is rolled into a cylinder, the shorter rectangle will be on the inside of the hat and will even out with the 58-cm (23-in) rectangle. Sandwich the interfacing between both layers of corresponding felt for all three cutouts.

Pin the three layers of 18-cm (7-in) circles along the 58 x 57.5-cm (23 x 22⅜-in) rectangle edge, making sure the rectangle is on the inside. With black embroidery thread, whip stitch all along the top 18-cm (7-in) circle and backstitch down the 18-cm (7-in) seam of the rectangle, 0.25cm (⅛ in) from the edge. Turn the hat upside down with the 18-cm (7-in) circle you just sewed on the bottom. Pin the three layers of the 25-cm (10-in) brim to the bottom edge of the hat and whip stitch around the edge, with black embroidery thread, and with the stitches on the inside of the hat.

white band

With 4.5 mm needles and yarn, CO 8 sts. Work in st st for 55cm (22 in) BO and weave in ends. Block flat and pin to the base of the hat. Make a running stitch along the top and bottom of the band with white thread, and stitch just to the first layer of felt not all the way to the inside layer.

knitted bow tie

see variations page 184

materials

- yarn: Brown Sheep Shepherd's Shades (100% wool, 100g (3½ oz), 120m (131 yds)), 1 skein of Blue Sky
- 6.5 mm (US size 10.5) knitting needles
- tapestry needle
- round black elastic cord

tension: 4 sts over 5 rows = 2.5cm (1 in)

instructions

With yarn and 6.5 mm knitting needles, CO 10 sts. Work in st st for 25cm (10 in) and sl st the first st knitwise of each knit row, and purlwise of each purl row to create a nice edge. BO and leave enough sewing yarn.

Mattress stitch the short sides together, making a ring.

Flatten the piece lengthwise with the seam on one end, and make a running stitch along the top and bottom of the bow tie. Weave in the ends.

Cinch the centre together like a fan, and so that there's a crease in the centre. Wrap the yarn around the cinch and knot together, securing the centre cinch.

With yarn and 6.5 mm knitting needles, CO 5 sts. Work in st st for 7.5cm (3 in), BO, and leave enough sewing yarn. Wrap this piece around the centre of the bow tie, stitch the ends together, and secure to the bow tie. Weave in the ends.

Cut a 38-cm (15-in) length of elastic cord (adjust cord length as needed) and thread through a tapestry needle. Pull the cord through the centre back loop that you just secured to the bow tie, and knot the cord ends together.

crochet spectacles

see variations page 185

materials

- yarn: Brown Sheep Cotton Fleece (80% cotton, 20% merino wool, 100g (3½ oz), 196m (215 yds)), 1 skein of Cavern
- 2–3 black pipe cleaners
- wire cutters/scissors
- 4 mm (US size G/6) crochet hook
- tapestry needle
- fabric glue

finished dimensions:
12cm (5 in) long,
12cm (5 in) wide,
5cm (2 in) high

instructions

Bend 14cm (5½ in) of one end of a pipe cleaner so that you have a 4.5-cm (1¾-in)-diameter circle. Wrap about 0.5cm (¼ in) of the end around the circle base to join, making sure the pointy edge is secure. Bend another pipe cleaner in the same way. To make a 2.5-cm (1-in) bridge for the glasses, cut a 5-cm (2-in) piece of pipe cleaner and wrap 0.5cm (¼ in) of each end around the centre of both rims directly opposite each circle joint.

Start at the back earpiece end of the spectacles on the right. Make a slip knot with your yarn and loop onto the hook. Treat the pipe cleaner as a working row. Pull a loop up in front of the pipe cleaner so you have two loops on the hook. Yarn over and pull the yarn through both loops to make a single crochet. Continue to dc across the length of the pipe cleaner and around the spectacle rim. Break yarn, fasten off, and weave in ends when you complete the circle.

Begin to dc again at the bridge, closest to the rim you just finished. Dc across the bridge and around the next circular rim. Break yarn, fasten off, and weave in ends when you complete the circle.
Dc straight across the last side of the spectacles and begin at the hinge next to the rim you just finished.

Secure the ends with a dab of glue and go back over with a tapestry needle and yarn to knot all the joints to make them stronger. Curve the back earpieces to fit your head.

MAGIC

felt raccoon mask

see variations page 186

materials

- felt, one 20 x 25-cm (8 x 10-in) sheet each of grey and black
- tracing paper
- sewing thread to match felt
- black elastic cord

finished dimensions:
21.5cm ($8\frac{1}{2}$ in) wide, 11.5cm (4 1/2 in) high

instructions

Trace and cut two masks out of grey felt, and two ears, one nose, and one eye piece out of black felt. Lay the black eye piece over both layers of the grey mask and line up the eyes. Baste and backstitch the three pieces together and blanket stitch around both eyes with black thread. Sew around the outer edges of the black eye piece with black thread.

Cut 35.5cm (14 in) of elastic cord and knot at both ends. Place in between the grey felt layers and pin to either side of the mask. Sew around the edge of the mask with grey thread and reinforce the elastic with extra stitches, pushing the thread through the elastic. With the same grey thread, sew a line under each ear connecting with the outer edge seam. Centre the ears and nose and sew in place with black thread.

Enlarge to 400%
to make to actual size.

grey mask (2)

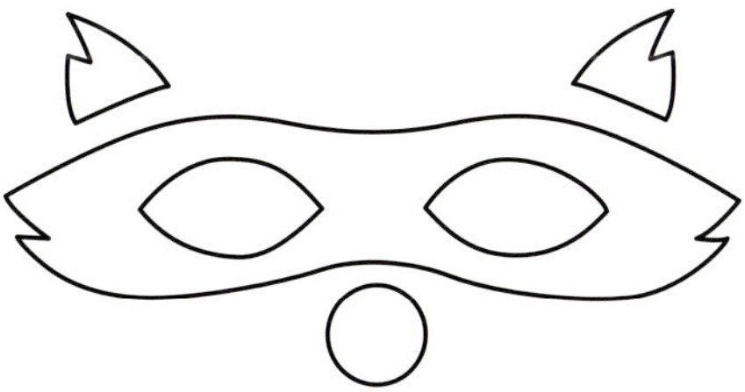

black mask with ears and nose (1 of each)

clown hat

see variations page 187

materials

- yarn: Brown Sheep Nature Spun Worsted (100% wool, 100g (3½ oz), 224m (245 yds)), 1 skein of Natural
- felt, 25cm (¼ yd) of red
- sew-in interfacing, 25cm (¼ yd)
- fork
- cardstock
- fabric marker
- sewing thread in white and red
- sewing machine (optional)
- thick white elastic

finished dimensions:
16.5cm (6½ in) high, 11.5cm (4½ in) wide

instructions

pompoms (make 3)

Cut 2.75m (3 yds) of yarn per pompom, and a 12-cm (5-in) piece of yarn to tie the centre together. Hold a fork horizontally in one hand and wrap the yarn around the base of the fork like spaghetti, then loop the 12-cm (5-in) yarn through the centre prong space. Knot tightly around the centre of the yarn wrap. With scissors, snip the top and bottom loops of the wrapped yarn. Slide off the fork and fluff up your pompom. Trim off any uneven ends.

hat

Print the hat pattern onto cardstock, trace around it onto the red felt and the interfacing with a fabric marker, and cut. Align the interfacing piece with the wrong side of the felt piece and pin together. Sew along the bottom with red thread, 0.5cm (¼ in) from the edge. Pin the straight edges together with 0.5cm (¼ in) overlapping, creating a cone shape. Trim the interfacing if necessary. Backstitch 0.5cm (¼ in) from the edge from top to bottom.

Stitch one pompom to the tip of the hat, and stitch the other two as shown (right). For an older child, cut a 55-cm (22-in) piece of elastic as a chin strap. Tie a knot at each end, and with red thread, stitch just below the knot to fix to both sides of the hat.

Enlarge to 500% to make to actual size.

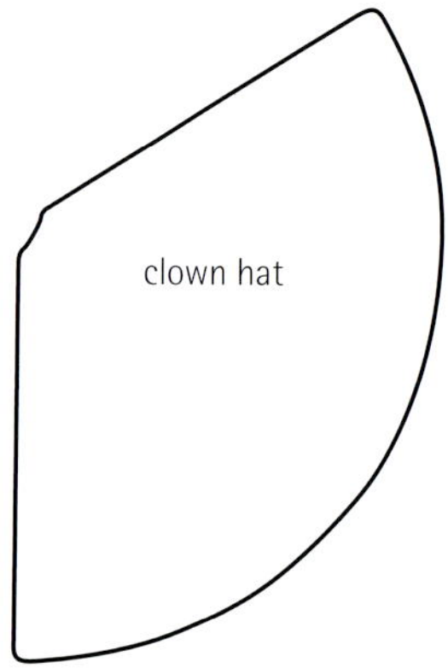

variations

superhero cape

see base design page 159

royal cape

Follow the main cape instructions using red satin fabric for the outside, and gold-coloured satin to line.

zorro cape

Follow the superhero cape instructions and use black satin fabric to make a Zorro cape. Lengthen the cape to reach the ankles of your little hero. Use black ribbon for the necktie.

magician's cape

Use black satin for the outside, and red satin to line. Sew with the right sides facing, leaving one end open. Turn right side out, turn in the edges by 1.25cm (½-in), and press. Topstitch 0.5cm (¼ in) from the closed edge and continue all around the cape edges. Sew two parallel lines – one 5cm (2 in) from the top edge and one 7.5cm (3 in) from the top edge. Make buttonholes on the right side of the cape at each end between the parallel stitches, large enough for the cord to fit through. Feed the cord through.

little red riding hood cape

With red fabric, add 38cm (15 in) length to the top edge of the superhero cape to make a hood. Cut a matching piece of the same fabric to line. Sew 1.25-cm (½-in) seam allowance around the edges with the right sides together, leaving one end open. Turn right side out and press. Turn the open edges in and press. Topstitch 0.5cm (¼ in) from the edge all around the cape. For the cord, sew two parallel lines – one at 35cm (14 in) from the top edge, and one at 38cm (15 in). Make buttonholes on the right side of the cape at each end between the parallel stitches. Feed the cord through. Fold the top edge in half and pin to make the hood. Invisible stitch together. Put on the hood and pull the cord, bunching up the fabric.

initial cape

Personalise the superhero cape with the first letter of your hero's name. Using a word processing program, select a simple font, enlarge it to the desired size, and print it out. Follow the instructions for the lightning bolt appliqué (see page 159) to appliqué the initial to the centre back of the cape.

variations

felt crown

see base design page 160

tiara

Following the crown pattern, use the same length to make a tiara, but only use the three points in the centre of the pattern. Trim the rest of the points down and taper to 4cm (1½ in) high at the back. Follow the sewing instructions from the crown pattern and add more jewels.

felt belt

Use the same yellow felt as the crown to make a matching belt. Measure the waist of your king or queen and add 7.5cm (3 in) to the end to overlap with hook-and-eye fastener. Cut two strips of felt 7.5cm (3 in) wide and as long as the waist measurement. Add felt 'jewels' to the belt and topstitch around the edges. Sew 7.5-cm (3-in)-square hook-and-eye fastener to the ends so that the belt comes together when wrapped round the waist.

crown of flowers

Make a fairy flower crown using wire; wrap it with strips of green fabric and secure with fabric glue. Bend the wire to wrap around the head at least three times, pulling the wire in different directions so it doesn't all sit on top of itself. Cut 4 x 2.5-cm (1½ x 1-in) felt leaves and stitch or glue randomly around the crown.

laurel wreath crown (pictured)

Use a thick-tension wire to make a laurel wreath crown. Cut the wire to the child's head size, between 46–55cm (18–22 in) around, and leave about 7.5cm (3 in) extra for twisting the ends together. Bend the wire into a circle and twist the ends together over each other. Crochet over the wire with olive green yarn as in the glasses instructions. Hide ends on the inside. Cut 4 x 6-cm (1½ x 2½-in) leaves and stitch all around the crown until it's full.

crown appliqué

Use the centre section with three points of the crown pattern to make a flat appliqué for a royal cape. Follow the superhero cape instructions on page 159 for the appliqué and cape.

variations

crochet sceptre

see base design page 163

torch

Follow the sceptre pattern but omit the four yellow chains and yellow felt ball at the end. Cut enough 7.5–12.5-cm (3–5-in) 'flames' out of orange and red felt to layer around the bulb, and stitch into place.

needle felt wizard wand (not suitable for young children)

Roll a 30-cm (12-in) length of wool roving into a thin tube, and needle felt. Add more wool to one end for the handle. Felt until solid. Insert a cut-down bamboo skewer, making sure the ends are covered.

fairy wand (pictured)

With pink yarn, make 8 dc in a magic ring and dc in each stitch around until piece measures 25cm (10 in) Insert a 0.5-cm (¼-in)-diameter x 25-cm (10-in) dowel inside the crochet tube and loop yarn through the last 8 sts and knot closed. Hide ends on the inside. Cut two 10 x 10-cm (4 x 4-in) stars from yellow felt and stitch together, leaving an opening at the bottom for the end of the crocheted stick to fit inside. Stuff and insert the crocheted handle and add a few ribbon tails at the base of the star before stitching closed.

magician's wand

Make 8 dc in a magic ring with white yarn and dc in each st around until the piece measures 2.5cm (1 in) Fasten off white and join black yarn and dc in each st around until the piece measures 28cm (11 in) Fasten off black and join white and dc in each st around for one more in. Insert a 0.5 x 30-cm (¼ x 12-in) dowel, loop yarn in last 8 sts, and pull closed. Knot the end to secure and hide the ends on the inside.

trident

Follow the main handle pattern, but extend by 38cm (15 in); insert thick-tension wire inside for support. Crochet two 25-cm (10-in) tubes from the same yarn, insert wire, and stuff. Loop yarn through the last row of stitches, pull, and knot together closed. Bend wire to a curved right angle at one end and stitch to the handle with 7.5cm (3 in) of the handle taller than the top of the prong. Repeat with the second tube on the other side.

variations

bandit mask

see base design page 164

western bandana facemask

Make an old Western bandit mask to tie over the nose and mouth with a 52-cm (20½-in) square of red cotton fabric. Make a rolled hem around all four sides on the wrong side of the fabric. Fold the bandana in half, diagonally, making a triangle. To wear, place over the nose and mouth, and knot in the back of the head to secure.

karate belt

Follow the bandit mask instructions to make a karate belt. Omit the eye cutouts and cut two straight 2.5m x 6-cm (100 x 2½-in) lengths of fabric. Sew with the right sides together and a 1.25-cm (½-in) seam allowance. Leave one short end open and turn right side out. Turn the last edge in 1.25cm (½-in) and invisible stitch closed.

pirate sash

Cut two pieces of 2.5m x 23-cm (100 x 9-in) red fabric to make a pirate sash, and cut the ends at an angle. Follow the sewing instructions for the karate belt variation. Wrap the belt around the waist twice and knot at the side of the body.

blindfold

Follow the bandit mask pattern but don't cut out the eyeholes, to make a blindfold. Use the blindfold for games such as pin the tail on the donkey, and hitting a piñata.

knitted aviator scarf

Use a lightweight white yarn to knit a 25 x 165-cm (10 x 65-in) scarf in stockinette stitch. The edges will curl in a bit.

masquerade ball mask

Follow the instructions for the bandit mask, and sew sequins or glue on rhinestones to decorate.

variations

needle felt moustache

see base design page 167

needle felt beard

Make a lightly needle felted wool beard to connect to the moustache. Lay out wool roving to your desired beard length and width. Roll the top edge of the wool down and needle felt. Pull the left and right side up so you have a 'U' shape in the middle, and needle felt the two sides to the bottom of the moustache. Lightly needle felt the rest of the beard so it holds together but is still fluffy.

needle felt sideburns

Needle felt two 2.5 x 5-cm (1 x 2-in) rectangles to make sideburns. Cut a strip of matching felt to the sideburn size and stitch together, keeping the stitches on the back and not sewing all the way through to the front. Attach the sideburns with a bit of double-sided sticky tape.

fuzzy eyebrows

Needle felt fuzzy black eyebrows like Groucho Marx's. Make them 5cm (2 in) wide and keep it wispy for the top 2.5–4cm (1–1½ in). Cut a 1.25 x 5-cm (½ x 2-in) strip of black felt and stitch to the back of each eyebrow. Attach the eyebrows with double-sided sticky tape just above your actual eyebrows.

felt goatee

Cut two layers of your chosen colour of felt 6cm (2½ in) wide and 5.5cm (2¼ in) tall. Adjust the size as required. Round the corners and fold the centre enough to snip. Cut out the centre of both pieces, leaving a 0.75-mm (⅜-in) border. Make vertical stitches with matching thread all over both pieces to simulate facial hair, and to sew the pieces together. Attach the goatee with double-sided sticky tape.

needle felt unibrow

Make a unibrow like that of artist Frida Kahlo. Follow the moustache instructions and turn it upside down to make a unibrow. Felt it a bit thinner than the moustache and wide enough to stretch between the outer corners of the eyes. Sew a strip of matching felt to the back and attach with double-sided tape.

variations

felt magician's hat

see base design page 168

mad hatter hat

Use green felt to follow the magician's hat pattern, but extend the top rectangle edge 12cm (5 in) longer than the bottom edge, to make the Mad Hatter's hat (from *Alice's Adventures in Wonderland*). The hat will be larger at the top and taper in at the base. Pin the rectangle together and measure the new top diameter to cut the top circles. Trim off the excess felt at the short edge after pinning, leaving a 1.25-cm (½-in) seam allowance. Follow the magician's hat sewing instructions to finish the Mad Hatter's hat.

mary poppins hat

Follow the magician's hat instructions but shorten the height of the rectangle by 2cm (¾ in) to make a hat fit for Mary Poppins. Add 5-cm (2-in)-diameter white felt daisies and 1.25-cm (½-in)-diameter red felt ball 'berries' around the base of the hat to complete the costume.

uncle sam hat

Use the magician's hat pattern and red felt for the base of the hat to create a stars and stripes hat. Cut a 56 x 5-cm (22 x 2-in) strip of royal blue felt for the hat base. Use fabric glue to secure in place. Cut 4cm (1½-in) white felt stars and glue all around the blue stripe. Cut seven 4cm (1½-in)-wide white felt stripes to fit flush above the blue stripe and to the top edge of the hat. Space evenly and glue in place.

willy wonka hat

Create the classic Willy Wonka hat with a rust-coloured felt, following the magician's hat instructions. Add a medium-tension wire between the two layers of felt around brim of the hat to bend the sides up.

charlie chaplin bowler hat

Follow the magician's hat pattern but make the top circle 15cm (6 in) in diameter instead of 18cm (7 in) Cut four vertical slits 5–7.5cm (2–3 in) long, spaced evenly around the top edge of the rectangle. Pull the slits together to make the hat curve in at the top to fit around the 15-cm (6-in). circle. Stitch the pulled-in slits together, and whip stitch the circle on top. Knit the base strip with black yarn instead of white.

variations

knitted bow tie

see base design page 171

crochet bow tie

With a 6.5 mm (US size K/10.5) crochet hook and the same yarn as the knit bow tie, ch 9 sts, turn, and begin 2nd ch from the hook. Dc in next 8 sts, turn, ch 1, and repeat until the piece measures 25cm (10 in). Fold the piece in half and stitch the short edges together. Pinch the centre together, wrap matching yarn tightly around the centre, and knot to secure. Hide the ends on the inside. Loop and knot an elastic cord through the back.

polka dot bow tie (pictured)

Follow the knit bow tie instructions and once you've finished knitting 25cm (10 in), use a tapestry needle and contrasting colour yarn to make random polka dots in duplicate stitch. Weave in the ends, and continue constructing the bow tie as stated.

crochet tie

Make a custom-sized tie by measuring the length from the base of the neck to just above the belt line. With a 6.5 mm (US size K/10.5) crochet hook and the same yarn as the knit bow tie, ch 8, turn, and begin 2nd ch from the hook. Dc in next 7 sts, turn, ch 1, and repeat until the piece fits your custom measurement. Weave in ends. To make the top 'knot', ch 8, turn, and begin 2nd ch from the hook. Dc in next 7 sts, turn, ch 1, and repeat until piece measures 7.5cm (3 in); break yarn with enough for sewing. Place this piece over the top edge of the tie with the long edge vertical on the tie. Turn both pieces over and fold the top of the 'knot' edge 1.25cm (½-in) down over the top of the tie edge. Pull in both bottom corners to the centre, pinching the base of the knot together, and stitch together. Stitch a tie clip to the back of the knot, or use elastic as in the knit bow tie.

striped knitted bow tie

Use the knit bow tie pattern and two colours of yarn to make a striped bow tie. Change the yarn colour every two rows and carry the previous yarn up the side as you knit, so you're not breaking the yarn after each change. Continue constructing the bow tie as stated.

variations

crochet spectacles

see base design page 172

crochet monocle (pictured)

Bend a pipe cleaner into a 5-cm (2-in) circle and crochet around it as in the glasses pattern. Attach a string to the monocle, and make it as long as needed to attach to clothing with a small clip.

crochet nerd spectacles

Follow the crochet spectacles instructions and bend the wire into rectangles instead of circles. Use black yarn for the frames and white yarn on the bridge of the spectacles to give the effect of white tape holding them together.

knitted cat-eye spectacles

Cast on three stitches on a double-pointed needle and make an I-cord for the length of each section of wire; slip over the wire before bending into shape. Bend wire to the same size as the circular spectacles and pinch the outside corners of the frames to a point to make cat-eye spectacles. Stitch the ends closed with a tapestry needle and hide them on the inside.

crochet eyeglasses chain

Chain stitch for 76cm (30 in) using a different colour than the glasses. Stitch the ends together to form a loop, and attach to either side of the spectacles. Attach to cat-eye spectacles to complete a librarian costume.

shutter shade sunglasses

Begin with the circular spectacles instructions and use more wire to make the frames larger and into aviator-shaped glasses with a straight connected top edge, and rounded bottom lenses. Cut thin slats with matching stiff felt for the horizontal shutter shades and stitch these, evenly spaced, to each 'lens'.

variations

felt raccoon mask

see base design page 175

felt owl mask

Use the basic raccoon mask to make an owl mask. Use taupe-coloured felt for the face and ears. Cut a yellow triangle beak 4 x 5cm (1½ x 2 in) from felt and sew in place of the black nose. Cut two cream-coloured circles to sew around the eyes, and cut holes in the centre for the eyeholes. Stitch 1.25 x 2.5-cm (½ x 1-in) taupe felt 'feathers' around the eyes.

felt masquerade mask

Use the raccoon mask pattern and omit the ears to make a masquerade mask. Use any colour felt you like and cut 7.5–10cm (3–4 in) felt 'feathers' in a contrasting colour and sew to one side of the mask. Add embellishment with embroidered flowers around the border. Sew elastic to either side to attach the mask.

mask with a stick

Turn any of the masks above into handheld masks or photo-booth props. Sew interfacing or stiff felt between the layers of felt to give it stiffness. Cut a 25-cm (10-in) dowel and a 4 x 5-cm (1½ x 2-in) piece of felt for the pocket. Turn the mask to the reverse side and place an end of the dowel on the right end of the mask. Pin the piece of felt over the dowel so it fits snugly and sew the felt to the mask. Insert the dowel once finished, and you're ready to play.

pig snout

Make a pig snout to fit over the nose with pink felt and an elastic band. Cut two layers of felt 5 x 7.5cm (2 x 3 in) Round the corners and sew together. Cut two black felt ovals, 2.5 x 1.25cm (1 x ½ in), for the nostrils and sew onto the snout.

felt lion mask

Round out the ears and cut and sew a 2.5-cm (1-in) black triangular felt nose. Cut 2.5 x 5-cm (1 x 2-in) orange felt strips and sew around the top of the head for the mane.

variations

clown hat

see base design page 176

party hat

Follow the instructions for the clown hat but stitch contrasting-coloured felt polka dots around it. Make enough pompoms to fit around the bottom border, and stitch into place. Stitch one pompom at the tip of the hat. Make enough hats for all partygoers, with different colour combinations and appliqués.

wizard hat

Enlarge the clown hat pattern so that the bottom edge measures 45–55cm (18-22 in), depending on your wizard's head size. Use royal blue felt for the hat and follow the clown hat instructions for sewing the hat together. Cut 5-cm (2-in) stars from white felt and either stitch or glue to the hat.

princess hat

Enlarge the pattern so the bottom edge measures 45–55cm (18-22 in), depending on your princess's head size, and cut it out of pink felt. Sew pink sequin ribbon trim to the bottom edge of the hat. Cut a 50 x 12.5-cm (20 x 5-in) length of pink tulle, bunch together at one end, pin to the tip of the hat, and follow the clown hat instructions for sewing the hat together. Add fabric flowers, faux fur trim or ribbon cascading with the tulle.

gnome hat

Follow the clown hat instructions but omit the pompoms to make a red gnome hat. Enlarge the pattern to the desired hat size and sew together. If you'd like the tip of the hat to curl downward, cut the interfacing a few inches below the tip of the hat so it'll flop over and not stick straight up. Follow the needle felt beard variation of the needle felt moustache (see page 167) to complete the gnome costume.

witch hat

Combine the clown hat pattern with the magician hat's brim (see page 168) to make a witch's hat. Enlarge the clown hat pattern to 55cm (22 in) at the base edge, cut out of black felt, and sew. Follow the magician hat brim pattern and sewing instructions to sew to the base of the black cone.

everyday objects

Drive through the streets with a knitted car, or call your mum with a crochet mobile phone. Arrange a bouquet of peonies or play a tune on a knitted keyboard. You can do all these things and more with the everyday objects from this chapter.

plushie sewing machine

see variations page 222

materials

- 25cm (1/4 yd) floral fabric
- wool felt in contrast colour
- tracing paper
- felt scraps
- sewing thread
- 4 mm (US size 6) crochet hook
- worsted weight yarn in white and tan
- 4.5 mm (US size 7) double-pointed knitting needles
- fabric glue

finished dimensions:
23cm (9 in) long x 7.5cm (3 in) wide x 20cm (8 in) high after stuffing

instructions

sewing machine body

Trace and cut out the sewing machine pattern from fabric. Cut another strip of 9 x 95-cm (3 1/2 x 37 1/2-in) felt for the width of the machine. If you don't have a continuous piece of 9 x 95-cm (3 1/2 x 37 1/2-in) felt, you can sew two shorter strips together. Pin the 9 x 95-cm (3 1/2 x 37 1/2-in) strip of felt along the edge of one of the sewing machine cutouts with the front sides facing each other. With your sewing machine, sew a 0.5-cm (1/4-in) seam. Once you finish, pin the second sewing machine cutout to the strip with the right side on the inside, and sew with a 0.5-cm (1/4-in) seam. You'll have an opening where the 9 x 95-cm (3 1/2 x 37 1/2-in) strip of fabric meets. Use this opening to stuff your toy sewing machine. Once it's stuffed, turn the edges in 0.5cm (1/4 in) each, and hand-sew an invisible seam.

embellishments

crochet knobs:
With a size 6 crochet hook and white yarn, make 6 dc in a magic ring, sl st.
Rnd 1: ch 2, dc 6 in 2nd ch from hook.
Rnd 2: 2 dc in each st – 12 sts.
Rnd 3: *tr 1, 2 tr in next st* rep to end – 24 sts. (Stop here for smaller knob.)
Rnd 4: *tr 2, 2 tr in next st* – 30 sts. (Larger right-hand side knob.) Stitch or glue crochet knobs in place.

Cut out a small circle, rectangle, and sewing needle shape from white felt. Hand-sew the needle in place as shown and glue the button embellishments on. Crochet a 7.5-cm (3-in) chain in white and stitch in place above the sewing needle.

knitted spool of thread

With 4.5 mm knitting needles and tan yarn, CO 15 sts. Join and knit in the round for 3cm (1 1/4 in.) BO and weave in ends. Cut out two circles from white felt for the spool top and bottom. Stuff and stitch together then stitch in place on top of the machine.

knitted camera

see variations page 223

materials

- yarn: Brown Sheep Cotton Fleece (80% cotton, 20% merino wool, 100g (3½ oz), 196m (215 yds)), 1 skein each of (A) Lime Light, (B) Cavern, (C) Cotton Ball
- wool felt in black and white
- 4 mm (US size 6) knitting needles
- sewing thread in black and white
- 4 mm (US size G/6) crochet hook
- stuffing

tension (for seed stitch):
5 sts over 8 rows = 2.5cm (1 in)

finished dimensions:
12cm (5 in) long, 9cm (3½ in) high, 5cm (2 in) wide

instructions

camera body

With size 6 needles and A, CO 25 sts and knit in moss st for 19 rows. BO and repeat to make a matching piece. With A, CO 8 sts and knit in moss st for 24cm (9½ in). BO and weave in ends. Using A, sew the 24cm (9½ in) strip along both sides and bottom of each rectangle with a running stitch, with the edges on the outside. Cut two pieces of black felt 2.5 x 12cm (1 x 5 in), one 4 x 12cm (1½ x 5 in), and two pieces 2.5 x 4cm (1 x 1½ in) for the top of the camera. The 4 x 12-cm (1½ x 5-in) strip is the camera top. Sew the 4cm (1½ in) and 12cm (5 in) edges together around this top piece and down the 2.5-cm (1-in) sides.

lens

With a 4 mm hook and C:

Rnd 1: ch 2, 6 dc in 2nd ch from hook. Sl st in the first chain to join.

Rnd 2: ch 1, 2 dc in each st across, sl st in first st to join – 12 sts.

Rnd 3: ch 1, [2 dc in next st, dc in next st] across, sl st in first st to join – 18 sts.

Rnd 4: ch 1, [2 dc in next st, dc in next 2 sts] across, sl st in first st to join. Fasten off C, join B – 24 sts.

Rnd 5: ch 1 [2 dc in next st, dc in next 3 sts] across, sl st in first st to join – 36 sts.

Break yarn and make two diagonal lines across the lens for the glass shine. Weave in ends.

shutter release

With a 4 mm hook and B:

Rnd 1: ch 2, 6 dc in 2nd ch from hook. Sl st in the first chain to join.

Rnd 2: ch 1, 2 dc in each st across, sl st in first st to join – 12 sts. Break yarn and weave in ends. Sew on the top left-hand corner at the top of the camera. Cut a 2 x 1.25-cm (¾ x ½-in) rectangle out of white felt and sew to the top right-hand corner on the front of the camera. Stuff and pin the camera body and top felt piece together. Stitch the lens onto the front of the camera.

crochet mobile phone

see variations page 224

materials

- yarn: Brown Sheep Cotton Fleece (80% cotton, 20% merino wool, 100g (3½ oz), 196m (215 yds)), 1 skein of Caribbean Sea
- scraps of felt in black and an assortment of bright colours
- embroidery thread in black, white, and an assortment of bright colours
- 4 mm (US size G/6) crochet hook
- sewing thread to match fabric
- stuffing
- fabric glue

tension: 4½ sts over 5 rows = 2.5cm (1 in)
finished dimensions: 7.5cm (3 in) wide, 10cm (4 in) high

instructions

With the crochet hook and yarn, ch 14.
Row 1: Dc in 2nd ch from hook, dc in each ch across, turn – 13 sts.
Row 2: Dc across each st.
Rep prev row until the rectangle measures 12cm (5 in). Break yarn, fasten off, and weave in ends. Crochet another matching piece and leave enough sewing yarn before breaking.

Cut a 9 x 5.5-cm (3½ x 2¼-in) piece of black felt for the face of the phone. Centre onto one of the crocheted rectangles, baste and blanket stitch in place. Sew the two crocheted pieces together, and stuff.

Cut 12 1.25-cm (½-in) felt squares in different colours and embroider different 'apps'. Glue the apps into four rows and three columns. Use your imagination to create interesting buttons and icons.

felt clock

see variations page 225

materials

- felt in red and turquoise
- stiff felt in white
- tracing paper
- 25-cm (10-in) embroidery hoop
- sewing needle
- sewing thread
- embroidery thread in white and purple
- tweezers
- tailor's chalk
- 2.5-cm (1-in) white plastic button

finished dimensions:
25-cm (10-in)-diameter circle

instructions

Trace the clock numbers onto tracing paper and stretch the red felt over the embroidery hoop. Centre the clock numbers over your felt and hoop. Baste in place with a few stitches around the perimeter.

With white embroidery thread, chain stitch the numbers directly over the tracing paper pattern onto the felt. Once you've finished, carefully cut the tracing paper away from the embroidery. Use tweezers to pull out small bits if necessary.

Take the felt out of the embroidery hoop and cut along the innermost hoop crease to make a 25-cm (10-in)-diameter clock. Using the inner hoop as a stencil, trace along the outside edge of the stiff felt with tailor's chalk. Cut out and topstitch the clock and the stiff felt backing together with white thread, 1cm (5/16 in) from the edge.

Trace and cut out two layers of each clock hand in turquoise felt. Blanket stitch each hand together with purple thread. Snip and cut a 0.5-cm (1/4-in) hole 0.5cm (1/4 in) from the bottom edge of each hand, then buttonhole stitch around.

Measure the centre of the clock, and sew the clock hands from back to front and the button on top. Make sure the thread goes through both of the clock hand holes. Sew the button loose enough that the hands can be turned.

Enlarge to 230% to make to actual size.

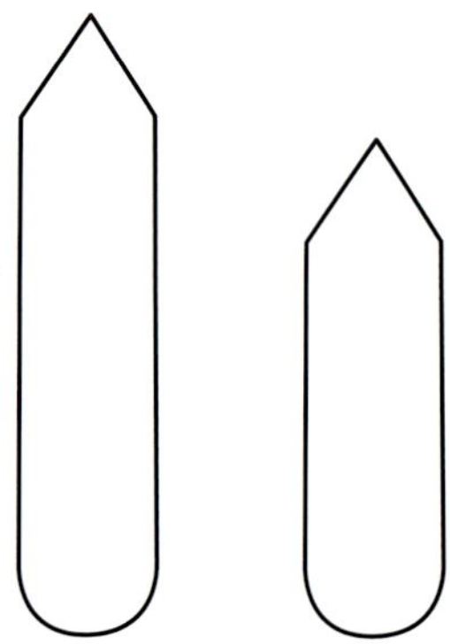

minute hand hour hand

Q 33

materials

- yarn: Brown Sheep Nature Spun Worsted (100% wool, 100g (3½ oz), 224m (245 yds)), 1 skein each of (A) Turquoise Wonder, (B) Snow, (C) Pepper
- wool felt in white and yellow
- 4.5 mm (US size 7) knitting needles
- tapestry needle
- 4 mm (US size G/6) crochet hook
- size 38 felting needle
- stuffing
- sewing thread in white
- tracing paper

tension:
5 sts over 7 rows = 2.5cm (1 in)

finished dimensions:
13cm (5½ in) long,
12cm (5 in) wide,
7.5cm (3 in) high

Enlarge to 320% to make to actual size.

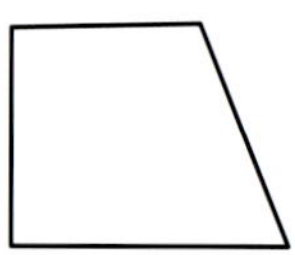

side window (4)

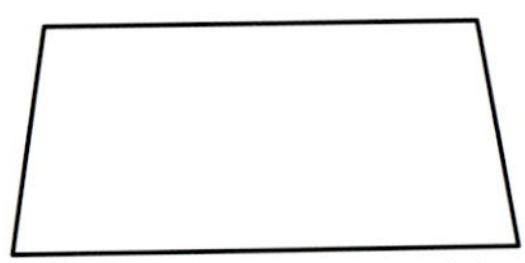

front and back window (2)

knitted car

see variations page 226

instructions

wheels

With B, and a 4 mm hook, ch 4 sts in a magic ring. Sl st in first ch to join.

Rnd 1: ch 1, 2 dc in each st around, sl st in first ch to join. Fasten off B, join C – 8 sts.

Rnd 2: ch 1, [dc in next st, 2 dc in next st] around, sl st in first ch to join – 12 sts.

Rnd 3: ch 1, [dc in next 2 sts sts, 2 dc in next st] around, sl st in first ch to join – 16 sts.

Rnd 4: ch 1, dc in each st across, sl st in first ch to join.

Rnd 5: ch 1, [dc in next 2 sts, dc2tog] around, sl st in first ch to join – 12 sts.

Rnd 6: ch 1, [dc in next st, dc2tog] around, sl st in first ch to join – 8 sts.

Rnd 7: ch 1, dc2tog across, sl st in first ch to join – 4 sts.

Break yarn with enough to sew. Make three more wheels.

car sides

With A, and US 7 needles, CO 25 sts.

R1–10: Starting with a k row, work in st st.

R11 (RS): BO 5 sts, k 15, BO 5 sts, break yarn, and weave in end.

R12 (WS): attach yarn to remaining sts and p.

R13–20: Starting with a k row, work in st st.

BO and weave in ends. Knit another piece for the other side of the car.

car bottom

With C, and 4.5 mm needles, CO 15 sts. Starting with a k row, work 32 rows in st st, BO, and weave in ends.

car midsection

With A, and 4.5 mm needles, CO 15 sts. Starting with a k row, work in st st for 23cm (9 in) BO and leave enough for sewing.

assembly

Pin the bottom car edge to the edge of the car sides. With A, backstitch with the seams on outside and weave in ends. Pin the 23-cm (9-in) midsection strip starting at the 7.5-cm (3-in) edge, moving around the top of the car on both sides. Leave the other edge open for stuffing. Backstitch with A – seams on the outside – and stuff. Stitch the last edge closed and weave in ends. With a felting needle, push in any loose edges along the outside seam. With C, stitch the wheels onto the bottom of both sides of the car, 2.5cm (1 in) in from the front and back.

Trace and cut the windscreens, plus four other windows from white felt. Baste and blanket stitch the windscreen and back window 5cm (2 in) from the bottom on the midsection of the car. Baste and blanket stitch two windows 4cm (1½ in) from the bottom, on either side of the car. Place the windows so the straight edges are centred and 0.5cm (¼ in) away from each other. Cut out two 5-cm (2-in)-diameter circle headlights from yellow felt. Sew 2.5cm (1 in) apart, and 1.25cm (½ in) from the bottom of the front of the car.

sewn ukulele

see variations page 227

materials

- fabric: 100% cotton, 25cm (1/4 yd) each of green and black
- felt in white and black
- yarn: Brown Sheep Cotton Fleece (80% cotton, 20% merino wool, 100g (3 1/2 oz), 196m (215 yds)), 1 skein each of (A) Cavern, (B) Cotton Ball; Lion Brand Cotton Bamboo (52% cotton, 48% bamboo, 100g (3 1/2 oz), 224m (245 yds)), 1 skein of (C) Gardenia
- tracing paper
- tailor's chalk
- sewing needle
- sewing thread to match fabrics
- stuffing
- 4 mm (US size G/6) crochet hook
- embroidery thread

tension: 5 sts/2.5cm (1 in)
finished dimensions: 20cm (8 in) long, 6cm (2 1/2 in) wide, 55cm (22 in) high

instructions

body

Cut two ukulele body pieces, and use a ruler and fabric chalk to measure and draw a 81 x 1.25-cm (32 x 1/2-in) strip on green fabric. Pin the length of the 81 x 1.25-cm (32 x 1/2-in) strip along the edges of both body pieces with the right sides together, leaving an opening at the bottom.

Sew around one body edge beginning at the bottom opening, and ending where you started, then repeat for the other side.

Cut V shapes out of the seam allowance all along both edges, being careful not to cut in or too close to the seam. This will give the fabric room on the inside so your seam won't bunch up. Turn the body inside out and stuff firmly. The body needs to be firm enough to hold the neck up. Sew the opening closed using an invisible stitch.

neck

Cut two neck pieces out of black fabric and be sure to transfer all the fret lines. Stitch over the fret lines with yellow thread with a straight stitch.

Pin the neck pieces with the right sides together. Sew around the edge with a 1-cm (3/8-in) seam allowance, leaving the bottom 8-cm (3 1/4-in) edge open. Turn inside out and stuff firmly.

Fold the open edge in 0.5cm (1/4 in) and pin to the centre top of the ukulele body. Hand-sew together with black thread.

sound hole

With A and 4 mm hook
Rnd 1: Make 6 dc in a magic ring. Sl st in the first ch to join.
Rnd 2: Ch 1, 2 dc in each st around, sl st to join – 12 sts
Rnd 3: Ch 1, [dc in next st, 2 dc in next st] around, sl st to join – 18 sts
Rnd 4: Ch 1, [dc in next 2 sts,

2 dc in next st] around, sl st to join – 24 sts
Rnd 5: Ch 1, [dc in next 3 sts, 2 dc in next st] around, sl st to join – 30 sts
Rnd 6: Ch 1, [dc in next 4 sts, 2 dc in next st] around, sl st to join. Fasten off A, join C – 36 sts
Rnd 7: Ch 1, [dc in next 5 sts, 2 dc in next st] around, sl st to join – 42 sts
Break yarn and weave in ends. Pin the sound hole 12cm (4¾ in) from the bottom, 6cm (2 ½ in) from the top, and 3cm (1¼ in) from both sides of the body. Sew around the edge with yellow thread.

tuning heads

With A and 4 mm hook
Rnd 1: Ch 2, 4 dc in 2nd ch from hook, sl st in first ch to join.
Rnd 2: Ch 1, 2 dc in each st around, sl st to join – 8 sts
Rnds 3–4: Ch 1, dc in each st around, sl st to join – 8 sts
Break yarn and hide ends inside. Make three more.

Sew a tuning head 1.25cm (½-in) below the top edge of the head on the left side. Sew the second tuning head 0.5cm (¼ in) below the first head. Repeat for the right side.

strings

With B, cut four 50-cm (20-in)-long strings. Make a knot at one end of each string.

Starting 6.5cm (2¾ in) from the left edge and 5.5cm (2¼ in) from the bottom, pin the knotted end of one string to the body. Align the rest of the strings 1.25cm (½-in) apart to the right of the first string, and pin. Stitch each string in place right above the knot with white thread. Lay the ukulele flat on its back and stretch the leftmost string up to the closest tuning head. The yarn will have some stretch to it, so pull it tight, but not too tight. Make a knot where the string meets the tuning head, and trim off the excess yarn. Pin the knot 1.5cm (⅝ in) from the edge and centred from the tuning head, and stitch just below the knot. Repeat for the rightmost string. Follow the instructions above

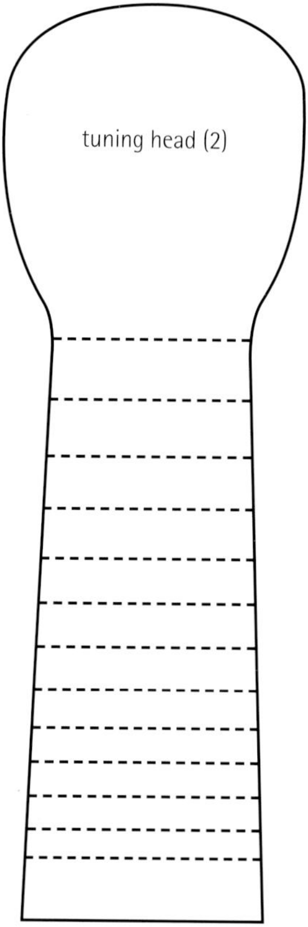

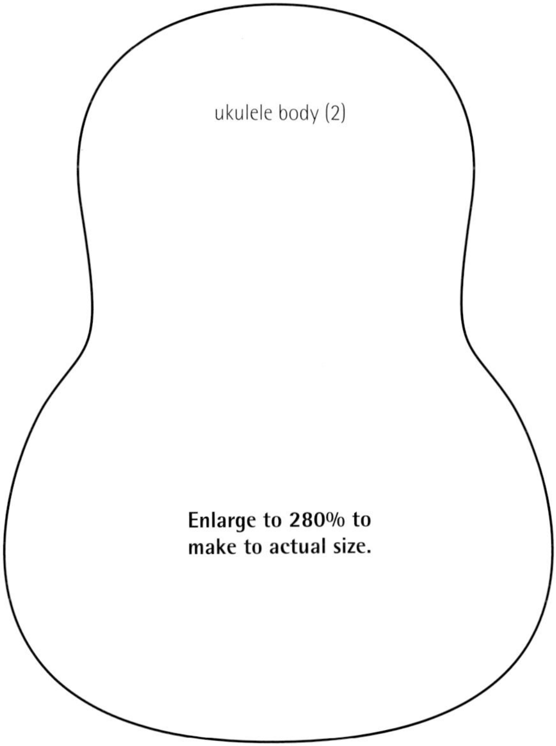

for the centre strings, sewing 2cm (3/4 in) from either edge. Pull the outside strings in 1.5cm (5/8 in) and pin 1.25cm (1/2-in) above the top fret. Align the inside strings in between the outside ones and 0.5cm (1/4 in) apart. Stitch the strings at the pins.

Cut a 1 x 6-cm (3/8 x 2 1/2-in) piece of white felt and sew it over what you just stitched. Cut a 2.5 x 7.5-cm (1 x 3-in) piece of black felt and centre and sew over the bottom strings.

With C and 4 mm hook, make 6 dc in a magic ring and sl st to join. Pull the centre string to make the hole tight. Make three more and sew over the string knots on the head. Cut a 2.5 x 7.5-cm (1 x 3-in) piece of black felt and centre it over the bottom strings. Backstitch around the edge with black thread.

With C, and the 4 mm hook, make 6 dc in a magic ring. Sl st in first ch to join. Pull the centre string to make the centre hole tight. Knot this together with the end string and trim off the excess. Make three more of these and sew over the white string knots on the head with yellow thread.

needle felt toadstool

see variations page 228

materials

- wool roving in red and white, approx. 15g ($^1/_2$ oz) of each
- size 38 felting needle
- felt foam pad
- scrap fabric: white for dots, plaid for grass
- embroidery thread
- sewing needle
- stuffing

finished dimensions:
10cm (4 in) high, 5cm (2 in) wide

instructions

toadstool base

Pull off a 30 x 7.5-cm (12 x 3-in) section of white roving, and roll it into a tube. Start at one end and roll tightly, tucking in both sides as you go. You should end with a 3 x 7.5-cm (1$^1/_4$ x 3-in) tube. Hold it in place and lay it lengthwise on top of your foam pad. Stab all over with your felting needle until it feels firm, including the top and bottom of the tube, which you should stab flat. To make the base a little wider than the top, pull off a smaller section of the white roving and wrap it around the base. Stab and smooth this in place with your needle until the base measures 3cm (1$^1/_4$ in.), and the top measures 2.25cm ($^7/_8$ in) in diameter. Stab the base as flat as you can.

toadstool cap

Pull off a 76 x 5-cm (30 x 2$^1/_2$-in) section of red roving, and roll it into an oval. Hold it together and place on top of your foam pad, then stab all over with the felting needle. When it starts to firm up but is not completely firm, shape your cap by rounding out the top and flattening out the bottom with your needle. Keep stabbing and shaping to get the correct shape.

attaching

Hold the toadstool cap upside down and place the smaller end of the base on the upside-down cap. Stab the felting needle at an angle through the base and cap. Keep stabbing the two pieces together until you have a strong join.

details

Cut small three circles of different sizes from the white fabric and blanket stitch them to the mushroom cap. Cut two layers of grass leaves for each blade and blanket stitch, stuff, and stitch them to the base.

sewn boat

see variations page 229

materials

- fabric: Robert Kaufman Kona Cotton (100% cotton), 25cm ($\frac{1}{4}$ yd) of Bone; P&B Spectrum Solids (100% cotton), 25cm ($\frac{1}{4}$ yd) of Camel
- wool felt in cream
- tracing paper
- dressmaking pins
- sewing needle
- sewing thread to match fabric
- sewing machine (optional)
- stuffing
- 1 bamboo skewer
- masking tape
- fabric glue
- blue 0.5-cm ($\frac{1}{4}$-in)-wide ribbon

finished dimensions:
18cm (7 in) long, 10cm (4 in) wide, 28cm (11 in) high

instructions

boat

Trace and cut out the boat pattern from the Camel fabric. Pin the sides around the bottom cutout of the boat and sew together with a 0.5-cm ($\frac{1}{4}$-in) seam allowance. Pin the three 6-cm ($2\frac{1}{2}$-in) boat corners together, and sew with a 0.75-cm ($\frac{5}{16}$-in) seam allowance. Pin the last cutout to the top and sew around the edges, leaving the back 9.5cm ($3\frac{3}{4}$-in) edge open.

Turn the boat right side out and stuff. Make an invisible stitch to close. Snip a small hole 4.5cm ($1\frac{3}{4}$ in) from the back and sides of the boat.

Cut a 2-cm ($\frac{3}{4}$-in)-diameter circle out of wool felt and snip a small hole in the centre. Cut the bamboo skewer to 26.5cm ($10\frac{1}{2}$ in), cutting the pointed end off, and wrap a bit of masking tape around the cut end. Insert the skewer, with the masking tape end down, through the felt circle and through the hole on top of the boat. Glue the felt and skewer to the boat.

Cut an 46-cm (18-in) length of blue ribbon and glue around the boat, 1.25cm ($\frac{1}{2}$-in) below the top. Add a thin dab of glue along the cut edges to keep it from fraying.

sail

Trace and cut out two layers of the sail from the Bone fabric. Pin and sew all three edges together with the wrong side facing, leaving 5cm (2 in) open at bottom right, and with a 1-cm ($\frac{5}{16}$-in) seam allowance.

Turn right side out and fold the 5-cm (2-in) opening in. Press.

Sew straight along the side of the sail, 1cm ($\frac{3}{8}$ in) from the edge, to make a pocket for the skewer. Invisible stitch the 5-cm (2-in) opening closed and insert the sail over the skewer. Add a dab of glue at the base of the sail and skewer to secure.

Enlarge to 600%
to make to actual size.

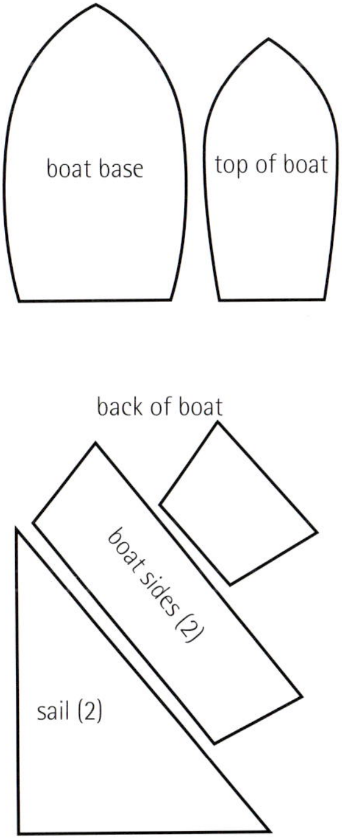

materials

- yarn: Brown Sheep Shepherd's Shades (100% wool, 100g (3½ oz), 120m (131 yds)), 1 skein each of (A) Pearl, (B) Fire; Brown Sheep Nature Spun Worsted (100% wool, 100g (3½ oz), 224m (245 yds)), 1 skein of (C) Pepper
- 6.5 mm (US size K/10.5) crochet hook
- stuffing
- tapestry needle
- dressmaking pins

tension:
3 sts over 4 rows = 2.5cm (1 in)
finished dimensions:
12cm (5 in) high, 12-cm (5-in) diameter

crochet drum

see variations page 230

instructions

With A, ch 2.

Rnd 1: 8 dc in 2nd ch from hook.

Rnd 2: 2 dc in each st, sl st to join – 16 sts.

Rnd 3: ch 1, [dc in next st, 2 dc in next st] around, sl st to join – 24 sts.

Rnd 4: ch 1, [dc in next 2 sts, 2 dc in next st] around, sl st to join – 32 sts.

Rnd 5: ch 1, [dc in next 3 sts, 2 dc in next st] around, sl st to join – 40 sts.

Rnd 6: ch 1, [dc in next 4 sts, 2 dc in next st] around, sl st to join – 48 sts.

Rnd 7: ch 1, [dc in next 5 sts, 2 dc in next st] around, sl st to join – 56 sts.

The next round will start the body of the drum.

Rnd 8: ch 1, dc on the back loop only in each st around, sl st to join.

Rnd 9: ch 1, dc in each st around, sl st to join.

Rnd 10: ch 1, dc in each st around, sl st to join. Fasten off A, join B.

Rnd 11: repeat rnd 8.

Rnds 12–19: ch 1, dc in each st around, sl st to join.

Rnd 20: ch 1, dc in each st around, sl st to join. Fasten off B, join A.

Rnd 21: ch 1, sl st loosely in the front loop only in each st around, sl st to join.

Rnd 22: ch 1, dc in the back loop only in each st around, sl st to join.

Rnds 23–24: ch 1, dc in each st around, sl st to join.

Rnd 25: ch 1, in the back loop only [dc in next 5 sts, dc2tog] around, sl st to join – 48 sts.

Rnd 26: ch 1, [dc in next 4 sts, dc2tog] around, sl st to join – 40 sts.

Rnd 27: ch 1, [dc in next 3 sts, dc2tog] around, sl st to join – 32 sts.

Rnd 28: ch 1, [dc in next 2 sts, dc2tog] around, sl st to join – 24 sts.

Begin to stuff and continue stuffing to end.

Rnd 29: ch 1, [dc in next st, dc2tog] around, sl st to join – 16 sts.

Rnd 30: ch 1, dc2tog around, sl st to join – 8 sts.

Break yarn, weave around the circle, and pull tightly closed. Fasten off and hide ends on the inside.

The diameter of the drum should be 40cm (16 in) Measure out four points 10cm (4 in) apart just below the white ridge and place a pin at each point. Do the same for the bottom ridge, but centre the points between the top points. Cut a 89-cm (35-in) length of C and, with a tapestry needle, make a knot at each point. Thread starting at a top point, then moving to the bottom, and back up to form 'V's. Once you're finished, tie off and hide ends on the inside.

knitted money plant

see variations page 231

materials

- yarn: Brown Sheep Shepherd's Shades (100% wool, 100g (3½ oz), 120m (131 yds)), 1 skein each of (A) Wintergreen, (B) Chestnut; Brown Sheep Lamb's Pride Worsted (85% wool, 15% mohair, 100g (4 oz), 175m (190 yds), 1 skein of (C) Oregano
- wool and rayon blend felt in olive
- 6.5 mm and 5 mm (US size 10.5 and 8) dpns
- stuffing
- pipe cleaner

gauge: 4 sts over 5 rows = 2.5cm (1 in)
finished dimensions: 25cm (10 in) high, 9cm (3½ in) wide

instructions

plant pot

With A and 6.5 mm dpns, CO 8 sts and divide between three needles. Join in the round.

Rnd 1: k.
Rnd 2: k1f&tb in each st – 16 sts.
Rnds 3–5: k.
Rnd 6: k1f&tb in each st – 32 sts.
Rnd 7: p.
Rnds 8–20: k.
Rnds 21–23: p.
Rnds 24–26: change to B and k.
Begin to stuff and continue stuffing to end.
Rnd 27: k2tog around – 16 sts.
Rnds 28–30: k.
R31: k2tog around – 8 sts.
BO and break yarn with enough to sew stem on.

plant

With C and 5 mm dpns, CO 4 sts. Knit in I-cord for 10cm (4 in) BO and weave in ends. Bend the tip of the pipe cleaner and insert into the cord. Leave the rest of the pipe cleaner hanging out.

Trace the leaf pattern and cut a double layer of felt for 10 leaves. With embroidery thread, backstitch the edges of each leaf together, beginning and ending at the base. Stitch each leaf on with the waste thread as you finish it. Sew the leaves in opposing pairs about 1.25cm (½-in) apart. Hide the ends inside the stem. Bend the bottom pipe cleaner and push into the centre hole of the pot and dirt. Make a few stitches with rest of the brown yarn to fix the stem in place.

Pattern is actual size.

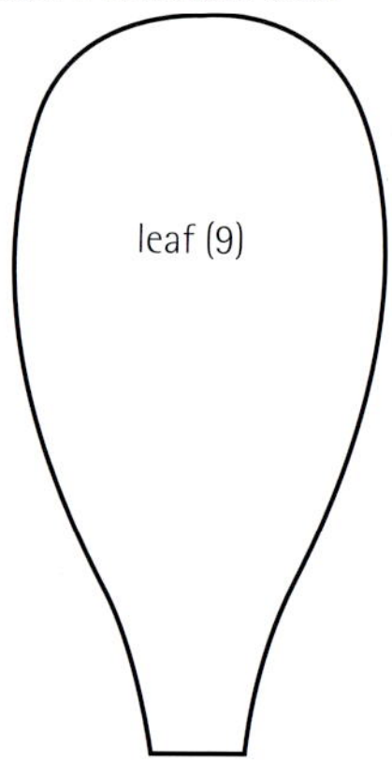

b
3
j

crochet/sewn hammer

see variations page 232

materials

- yarn: Brown Sheep Nature Spun Worsted (100% wool, 100g (3½ oz), 224m (245 yds)), 1 skein of Red Fox
- felt, one 23 x 30-cm (9 x 12-in) sheet in light grey
- 4 mm (US size G/6) crochet hook
- tapestry needle
- stuffing
- tracing paper
- dressmaking pins
- sewing machine (optional)
- sewing needle
- sewing thread in grey and red

tension:
5 sts over 6 rows = 2.5cm (1 in)

finished dimensions:
12cm (4¾ in) long, 3cm (1¼ in) wide, 28cm (11 in) high

instructions

handle

With yarn and crochet hook, ch 6.

Rnd 1: begin 2nd ch from hook, dc in next 5 ch, 2 dc in last ch.

Rnd 2: continue down the back of chain, dc in next 5 ch, 2 dc in last ch.

Rnd 3: work in the round to make an oval. [Dc in next 5 sts, 2 dc in next 2 sts] twice – 18 sts.

Dc in each st around until piece measures 14cm (5½ in) Break yarn, weave in ends, and stuff.

head

Trace the hammer head pattern. Fold the felt in half with the right sides together and cut two layers of the hammer head. Pin along the edges, leaving the bottom edge open. Sew around the edge with a 0.5cm (5/16-in) seam allowance.

Turn right side out and push the corners out. Stuff and pin to the inside top of the handle with the felt edge 1.25cm (½-in) below the handle opening.

With red thread, stitch the two pieces together. Hide the ends on the inside.

Enlarge to 330% to make to actual size.

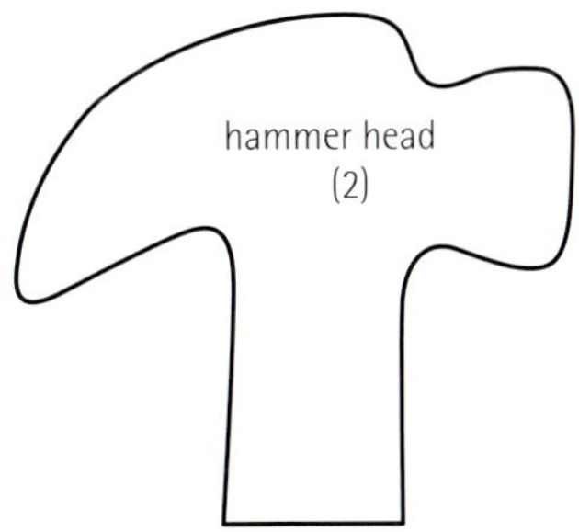

knitted airship

see variations page 233

materials

- yarn: Brown Sheep Lamb's Pride Bulky (85% wool, 15% mohair, 100g (4 oz), 114m (125 yds)), 1 skein of Pumpkin
- 6.5 mm (US size 10.5) double-pointed needles
- stitch marker
- stuffing
- tapestry needle

tension:
3.5 sts over 4.5 rows = 2.5cm (1 in)

finished dimensions:
16.5cm (6½ in) long,
8.25cm (3¼ in) wide,
8.25cm (3¼ in) high

instructions

CO 8 sts, divide between three needles, pm, and join in the round.
Rnd 1 and all odd rows: k.
Rnd 2: [k4, m1] two times – 10 sts.
Rnd 4: [k5, m1] two times – 12 sts.
Rnd 6: [k6, m1] two times – 14 sts.
Rnd 8: [k7, m1] two times – 16 sts.
Rnd 10: [k8, m1] two times – 18 sts.
Rnd 12: [k9, m1] two times – 20 sts.
Rnd 14: [k10, m1] two times – 22 sts.
Rnd 16: [k11, m1] two times – 24 sts.
Rnd 18: [k12, m1] two times – 26 sts.
Rnd 20: [k13, m1] two times – 28 sts.
Rnd 22: [k14, m1] two times – 30 sts.
Rnd 24: k.
Rnd 26: [k3, k2tog] six times – 24 sts.
Rnd 28: [k2, k2tog] six times – 18 sts.
Begin to stuff and continue stuffing to end.
Rnd 30: [k1, k2tog] six times – 12 sts
Rnd 32: k2tog around – 6 sts
Break yarn and thread yarn through the 6 sts, and weave in ends.

fins

CO 5 sts and knit 5 rows in garter st. BO with enough sewing yarn. Knit three more fins, space evenly, and sew around the pointed tip of the airship. Weave in ends.

fabric peonies

see variations page 234

materials

- yarn: Brown Sheep Nature Spun Worsted (100% wool, 100g (3½ oz), 224m (245 yds)), 1 skein of Lemon Grass
- 100% cotton fabric, 25cm (¼ yd) in dusty rose
- wool roving, 7g (¼ oz)
- size 38 felting needle
- felting foam pad
- sewing thread in pink
- 4.5 mm (US size 7) double-pointed needles
- 18-tension wire
- embroidery thread in olive green

finished dimensions:
10cm (16 in) long, 15cm (6 in) wide

instructions

peony

Follow the needle felt ball instructions on page 48 to felt a 5-cm (2-in) diameter ball with white roving. This will be the centre of the peony. Trace and cut 10 petals out of the dusty rose fabric. Arrange them so they don't line up directly on top of one another. Place the felt ball in the centre and scrunch the petals around it. Use a light pink thread to stitch from the bottom outside base of the flower midway up the ball, and ruffle the petals around the ball. Push the petals around the inside of the peony around the ball, and make a few small stitches to secure. Hide the ends on the inside.

stem

With yarn, and size 7 dpns, CO 4 sts. Knit in I-cord for 25cm (10 in).

Enlarge to 480% to make to actual size.

Continue below to make the area where the stem and the flower join.

R1: k1f&b in each st across and divide between 3 dpns and join for working in the round – 8 sts.
Rnd 2: k.
Rnd 3: k1f&b in each st across – 16 sts.
Rnd 4: k.
Rnd 5: k1f&b in each st across – 32 sts.
Rnds 6–10: k.
BO and weave in ends.

Cut a 50-cm (20-in) length of wire. Use a large, pointy needle to make a hole at the base of the flower petals and push the wire through. Bend 5cm (2 in) of wire together and wrap around the stem. Bend the other end of the wire so that it's rounded. Push the knitted stem through the wire with the wider end at the top. Stitch the stem to the flower base with olive green thread. Bend the wire at the bottom of the stem and push through a loop of yarn at the bottom to secure.

knitted keyboard

see variations page 235

materials

- yarn: Brown Sheep Shepherd's Shades (100% wool, 100g (3½ oz), 120m (131 yds)), 1 skein each of (A) Fire, (B) Pearl; Brown Sheep Cotton Fleece (80% cotton, 20% merino wool, 100g (3½ oz), 196m (215 yds)), 1 skein of (C) Cavern
- felt in black
- 6.5 mm (US size 10½) knitting needles
- stuffing
- tapestry needle
- 3.75 mm (US size F/5) crochet hook
- tailor's chalk
- sewing thread in black
- fabric glue (optional)

tension:
4 sts over 5 rows = 2.5cm (1 in)

finished dimensions:
33cm (13 in) long, 6cm (2½ in) wide,14cm (5½ in) high

instructions

front

With A, CO 48 sts.
R1–10: Starting with a k row, work in st st.
R11 (RS): k6, change to B and k36, change to A and k6.
R12–30: Continue in st st as set keeping the colour pattern set in row 11.
BO with A and leave enough yarn for sewing.

back

With A, CO 48 sts and starting with a k row, work 30 rows in st st. BO and weave in ends.

With the wrong sides together, mattress stitch the edges together (the seam will turn and be on the inside). Leave one of the short edges open. Stuff and stitch closed. Hide the ends inside.

keys

With crochet hook and C, ch 12 and break yarn with tail long enough for knotting. Make six of these short key lines. With C, ch 20 and break yarn with enough for knotting. Make two of these long key lines.

Pin these key lines 2.5cm (1 in) apart on the white section of the keyboard. Line up with the bottom bound-off edge. Pin the lines in this order, beginning on the left side: 2 short, 1 long, 3 short, 1 long, 1 short. Knot the excess yarn at each end onto the keyboard, stretching it a little. Hand-sew with black thread over these lines onto the keyboard, to secure.

Measure, draw, and cut six 5.5 x 2-cm (2¼ x ¾-in) keys out of black felt. Place each key above each short key line and either dab a line of glue underneath each key to hold in place, or baste in place. Blanket stitch around the edges of each key with black thread.

PIANO CONDUCTEUR
MENUET

Enlarge to 200% to make to actual size.

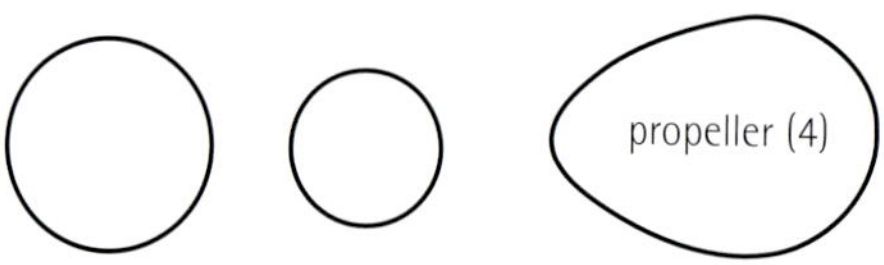

window (6) propeller centre

materials

- yarn: Brown Sheep Shepherd's Shades (100% wool, 100g (3½ oz), 120m (131 yds)), 1 skein of Sunshine
- wool felt in grey
- 6.5 mm (US size K/10.5) crochet hook
- stuffing
- tapestry needle
- fabric glue
- embroidery thread in white
- sewing needle

tension:
3 sts over 4 rows = 2.5cm (1 in)

finished dimensions: 18cm (7 in) long, 7.5cm (3 in) wide, 10cm (4 in) high

crochet submarine

see variations page 236

instructions

submarine

With yarn and crochet hook, make 8 dc in a magic ring, sl st in first dc to join.

Rnd 1: ch 1, 2 dc in each ch across, sl st in first dc to join – 16 sts.

Rnd 2: ch 1, [dc in next st, 2 dc in next st] around, sl st in first dc to join – 24 sts.

Rnd 3: ch 1, [dc in next 2 sts, 2 dc in next st] around, sl st in first dc to join – 32 sts.

Rnds 4–25: ch 1, dc in each st across, sl st in first dc to join. Begin to stuff and continue to end.

Rnd 26: ch 1, [dc in next 2 sts, dc2tog] across, sl st in first dc to join – 24 sts.

Rnd 27: ch 1, [dc in next st, dc2tog] across, sl st in first dc to join – 16 sts.

Rnd 28: ch 1, dc2tog across, sl st in first dc to join – 8 sts. Break yarn and weave in ends.

tower

With yarn and crochet hook, ch 7, turn.

R1: begin 2nd ch from hook, dc in next 6 sts, 2 dc in last st, turn.

R2: continue on back edge of chain, dc 6, 2 dc in last st.

Rnd 3: continue in the round, dc 6, 2 dc in next 2 sts, dc 5, 2 dc in next 2 sts, sl st in first dc to join – 20 sts.

Rnds 4–7: ch 1, dc in each st across, sl st in first dc to join. Break yarn with enough to sew.

fins

With A, ch 5, turn.

R1: begin 2nd from the hook, dc in next 4 sts, turn.

R2–4: ch 1, dc in next 4 sts, turn.

Break yarn with enough to sew, and make three more.

assembly

Centre a fin on either side of the tower and sew on with the waste yarn. Weave in ends. Stuff the tower and sew to the top of the submarine, beginning 4cm (1½ in) from the front. Hide ends on the inside. Centre a fin on either side of the submarine, and sew 1.25cm (½-in) from the back. Hide ends on the inside.

Trace and cut four propellers out of grey felt. Pinch the pointed ends of each propeller and sew together. Stitch to the centre back of the submarine. Cut a 1.25-cm (½-in)-diameter circle out of grey felt and glue to the centre of the propeller, covering up centre stitches. Trace and cut out six portholes out of grey felt. Centre three portholes evenly 3cm (1¼ in) below the tower. Pin and backstitch around with white thread. Repeat for the other side.

crochet cactus

see variations page 237

materials

- yarn: Brown Sheep Nature Spun Worsted (100% wool, 100g (3½ oz), 224m (245 yds)), 1 skein each of (A) French Clay, (B) Lemon Grass, (C) Peruvian Pink
- 4 mm (US size G/6) crochet hook
- sewing thread
- stuffing

tension: 5 sts over 6 rows = 2.5cm (1 in)
finished dimensions: 12cm (5 in) high, 7.5cm (3 in) wide

instructions

cactus

With B, ch 16.
R1: dc 2nd ch from hook, dc in the back loop only in next 15 ch, turn – 15 sts.
R2–25: ch 1, dc in the back loop only in next 15 sts, turn.
Sl st both 7.5-cm (3-in) edges together, making the seam ridge blend in with the ribbing. Make a running stitch along one edge and pull the edge tight to make the top of cactus, and secure. Hide the ends inside.

clay pot

With A, ch 2.
R1: 8 dc in 2nd ch from hook.
R2: 2 htr in each st, sl st to join – 16 sts.
Rnd 3: ch 2, htr in same st, (2 htr in next st, htr in next st) around, sl st to join – 24 sts.
Rnd 4: ch 1, dc under the ridge on the back of the first st of previous round. Work under this ridge, not into the regular 'V's. This will make the base lie flat.
Rnds 5–8: ch 2, htr in same st, htr in next 23 sts, sl st to join.
Rnd 9: ch 2, hc in same st, htr in next st, [2 htr in next st, htr in next 2 sts] around, sl st in 2nd turning ch to join – 32 sts.
Rnd 10: ch 2, htr in same st, htr in next 31 sts, sl st to join.
Rnd 11: ch 2, htr in same st, htr in 2 next sts, [2 htr in next st, htr in next 3 sts] around, sl st in 2nd turning ch to join – 40 sts.
Rnd 12: ch 2, htr in same st, htr in next 39 sts, sl st to join.
Break yarn with enough to sew.

cactus flower

With C, make 6 dc in a magic ring, sl st in the first dc to join.
Rnd 1: ch 1, [dc in next st, ch 5, dc in same st] around, sl st to join.
Break yarn with enough to sew.
Make another flower.

assembly

Fold the clay pot ridge down 2cm (¾ in) and sew the bottom edge to the body of the pot with a running stitch. Stuff the pot and cactus and sew the base of the cactus to the top ridge of the pot with a running stitch. Use the clay yarn to sew through the cactus to the front of the pot. Once you've finished, pull the yarn through the centre bottom of the pot to the top of the cactus to flatten out the bottom so the pot will sit flat. Secure with a small knot at the top. The flowers will hide the knot. Sew both flowers to the top. Hide the ends inside.

variations

plushie sewing machine

see base design page 189

patchwork sewing machine

Use up scrap fabric to make a patchwork sewing machine. Press the edges and sew together to make a 'sheet' of fabric big enough for the pattern. Trace, cut and sew following the plushie sewing machine instructions.

felt buttons

Cut two 5-cm (2-in)-diameter circles out of felt and use a hole punch to make two holes evenly in the centre. Stitch these two pieces together along the outer edge using a running stitch in a contrasting colour thread. Make tiny whip stitches all around each of the two holes in the same thread.

plushie scissors

Make scissors out of fabric by tracing an actual pair of scissors (closed or open, depending on how ambitious you are) on tracing paper and leaving an extra 0.5cm (¼ in) around for the seam. Pin and sew with the wrong side facing you, leaving 5–7.5cm (2–3 in) open. Turn right side out, stuff, and invisible stitch to close.

felt thimble

Cut a strip of felt 6 x 3cm (2½ x 1¼ in.) Hand stitch the 3-cm (1¼-in) edges together to form a tube. Cut a 2-cm (¾-in) circle out of felt, and sew to the top of the tube. Make little stitches around the top of the thimble to resemble the texture of a metal thimble.

button knobs

Hand-sew vintage buttons onto the sewing machine in place of the crochet and felt knobs to give it some flair.

variations

knitted camera

see base design page 190

crochet camera

Single crochet two 7.5 x 12.5-cm (3 x 5-in) rectangles and one 4 x 40-cm (1½ x 16-in) strip. Pin and stitch the strip along both rectangle edges and stuff before closing. Follow the lens, button, and flash details as for the knit camera.

knitted & crochet slr camera

Follow the knit camera instructions but add to the lens height to make an SLR camera. Follow the lens instructions, and continue crocheting after round 5 as follows. Rnd 6: ch 1, sc in the back loop only in each st around, sl st to join (36 sts). Continue to sc in each st around until the piece measures 5cm (2 in) high. Break yarn with enough for sewing, and stitch to the centre front of the camera. Stuff before closing.

camera strap

Crochet a 5 x 63-cm (2 x 25-in) strap for your camera. Cut four 5-cm (2-in)-square pieces of felt, and cut the bottom half into a triangle. Sew two layers together and stitch the top 5-cm (2-in) edge to the 5-cm (2-in) end of the crochet strap. Repeat for the other end. Make buttonholes above the triangle points. Sew a button to either side of your camera near the top, and button your strap on.

felt polaroid camera

Make a simplified square 'pillow' polaroid camera. Use white felt to make the 12.5-cm (5-in)-square main body, then cut a 12 x 3-cm (5 x 1¼-in) black strip and sew to the bottom edge. Follow the crochet lens instructions and sew to the centre of the square. Cut a 2.5-cm (1-in) black felt square for the viewfinder and sew to the top left-hand corner. Cut a 2.5-cm (1-in) black circle and a 2.5-cm (1-in) red circle from felt and stitch the black button on the left-hand side of the lens, and the red button on the right.

felt polaroid prints

Make polaroid prints using white felt with interfacing sewn in between. Cut the prints to 9 x 11cm (3½ x 4¼ in), and the actual print to be 7.5-cm (3-in) square, placed closer to the top of the frame. Cut and stitch different scenes in the 7.5-cm (3-in) frame, such as a house, a sun, or a puppy.

variations

crochet mobile phone

see base design page 193

tablet

Enlarge the mobile phone measurements by 100 percent to make a tablet. Use black yarn in place of the blue for the base of the tablet.

knitted smartphone

Knit two 7.5 x 10-cm (3 x 4-in) rectangles and mattress stitch together. Stuff lightly before sewing closed. Follow the screen and app instructions from the crochet phone.

flip phone

Cut two 5 x 7.5–cm (2 x 3–in) pieces of felt for the screen and keypad. Stitch numbers onto the keypad and stitch a phone number onto the screen with a contrasting colour thread. Crochet two 5 x 7.5-cm (2 x 3-in) rectangles and stitch a felt rectangle to a crochet one; insert two strong magnets at the corners before stuffing so the flip phone will hold shut when closed.

embroidered game

Follow the mobile phone pattern and embroider your favourite game onto the screen.

ringing sound chip

Add a ringing phone sound chip in the centre of the phone before stitching closed to make an interactive phone.

felt clock

see base design page 194

watch
Resize the pattern to a 5-cm (2-in) circle and make tiny stitches for the numbers, and use a 0.5-cm (¼-in) button for the centre. Add a fabric band to the back to make a wristwatch. Sew hook-and-eye fastener to the ends of the band to hold them together.

velcro numbers clock
This learning toy becomes even more educational if you make the numbers detachable, so kids will need to be able to place the numbers in order. Embroider the clock numbers onto circles of felt and stitch hook-and-eye fastener to the backs, and onto the clock face where the numbers will go.

crochet clock
Crochet two 25-cm (10-in)-diameter circles and sandwich a 25-cm (10-in) circle of stiff felt between them. Stitch the crochet edges together and follow the rest of the felt clock instructions for the numbers and clock hands. Add a string in the back to hang on the wall.

cuckoo clock
Using stiff felt in a contrasting colour, cut the shape of a house 35.5cm (14 in) wide and 46cm (18 in) tall. Sew the clock in the centre of one of the felt pieces. Sandwich the stiff felt between the felt layers and sew together. Cut four 5 x 10-cm (2 x 4-in) pinecone-shapes from yellow felt and sew two layers together to make two 'weights'. Hang them at different lengths from the bottom of the cuckoo clock with cotton yarn.

pocket watch
Create the White Rabbit's giant pocket watch (from *Alice's Adventures in Wonderland*) by resizing the clock pattern to a 15-cm (6-in) circle, and following the embroidery pattern for the numbers. Resize the clock hands to fit the pocket watch. Add a loop of yarn at the top of the watch and crochet chain stitch a 64-cm (25-in) chain to attach to the watch loop and clip onto your clothing.

variations

knitted car

see base design page 197

crochet school bus

Crochet two yellow 18 x 7.5-cm (7 x 3-in) rectangles for the bus sides, and a 33 x 7.5-cm (13 x 3-in) yellow strip to sew along both 7.5-cm (3-in) edges and one 18-cm (7-in) edge of both rectangles for the front, top, and back. Crochet a 18 x 7.5-cm (7 x 3-in) black rectangle for the base. Stitch together and stuff. Cut and sew black felt windows for the windscreen, door, back window, and smaller side windows. Chain stitch two black chains along the bus's sides. Knit wheels as for the knit car and sew to the bus. Add other details too, such as headlights and a stop sign.

camping trailer

Make a trailer for your car. Cut two 7.5 x 10-cm (3 x 4-in) felt rectangles and round out the corners to make the sides of the camper. Cut a 7.5-cm (3-in)-wide felt strip, long enough to sew along the edges of the side cutouts. Stitch together and stuff before closing. Sew on felt windows and a door. Make two tyres as for the knit car. Sew them two-thirds along the length of the camper from the front. Make a felt latch on the bottom front of the camper to hook onto the car, and add a little loop on the car to attach.

wooden wheels

Insert two 15-cm (6-in) wooden dowels through the width of the car, and secure wooden wheels at each end of the dowels. You have an instant moving car!

police car

Follow the knit car instructions and use black for the bonnet and boot sections, and white yarn for the middle door and roof sections. Add little needle felt blue, white, and red lights to the roof of the car.

taxicab

Use a bright yellow yarn to make a taxicab. Use a black-and-white checkered ribbon for the cab decoration, stitched to the sides below the side windows (or use black and white yarn to stitch on the design) Stitch the word 'TAXI' onto a piece of felt and sew to the roof of the cab, facing the front.

variations

sewn ukulele

see base design page 198

acoustic guitar

Multiply all measures and quantities by two to make a guitar. Include six strings and two extra tuning heads at the top for the extra strings.

electric guitar

Make an electric guitar following the ukulele pattern and cutting the top sides of the guitar to point upward like horns. Make the left side taller than the right side. Extend the length of the side strip as necessary to fit around the whole guitar. Make six strings and two more tuning heads at the top. Add stripes or lightning bolts as decoration.

violin

Follow the ukulele pattern but use brown fabric. Omit the fret lines and sew the base of the neck beginning one-third of the way down the body. Taper the head to half its size at the top. Omit the sound hole and embroider two 'f' holes on either side of the body. Cut two 6 x 5-cm (2½ x 2-in) pieces of felt and sew together with a piece of stiff felt between to make the bridge. Sew the bottom 6-cm (2½-in) edge sticking straight up and horizontal to the body on the centre of the body, where it will hold up the strings. Extend the black tailpiece that holds the ends of the strings from the bottom third of the body to the very end. Follow the fishing rod instructions from 'go fish!' on page 248 to make a bow.

banjo

To make a banjo, cut and sew two 25-cm (10-in) white circles and a 80 x 6-cm (32 x 2½-in) strip of fabric with the right sides together. Leave an opening at the end, turn right side out, and stuff before closing up. Follow the ukulele pattern for the neck and head, and sew together.

sound chip

Add a sound chip with a few different songs under the sound hole before you finish stuffing and sewing closed to make an interactive ukulele.

variations

needle felt toadstool

see base design page 203

mushroom rattle

Wrap red roving thickly around a jingle bell ball. Make sure you have enough wool so that your needle won't jab into the ball when felting. It'll end up being a bit larger than the pattern, depending on the size of your ball. Felt the mushroom following the rest of the toadstool instructions. Make two to make mushroom maracas!

toadstool gnome dollhouse

Cut two 15-cm (6-in)-diameter white felt circles, and interfacing to sew in between. Cut two rectangles of white felt, 12cm (5 in) tall, to wrap around the 15-cm (6-in) circle with interfacing to sew in between. Cut a 6 x 7.5-cm (2½ x 3-in) doorway on the bottom of the rectangle, and cut a piece of red felt slightly bigger for the door itself. Sew the door hinge on the right-hand edge, and add a button for the doorknob. Needle felt a lightweight toadstool cap to fit on top of the house. It needs to be light enough to sit on the house without pushing it in. Sew together at the edges. Cut and sew windows and furnishing details.

cremini mushrooms

Needle felt 5 x 4cm (2 x 1½-in)-wide cremini mushrooms, following the toadstool instructions, for play food. Use medium brown wool for the mushroom cap and white wool for the stem.

enoki mushrooms

Needle felt long, thin white stems and small white mushroom caps to make a bunch of enoki mushrooms. Felt the stems together at the bottom to make the bunch and add to your collection of play food.

portobello mushroom

Needle felt a 12.5-cm (5-in)-wide mushroom cap and a 5-cm (2-in)-wide stem to make a portobello mushroom. Use light brown wool for the top of the cap, and dark brown wool for the underside. Stitch the gills with brown thread from the centre and out to the edges of the underside.

variations

sewn boat

see base design page 204

rowing boat

Follow the boat pattern but omit the top section of fabric and the sail to make a rowing boat. Cut a double layer of felt and interfacing to sew between for support. Sew the side and back edges to the base of the boat, and embroider wood plank details with brown thread. Stitch one felt 'plank' of wood for seating inside. Cut two 12.5-cm (5-in) oars from felt.

pirate ship

Turn the boat into a pirate ship by using black fabric for the sail, and appliquéing a white skull and crossbones to the sail. Follow the lightning bolt appliqué instructions on page 159 to sew the skull and crossbones on.

canoe

Follow the boat pattern, but make both ends of the bottom pointed to make a canoe. Stitch two felt planks inside for seating. Add 12.5-cm (5-in) felt oars for paddling.

tug

Omit the sail and add a wheelhouse on the top front section of the boat to make a tug. Cut and sew a 6-cm (2½-in) stuffed cube to the top of the boat for the wheelhouse. Stitch little windows on the front and sides of the cube.

motorboat

Add a felt propeller to the back of boat to turn it into a motorboat. Use the propeller pattern from the crochet submarine (see page 219).

variations

crochet drum

see base design page 207

tambourine

Follow the crochet drum pattern for the top white section and change to brown yarn for the lip. Extend the height a further 2.5cm (1 in) and weave in ends. Sew silver jingle bells around the lip of the tambourine.

bongos

Crochet two drums to make bongos. After changing to red, continue crocheting with it until the end. Omit the black strings and sew the bongos together with four strips of felt into a rectangular prism, connecting the sides of the bongos.

steel drum

Follow the crochet drum pattern but use the same colour yarn throughout. Stop before crocheting the base circle and break yarn. Weave in ends. Cut a circle of grey felt slightly bigger than the drum base so that it curves into the drum. Stitch the different sections for notes around the edges and centre of the steel. Whip stitch the steel and drum together and make two drumsticks following the fishing rod pattern from the 'go fish!' instructions on page 248.

snare drum

Add a crochet neck strap, attaching it at the top of the drum. Make the strap 5cm (2 in) wide and long enough for the drum to sit at the waist, and stitch onto the drum.

felt drum

Sew a felt drum to the same measurements as the crochet drum. Stitch the black V-shaped string details as stated in the pattern. Add a sound chip of drum sounds or a rattle inside before closing off.

variations

knitted money plant

see base design page 208

venus fly trap

Follow the knit money plant instructions for the pot, soil, and stem. Cut two 4 x 6-cm (1½ x 2½-in) pieces of felt and round the corners. Sew the 6-cm (2½-in) edge of both pieces of felt together to make the mouth of the Venus fly trap. Cut thin 2.5-cm (1-in) felt teeth and stitch to the edges of the mouth.

potted grass

Follow the knitting instructions for the yellow pot and cast off after knitting the yellow yarn. Cut thin strips of varying lengths of green grass from felt, and cut the tips to a point. Make enough grass to fill the pot, and insert the blades. This would be a good nesting place for the grasshopper on page 80.

bonsai tree

Make a shallower pot and follow the money plant's stem instructions to make a brown tree trunk for a bonsai tree. Make knitted I-cord branches with pipe cleaners inserted in the centre and stitch to the main tree trunk. Use fluffy wool roving for the clumps of leaves on the branches. Lightly needle felt the leaf clusters and stitch to the branches.

sprout

Use the crochet cactus pattern on page 220 to make a small pot for a sprout. Fill the pot with brown wool roving for the dirt. Follow the money plant instructions for the stem and make it 5cm (2 in) tall. Make two money leaves and stitch the ends together at the top of the stem to make a sweet little sprout.

basil plant

Follow the money plant instructions and use the basil leaves pattern from the crochet pizza on page 124 to make a basil plant.

variations

crochet/sewn hammer

see base design page 211

crochet/sewn screwdriver

Make a screwdriver to match the hammer, using same yarn and felt. Begin with the crochet handle, and make 6 dc in a magic ring, 2 dc in each st around (12 sts). Dc in each st around until the piece measures 10cm (4 in) Stuff firmly. Cut two 11.5 x 4cm ($4\frac{1}{2}$ x $1\frac{1}{2}$-in) pieces of grey felt, and cut them to look like a flathead screwdriver. Sew with the right sides together and turn right side out. Stuff and tuck 1.25cm ($\frac{1}{2}$-in) of the end into the handle. Hand stitch together.

sewn wrench (pictured)

Cut two pieces of grey felt 25cm (10 in) tall to make a wrench. Make an exaggerated tracing of a real wrench to draw out your pattern. Add room for the seam allowance before cutting. Sew with the right sides facing and leave the bottom end open. Turn inside out and stuff firmly. Sew an invisible stitch to close.

felt saw

Cut a 25-cm (10-in) saw blade from grey stiff felt, with little triangles for the teeth. Cut a double layer of brown felt for the handle and stitch together with interfacing between. Sew the handle to the end of the saw.

crochet & needle felt mallet

Follow the hammer instructions and use tan yarn to make the mallet handle. Needle felt a 10-cm (4-in) long by 5-cm (2-in)-diameter black mallet head. Remember to roll the wool a little bigger than the finished dimensions, as it will shrink with felting. If it ends up smaller than it's supposed to be, just wrap more wool around the mallet head and continue felting until it's the right size.

tool belt

Sew a belt, following the ninja belt variation of the bandit mask on page 164. Attach metal D-rings to fasten the belt together. Sew loops onto the front of the belt to fit the tools above, minus the saw. Add two 10 x 7.5-cm (4 x 3-in) pockets hanging from the belt for small tools such as a tape measure and nails.

variations

knitted airship

see base design page 212

hot air balloon

Follow the needle felt ball instructions on page 48. Add more wool to the bottom to create the upside-down teardrop shape of a hot air balloon. Add stripes of different colours to the balloon by needle felting another colour directly onto the balloon. Cut and sew a little square basket using felt, string the four corners with yarn, and attach to the balloon. Your hot air balloon can hang on a mobile along with the needle felt clouds from page 54, or it can hang on its own with a doll or animals riding inside.

doll's parachute

Create a rectangular parachute for a doll. Use nylon fabric and cut a 11.5 x 19cm (4½ x 7½-in) rectangle. Fold the edges 0.5cm (¼ in) to the wrong side and sew along the edges. Attach 8-in. strings to each corner and connect the strings at the bottom, then tie into a loop that kids can loop around their dolls. Note: This toy may not actually float.

torpedo

Knit a torpedo by following the airship pattern but knit 30 stitches in the round after row 22 for a further 7.5cm (3 in) Knit rows 24–30 as normal, and follow the rest of the pattern for the stuffing and fine details.

rocket ship (pictured)

Follow the airship pattern and stitch the fins to the opposite pointed end of the body. Use blue yarn for the body and red yarn for the fins. Cut a felt circle for a window and sew to the centre of the body.

airship mobile

Needle felt four small 7.5-cm (3-in)-long airships for a mobile. Roll the felt into a tight cylinder slightly bigger than the intended size. Stab the wool all around and felt the tail to a rounded point, and smaller in diameter than the front. Compare the shape with the knit airship for reference. Make the tail fins out of felt and sew onto the tail. String the airships on two dowels like the fabric birds mobile on page 39.

variations

fabric peonies

see base design page 215

crochet daisy

Needle felt a 4–5-cm (1½–2-in) yellow ball for the centre of the daisy. Follow the crochet dragonfly's (page 84) wing pattern to make daisy petals using white yarn and a smaller crochet hook to tighten the stitches. Make enough petals to sew around the ball. Wrap a thick-tension wire with green fabric and secure at the top and bottom with fabric glue. Loop the top of the wire into the bottom of the felt ball and wrap green fabric around the flower base and stem join, then add fabric glue to secure.

felt tulip (pictured)

Cut six 5 x 7.5-cm (2 x 3-in) tulip petals from purple felt and round the top and bottom edges. Cut a 4cm (1½-in) circle from purple felt as the base, and lay three petals around the circle. Needle felt the base of each petal to the circle. Needle felt a 5-cm (2-in) white felt ball for the flower's inside structure. Place the ball in the centre of the three petals and needle felt the bottom of each petal around the ball. Arrange the last three petals around these centre petals and needle felt together. Cut a 3-cm (1¼-in) green felt circle and needle felt to the outside base of the flower. Knit an I-cord stem and insert wire inside. Attach the wire to the base of the tulip and stitch in place. Cut a 15-cm (6-in)-long by 3-cm (1¼-in)-wide leaf from felt and stitch to the stem.

felt sunflower

Needle felt a 7.5-cm (3-in) brown disk for the centre and enough 1.25 x 5-cm (½ x 2-in) yellow felt petals to sew around it. Follow the peonies stem pattern to make the stem.

fabric magnolia

Cut six 10 x 7.5-cm (4 x 3-in) petals from white cotton fabric for outside petals, and three 7.5 x 5-cm (3 x 2-in) white petals for inside petals. Needle felt a 2.5-cm (1-in) yellow ball for the centre and add French knots with yellow thread to make a pollen texture. Stitch the small petals around the ball, arrange three of the larger petals around the base, and stitch. Arrange the last three petals and stitch to secure. Follow the peony stem instructions for the stem.

variations

knitted keyboard

see base design page 216

knitted melodica

Follow the knit keyboard pattern but add a felt mouthpiece on the left-hand side. Cut a 2.5 x 12.5-cm (1 x 5-in) strip of white felt and sew the short ends to the centre back, to make the handle.

crochet xylophone

Crochet eight 2.5-cm (1-in)-wide keys in descending size beginning with 12cm (5 in) and ending with 6cm (2½ in) Make the keys in rainbow colours, beginning with red and ending with violet. Crochet two 2.5 x 25-cm (1 x 10-in) tubes and stuff as you crochet. Pull the ends closed and knot to secure. These will form the base of the xylophone. Space the keys evenly over the 25-cm (10-in) tubes and stitch through the key to the tube at the top and bottom of each key. Make two mallets (following the crochet maracas pattern on page 40) and extending the handle another 10cm (4 in) Insert a dowel or strong wire as required for support. Include jingle bell balls for sound and make the head of the mallet one solid colour.

sewn keyboard

Cut two pieces of black felt to the knit keyboard dimensions and sew a white rectangle with the same dimensions on one of the black felt pieces. Cut and stitch black felt keys and stitch black vertical lines for the white keys. Blanket stitch the top and bottom felt sides together, stuffing lightly before sewing closed.

piano sound chips

Add a few sound chips of your favourite piano tunes in a few stitched felt pockets in the back of the knit keyboard to give it some life! Close with a zipper or button. This is a great way for kids to learn new tunes, and you can change the sound chips whenever you like.

sheet music

Cut 21.5 x 28-cm (8½ x 11-in) sheets of white felt and embroider black staves and treble clefs on them. Stitch musical notes for a short song on each sheet. Add a felt pocket to the back of the keyboard to roll up and store the sheet music.

variations

crochet submarine

see base design page 219

periscope

Add a periscope by knitting a 10-cm (4-in) I-cord and inserting a pipe cleaner inside. Leave 2.5–4cm (1–1½ in) of pipe cleaner hanging out of the tube to anchor into the tower. Cut a small grey felt circle and stitch it to one end for the glass. Stitch the other end to the centre top of the submarine tower, pushing the pipe cleaner into it. Bend the periscope at a right angle 2.5cm (1 in) down from the glass, and you're ready to look out!

deepsea diver

Follow the crochet pirate pattern (see page 140), using yellow yarn for the main body to make a diving suit for a deepsea diver. Use black yarn for the boots and gloves at the ends of the arms and legs. Cut a black circle from felt for the facemask and stitch onto the face. Add a felt belt and oxygen pack on the diver's back.

giant squid

Use the squid variation from the crochet octopus pattern on page 87 to make a giant squid to use for play with the submarine. Crochet around 21.5cm (8½ in) of pipe cleaner for the tentacles so they can wrap around the submarine or other underwater objects.

underwater backdrop

Sew a felt underwater backdrop scene for the submarine and variations. Make the backdrop 76cm (30 in) wide by 50cm (20 in) tall, and hang it from the wall. Sew tan sand at the bottom edge, and add felt coral reefs, seaweed, and seashells on top. This makes a great backdrop for the knit mermaid (page 145) too!

giant sewn submarine backdrop

Sew a giant submarine 120cm (4 ft) wide by 90cm (3 ft) tall that can hang from a tree or be tied across a room. Cut out the circular window holes for the underwater explorers to look out through, and a slit for the entry door. Explorers can wear scuba masks and dive for seashells or buried treasure!

variations

crochet cactus

see base design page 220

saguaro cactus

The saguaro cactus has 'arms' curving out and up from the main body. Crochet a few rows following the cactus pattern to make these arms. Loop yarn through the stitches of the last row and knot closed. Insert a pipe cleaner, and stuff, leaving 5cm (2 in) of pipe cleaner sticking out of the arm. Bend 1.25cm ($^1/_2$-in) of the end of the pipe cleaner up to make an anchor, and push the bent end into the body of the cactus. Stitch the end of the arm to the body of the cactus, and bend the arm to stick up. Repeat for the other side.

needle felt cactus

Use green and burnt orange wool roving for a needle felt cactus. Roll the green wool into a tube and felt a 7.5-cm (3-in)-high cactus. Roll the orange wool into a shorter tube and felt a 5-cm (2-in)-high pot for the cactus to sit in. Hold the cactus on top of the pot and felt together. Add felt flowers to the top of the cactus.

prickly pear cactus

The prickly pear cactus has leaves shaped like those of the money plant (see page 208) – rounded, and wider at the top than the bottom. Crochet the pot as in the main pattern, and cut enough leaves to fill the pot. Use beige thread to make the cactus needles by knotting one end and pulling it through a felt leaf. Knot the thread on the opposite side of the felt and snip with about 2.5cm (1 in) left on the leaf. Repeat to make a few needles on each leaf. Sandwich two leaves together with the anchor knots on the inside and the long needles on the outside, and stitch together. Stitch the leaves together at different heights and use fabric glue to secure the cactus in the pot.

desert snake

Make a desert snake to go with your cactus by following the caterpillar variation on page 107 to make a knitted snake. Add spots with duplicate stitch or knit two different-coloured stripes as you work. Insert a medium-tension wire to wrap the snake around the base of your cactus.

games & fitness

Get active with fitness toys and games. These classic activities are sure to be family favourites for years to come.

crochet dumbbells

see variations page 270

materials

- yarn: Brown Sheep Shepherd's Shades (100% wool, 100g (3½ oz), 120m (131 yds)), 1 skein each of (A) Blue Sky, (B) Rose Petal
- 6 mm (US size J/10) crochet hook
- tapestry needle
- stuffing

tension: 4 sts over 11.5cm (4½ in) rows = 2.5cm (1 in)
finished dimensions: 16.5cm (6½ in) long, 5cm (2 in) wide, 5cm (2 in) high

instructions

With A, ch 2.
Rnd 1: make 8 dc in 2nd ch from hook, sl st to join.
Rnd 2: ch 1, 2 dc in each st around, sl st to join – 16 sts.
Rnd 3: ch 1, [dc in next st, 2 dc in next st] around, sl st to join – 24 sts.
Rnds 4–8: ch 1, dc in each st around, sl st to join.
Rnd 9: ch 1, [dc in next st, skp 1, dc in next st] around, sl st to join – 16 sts.
Begin to stuff and continue stuffing until end.
Rnd 10: ch 1, [skp 1, dc in next st] around, sl st to join – 8 sts.
Rnds 11–24: ch 1, dc in each st around, sl st to join.
Rnd 25: ch 1, 2 dc in each st around, sl st to join – 16 sts.
Rnd 26: ch 1, [dc in next st, 2 dc in next st] around, sl st to join.
Rnds 27–31: ch 1, dc in each st around, sl st to join.
Rnd 32: ch 1, [dc in next st, skp 1, dc in next st] around, sl st to join – 16 sts.
Rnd 33: ch 1, [skp 1, dc in next st] around, sl st to join – 8 sts.
Break yarn and weave in ends.
Crochet another dumbbell with B to make a set.

knitted skipping rope

see variations page 271

materials

- yarn: Brown Sheep Cotton Fleece (80% cotton, 20% merino wool, 100g ($3\frac{1}{2}$ oz), 196m (215 yds)), 1 skein in Prosperous Plum
- craft felt in red
- 3.75 mm (US size 5) double-pointed knitting needles
- non-stretch cording, 2.75m (3 yds)
- safety pin
- tailor's chalk
- tape measure
- compass
- sewing needle
- sewing thread in red
- dressmaking pins
- stuffing

to fit child height: up to 1.4 m, 1.6 m, 1.8m (4 ft 10 in, 5 ft 3 in, 5 ft 10 in) tall
finished measurement: 2.1 m, 2.4 m, 2.75m (7 ft, 8 ft, 9 ft) long

instructions

To customise skipping rope length: Stand on the middle of the non-stretch cording with one foot. Trim so that the cord ends reach up to the armpit. Knit I-cord to this length.

rope

With A, CO 4 sts and knit in I-cord for 2.1 m, 2.4 m, 2.75m (7 ft, 8 ft, 9 ft). BO and weave in ends. The knit I-cord is stretchy, so you'll need to add non-stretch cording to maintain a stable length. Attach a safety pin to one end of the length of non-stretch cording and push through the centre of the I-cord to the other side.

handles

With tailor's chalk and a tape measure, mark and cut two 12 x 7.5-cm (5 x 3-in) rectangles. Use a compass to draw two 2.25-cm ($\frac{7}{8}$-in) circles and four 3.5-cm ($1\frac{1}{4}$-in) circles onto red felt, and cut out.

Fold the rectangles in half lengthwise and sew the 12-cm (5-in) edge with a 0.75-cm ($\frac{5}{16}$-in) seam allowance for each handle. Turn both handles right side out and pin and blanket stitch a 2.25-cm ($\frac{7}{8}$-in) felt circle on the end of each handle with red thread. Stuff each handle tightly.

Blanket stitch two 2.25-cm ($1\frac{1}{4}$-in) circles together with red thread. Repeat for the other 2.25-cm ($1\frac{1}{4}$-in) circle set.

Stitch one end of the knit rope to the centre of a 2.25-cm ($1\frac{1}{4}$-in) circle. Repeat for the other end of the rope.

Centre the open end of the handle on the 2.25-cm ($1\frac{1}{4}$-in) circle and sew together. Repeat for the other handle.

woven chequers

see variations page 272

materials

- yarn: Brown Sheep Nature Spun Worsted (100% wool, 100g (3½ oz), 224m (245 yds)), 1 skein each of (A) Red Fox, (B) Pepper
- felt: 45cm (½ yd) red, 25cm (¼ yd) black, 25cm (¼ yd) white
- 30-cm (12-in) ruler
- tailor's chalk
- craft knife
- cutting board
- dressmaking pins
- sewing needle
- sewing machine (optional)
- sewing thread to match felt
- fabric glue
- 4 mm (US size G/6) crochet hook
- tapestry needle

finished board dimensions:
25-cm (10-in) square
finished piece dimensions:
2.5-cm (1-in)-diameter circles

instructions

game board

With ruler and chalk, mark and cut two 25-cm (10-in) squares out of red felt. Mark a 2.5-cm (1-in) border around the edge on the wrong side of one square. Mark out eight 2.5 x 20-cm (1 x 8-in) vertical columns inside the border lines. Fold the felt a little and cut the seven vertical lines on the inside of the border.

Cut eight 24 x 2.5-cm (9½ x 1-in) strips out of black felt.

Flip the red board to the right side, and weave the black strips backwards and forwards in between the columns, tucking the excess ends to the wrong side. Begin weaving on the opposite side from each preceding row to give a chequerboard effect. Make sure the strips sit flush against one another so they all fit inside the border comfortably.

Pin both ends of each black strip to hold them in place, and with red thread, make a running stitch along both sides, or sew along the black strip ends with a sewing machine. Backstitch at the beginning and end.

Cut four 21 x 0.5-cm (8¼ x ¼-in) strips of white felt and glue around the border of the checkerboard to hide the cut and seam lines. Place both 25-cm (10-in) felt squares with the wrong sides together, and topstitch 0.5cm (¼ in) from the edge with white thread. Topstitch just outside the white border.

game pieces

With A and 4 mm hook.
Rnd 1: make 6 dc in a magic ring, sl st to join.
Rnd 2: ch 1, 2 dc in each st, sl st to join – 12 sts.
Break yarn, fasten off, and weave in ends. Make 12 game pieces with A, and 12 with B.

knitted bowling set

see variations page 273

materials

- yarn: Brown Sheep Shepherd's Shades (100% wool, 100g (3½ oz), 120m (131 yds)), 5 skeins of (A) Pearl, 1 skein of (B) Fire
- wool roving, 50g (2 oz) of chocolate brown
- 6 mm (US size 10) double-pointed knitting needles
- stitch marker
- dried beans or rice
- fabric or plastic pouch
- stuffing
- tapestry needle
- size 38 felting needle
- felting foam pad

tension: 4½ sts over 6 rows = 2.5cm (1 in)
finished dimensions: 18cm (7 in) high, 7.5cm (3 in) wide

instructions

With A, CO 8 sts and divide onto 3 dpns. Place a stitch marker onto the end and join in the round.
Rnd 1: k.
Rnd 2: k1f&b in each st around – 16 sts.
Rnds 3–5: k.
Rnd 6: rep row 2 – 32 sts.
Rnd 7: p.
Rnds 8–27: k.
Rnd 28: [k6, k2tog] rep 4 times – 28 sts.
Rnd 29: [k5, k2tog] rep 4 times – 24 sts.
Rnd 30: [k4, k2tog] rep 4 times – 20 sts.
Add 25g (1 oz) of dried beans or rice in fabric or plastic pouch and seal tight. Begin to stuff and continue stuffing to end.
Rnd 31: k.
Rnd 32: Change to B, but do not break A, and k.
Rnds 33–35: k.
Rnd 36: change to A, and break B, and k.
Rnds 37–38: k.
Rnd 39: [k5, m1] rep 4 times – 24 sts.
Rnd 40: [k6, m1] rep 4 times – 28 sts.
Rnd 41: [k7, m1] rep 4 times – 32 sts.
Rnds 42–47: k.
Rnd 48: [k6, k2tog] rep 4 times – 28 sts.
Rnd 49: [k5, k2tog] rep 4 times – 24 sts.
Rnd 50: [k4, k2tog] rep 4 times – 20 sts.
Rnd 51: [k3, k2tog] rep 4 times – 16 sts.
Rnd 52: [k2, k2tog] rep 4 times – 12 sts.
Rnd 53: [k1, k2tog] rep 4 times – 8 sts.
Break yarn and pull through last 8 sts. Weave in ends.
Knit five more pins to make a mini set, or knit nine more pins to make a full set.

Needle felt a 10-cm (4-in)-diameter bowling ball with dark brown wool roving following the needle felt ball pattern on page 48.

baby yoga mat

see variations page 274

materials

- fabric: Robert Kaufman Roar (100% cotton), 45cm (45cm (1/2 yd)) Bermuda; Moda Muslin (100% cotton), 45cm (45cm (1/2 yd)) Natural
- tape measure
- tailor's chalk
- dressmaking pins
- sewing machine (recommended)
- sewing thread in off-white
- point turner

finished dimensions:
46cm (18 in) wide, 92cm (36 in) long

note: You may add a rubber backing, such as a rubber drawer liner, to keep the mat from slipping on hardwood floors.

instructions

Lay the Bermuda fabric on top of the Natural fabric with the wrong sides up. Measure and mark a 48 x 94cm (19 x 37-in) rectangle on the top fabric and cut out both layers.

With the right sides together, sew along three edges with a 1-cm (1/2-in) seam allowance. Leave one 48-cm (19-in) edge open.

Cut all four corners, being careful not to cut too close to the seam, and turn inside out. Push the corners out with a point turner.

Press the mat edges flat. Turn the open edge in 1.25cm (1/2-in), pin, and then press.

Topstitch 1cm (3/8 in) from the edge all around the mat, beginning with the pinned 48-cm (19-in) edge.

go fish!

see variations page 275

materials

- yarn: Brown Sheep Cotton Fleece (80% cotton, 20% merino wool, 100g (3½ oz), 196m (215 yds)), 1 skein each of (A) Emperor's Robe, (B) Caribbean Sea, (C) Robin Egg Blue, (D) Cotton Ball
- felt: 25cm (¼ yd) of tan, two 2.5-cm (1-in) circles of grey
- 4 mm (US size 6) knitting needles
- stuffing
- 4 1.25-cm (½-in) magnets
- bamboo skewer
- masking tape
- tape measure
- tailor's chalk
- white embroidery thread

tension: 5 sts over 6 rows = 2.5cm (1 in) in st st

finished fish dimensions: 9.5cm (3¾ in) long

finished rod dimensions: 63.5cm (25 in) long, 1.5-cm (5/8-in)-wide rod, 2.25-cm (15/16-in)-wide hook

instructions

fish

With A and size 6 needle, CO 10 sts.

R1 (WS): p.

R2 (RS): k1, ssk, k to last 3 sts, k2tog, k1 – 8 sts.

R3 and all odd rows: p.

R4 and 6: rep row 2 – 2 sts decreased per row.

R8: k1, m1, k to the last st, m1, k1 – 6 sts.

R10 and 12: rep row 8 – 2 sts increased per row.

R14–19: k st st.

R20: k1, ssk, k to last 3 sts, k2tog, k1 – 8 sts.

R22 and 24: rep row 20 – 2 sts decreased per row.

R26: k2tog twice – 2 sts.

BO. Repeat rows 1–26 to make the other side of the fish. Leave enough yarn for sewing at the end of one piece. Place the fish with the wrong sides together and mattress stitch beginning at the mouth and around the body. Stuff lightly when you have a 2.5-cm (1-in) opening left. Place a magnet at the inside tip of the mouth, close off, and hide ends on the inside. Repeat to make a set of three or more fish for the game using B and C.

fishing rod

Cut a 36-cm (15-in) length of D for the fishing line. Make a knot at both ends. Cut a 25-cm (10-in) thin bamboo skewer. Wrap masking tape around the cut end. With measuring tape and chalk, mark and cut a 3.5 x 28-cm (1¼ x 11-in) rectangle from tan felt. Fold in half lengthwise and topstitch 0.5cm (¼ in) from the edge. Stop at the bottom opening and insert the dowel or skewer. Place one knotted end of the fishing line inside and finish sewing closed. Cut two 2.5-cm (1-in) circles from grey felt for the 'hook+. Backstitch around the edge using an embroidery needle and double-stranded white embroidery thread. Insert a magnet and the other knotted end of the fishing line halfway through sewing. Continue sewing around and hide ends on the inside.

knitted & felt noughts and crosses

materials

- yarn: Brown Sheep Lamb's Pride Worsted (85% wool, 15% mohair, 100g (4 oz), 175m (190 yds), 1 skein of (A) Limeade, (B) White Frost
- felt, 25cm (¼ yd) of orange
- 5 mm (US size 8) knitting needles
- tapestry needle
- tailor's chalk or fabric marker
- cardstock
- embroidery thread in white
- embroidery needle

finished board measurements: 16.5-cm (6½-in) square
finished game pieces measurement: 4cm (1½ in) high

instructions

game board

With A, CO 29 sts.
R1–4: [k1, p1] in seed stitch across.
R5 (RS): k1, p1, k1, k23, k1, p1, k1.
R6 (WS): k1, p1, k1, p 23, k1, p1, k1
R7–40: repeat rows 5 and 6.
R41: repeat row 5.
R42–45: [k1, p1] in seed stitch across.
BO and weave in ends.

With a length of B and a tapestry needle, duplicate stitch two vertical lines beginning at row 5, and on the 11th stitch from both the left and right sides, all the way up to row 41. With another length of B and a tapestry needle, duplicate stitch horizontal lines at rows 15 and 16, and 28 and 29. The blocks inside the seed stitch border should be 4cm (1½ in) square inside the white lines. Block to make a 16.5-cm (6½-in) square.

game pieces

Print out the 'X's and 'O's on cardstock. Cut them out and draw around them onto felt with fabric chalk or marker; make five of each piece and cut out two layers. Backstitch with two strands of white embroidery thread and an embroidery needle around the edge of the 'O' and down the middle of the 'X'.

Enlarge to 300% to make to actual size.

'X' (5)

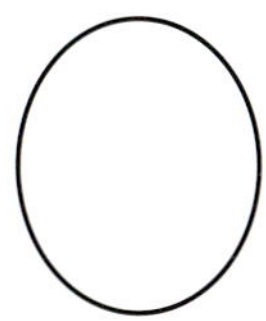

'O' (5)

see variations page 276

knitted sweatbands

see variations page 277

materials

- yarn: Brown Sheep Cotton Fleece (80% cotton, 20% merino wool, 100g (3½ oz), 196m (215 yds)), 1 skein each of (A) Hawaiian Sky, (B) Celery Leaves
- 4 mm (US size 6) knitting needles
- tapestry needle

tension: 5½ sts over 9 rows in garter st
wrist band sizes: child small (medium, large)
finished measurements: 10 cm, 12.5 cm, 15cm (4 in, 5 in, 6 in)
head band sizes: child small (medium, large)
finished measurements: 40.5 cm, 43 cm, 45.5cm (16 in, 17 in, 18 in)
note: This pattern is knit on straight needles so you can stop and measure your knitting against the wrist and head for custom sizing.

instructions

wristband

With A, CO 10 sts.
Knit in garter stitch for 4.5 cm (5.5 cm, 7cm) (1¾ in (2¼ in, 2¾ in)). Change to B, but do not fasten off A.

Knit the next row, purl the second row, and knit the third row. When you begin the third row of stockinette stitch, carry the blue yarn behind your knitting to bring it to the other side.

Change to A, fasten off B. Purl the next row, and continue to work purl rows for 4.5 cm (5.5 cm, 7cm) (1¾ in (2¼ in, 2¾ in)).

BO and mattress stitch ends together. Weave in ends. Knit another matching wrist band.

headband

With B, CO 10 sts.
Knit in garter stitch for 19 cm (20 cm, 21.5cm) (7½ in (8 in, 8½ in)).
Fasten off B, change to A. Knit the next row and continue in st st for the next six rows, ending with a knit row.

Fasten off A, change to B. Purl the next row, and continue to work purl rows for 19 cm (20 cm, 21.5cm) (7½ in (8 in, 8½ in)).

BO and mattress stitch together. Weave in ends and block the blue section.

sewn dominoes

see variations page 278

materials

- fabric: Robert Kaufman Kona Cotton (100% cotton), 45cm (45cm (½ yd)) of Ivory
- yarn: Brown Sheep Cotton Fleece (80% cotton, 20% merino wool, 100g (3½ oz), 196m (215 yds)) 1 skein of Cavern
- tape measure
- tailor's chalk
- dressmaking pins
- sewing needle
- sewing machine (optional)
- sewing thread to match fabric and yarn
- point turner
- stuffing
- 4 mm (US size G/6) crochet hook
- tapestry needle
- fabric glue

finished dimensions:
10cm (4 in) long, 20cm (8 in) high, 4cm (1½ in) wide

instructions

body

With tape measure and tailor's chalk, measure and cut two 22 x 12-cm (8¾ x 4¾-in) rectangles, and one 5.5 x 66-cm (2¼ x 26-in) strip out of Ivory fabric.

With the right sides facing, pin the 66-cm (26-in) strip along the edge of the rectangle, leaving 1.25cm (½-in) fabric to sew closed at the end. Sew along the edge with a 1-cm (⅜-in) seam allowance. Pin the other rectangle to the edge of the strip with the right sides facing, and sew with a 1-cm (⅜-in) seam allowance.

Clip corners and turn right side out. Use a point turner to push out the corners. Stuff and invisible stitch closed.

face

Black dots: With yarn and crochet hook, make 6 dc in a magic ring, sl st to join, ch 1, 2 dc in each st around, sl st, and break yarn. Weave in ends. Make multiple dots as needed for the numbers on each game piece.
Black dividing line: With A, ch 16 and weave in ends. Add a dab of fabric glue to secure ends. Make one chain for each game piece.

assembly

A classic set of dominoes has 26 pieces and two numbers on each piece, and uses the numbers one to six made up of dots. Each piece is a unique combination of the six numbers, and includes blank ends with no numbers. Arrange the dots as shown in the photograph and pin in place. Measure and mark the centre dividing line at 10cm (4 in) from the top and bottom of each piece. Pin the chain in place, stretching it so that it's 1cm (⅜ in) from both sides. Stitch the pieces in place with black thread and hide the knots underneath.

cup & ball

see variations page 279

materials

- yarn: Brown Sheep Lamb's Pride Superwash Bulky (100 % wool, 100g (3½ oz), 100m (110 yds)), 1 skein of (A) Charcoal Heather; Brown Sheep Shepherd's Shades (100% wool, 100g (3½ oz), 120m (131 yds)), 1 skein of (B) Wintergreen; Lion Brand Cotton Bamboo (52% cotton 48% bamboo, 100g (3½ oz), 224m (245 yds)), 1 skein of (C) Persimmon
- wool roving, white, 7g (¼ oz)
- stiff felt in white
- 5.5 mm (US size I/9) crochet hook
- bamboo skewer
- masking tape
- stuffing
- tapestry needle
- sewing needle with large eye
- size 38 felting needle
- felting foam pad

tension: 4 sts over 4½ rows = 2.5cm (1 in)
finished dimensions: 23.5cm (9¼ in) high, 6cm (2½ in) wide

instructions

handle

With A and 5.5 mm crochet hook, make 8 dc in a magic ring, sl st to join. Dc in each st around until piece measures 15cm (6 in) Break yarn with enough for sewing. Cut the bamboo skewer to 6 in and cover the rough end with masking tape. Insert the skewer in the handle, and stuff firmly.

cup

With B and 5 mm crochet hook, make 8 dc in a magic ring, sl st to join.
Rnd 1: ch 1, 2 dc in each st around, sl st to join – 16 sts.
Rnd 2: ch 1, [dc in next st, 2 dc in next st] around, sl st to join – 24 sts.
Rnd 3: ch 1, [dc in next 2 sts, 2 dc in next st] around, sl st to join – 32 sts.
Rnd 4: ch 1, dc in back loop only in each st, sl st to join.
Rnds 5–15: ch 1, dc in each st around, sl st to join.
Break yarn and weave in ends.

assembly

With a tapestry needle, stitch the handle to the centre base of the cup and secure with a knot. Hide the ends inside the handle. With a compass, draw a 5-cm (2-in) circle onto stiff felt and cut out. Place the circle on the bottom inside of the cup and stitch an 'X' in the centre, connecting it to the base and handle. This will give the cup more stability when playing the game.

Needle felt a 2.5-cm (1-in) white ball following the needle felt ball instructions on page 48. Cut an 46-cm (18-in) length of C, and knot at the base of the cup with a sharp needle, where the handle meets. Hide the end inside the handle. Thread the other end with the sharp needle and pierce the felt ball. Pull the yarn so it measures 30cm (12 in) Make a double knot to secure the yarn to the ball, and hide the end on the inside. Snip off excess yarn.

crochet & felt quoits

see variations page 280

materials

- yarn: Brown Sheep Nature Spun Worsted (100% wool, 100g ($3\frac{1}{2}$ oz), 224m (245 yds)), 1 skein each of (A) Turquoise Wonder, (B) Regal Purple, (C) Impasse Yellow
- felt, 25cm ($\frac{1}{4}$ yd) in chocolate brown
- tape measure
- tailor's chalk
- brown sewing thread
- dried beans or rice
- stuffing
- brown embroidery thread
- bamboo skewer
- 4 mm (US size G/6) crochet hook
- tapestry needle

tension: 5 sts over 6 rows = 2.5cm (1 in)
finished ring measurements: 9.5cm ($3\frac{3}{4}$ in)
finished stand measurements: 15cm (6 in) long, 38cm (15 in) high, 15cm (6 in) wide

instructions

stand

With measuring tape and chalk, measure, mark, and cut two 16.5-cm ($6\frac{5}{8}$-in) squares, one 68.5 x 7.5-cm (27 x 3-in) strip, one 10 x 28-cm (4 x 11-in) rectangle, and one 3-cm ($1\frac{1}{4}$-in)-diameter circle out of felt. Pin the 68.5-cm (27-in) strip along the edges of one square. Sew with a 0.75-cm ($\frac{5}{16}$-in) seam allowance. Stitch the 7.5-cm (3-in) strip opening closed. Pin the other square around the strip, lining it up with the bottom square. Sew with a 0.75-cm ($\frac{5}{16}$-in) seam allowance and leave a 10-cm (4-in) opening. Pour $1\frac{1}{2}$ cups of beans or rice into the square base for weight. Fill the rest of the base with stuffing. Invisible stitch to close up. Fold and sew the 10 x 28-cm (4 x 11-in) rectangle along the 28-cm (11-in) edge with a 0.75-cm ($\frac{5}{16}$-in) seam allowance. Turn right side out and blanket stitch the 3-cm ($1\frac{1}{4}$-in) circle to one end of the tube with brown embroidery thread. Stuff the tube firmly and insert a chopstick or skewer (with the point clipped and taped), leaving at least 5cm (2 in) hanging out to stick into the base. The stick doesn't need to reach to the top of the tube. Snip a small hole in the centre top of the square base and insert the stick and tube on top. Pin in place and backstitch around the base of the tube with brown embroidery thread to secure.

ring

With A, ch 8, sl st in first ch to join. Dc in each st around for 25cm (10 in) Stuff as you crochet and stitch the ends together to form a ring. Make 30-cm (12-in)- and 35.5-cm (14-in)-long rings following the same instructions with B and C. Needle felt any joins that look uneven. The different-sized rings will add extra challenge to the game. Crochet bigger rings as desired.

needle felt dice

see variations page 281

materials

- wool roving: 25g (1 oz) of red (plus 7g (1/4 oz) extra for finishing), 7g (1/4 oz) white
- size 38 felting needle
- felting foam pad

finished dimensions:
5-cm (2-in) cube

instructions

<u>cube</u>

Divide the red roving evenly into two 14-g (1/2-oz) sections. Each die will weigh 14-g (1/2-oz). Divide the 14-g (1/2-oz) roving again into two 7-g (1/4-oz) sections and roll into a ball, starting at one end and tucking in the sides as you go. The tighter you roll, the less work you'll have to do, because you want a hard mass in the end. Hold your rolled wool with the open ends on the left and right sides. Wrap the other 0.5-cm (1/4-in) section horizontally around the mid-section and right over the left-hand and right-hand open ends to make a cube shape.

Place your ball on the foam pad and hold the ends in place with your finger. Take your felting needle in your other hand and jab the ends together. Once you've tacked the ends in place, pull the loose ends around top and bottom to blend the wool in. They should be wispy. Gently tuck and stab lightly around until the wool is felted and blended in. If you have trouble smoothing it out, you can add a thin layer of extra wool over that side to cover any creases or wrinkles, and felt over it. Repeat for the other loose ends.

Stab all over the piece, felting six flat sides until you feel it firming up and holding together. If it's not a cube yet, keep jabbing any protruding area until the wool moves inwards and blends in. It's OK for the edges to be a little rounded, as shown. Repeat to make another die.

<u>dots</u>

Take a bit of white roving and lightly roll it between your fingers to make a dot. It doesn't have to be perfect – use your needletip to tuck in loose wisps. Place in the centre of one side of the red cube and hold in place with a finger. Push the felting needle through the white wool into the cube. Watch your finger as you do this. Keep felting the dot in place and gently using your needletip to tuck in any loose wisps so that you have a clearly defined dot. This side of the die will be number one.
Follow these steps to make numbers two to six on each side of the die.

crochet & felt darts

see variations page 282

materials

- yarn: Brown Sheep Cotton Fleece (80% cotton, 20% merino wool, 100g (3½ oz), 196m (215 yds)), 1 skein each (A) Gold Dust, (B) Provincial Rose
- felt: 45cm (45cm (½ yd)) of turquoise, 25cm (¼ yd) of navy
- stiff felt, 30-cm (12-in) square
- string
- fabric marker
- sewing needle
- sewing thread to match felt and in a contrasting colour for basting
- pink and white hook-and-loop fastener, 4cm (1½ in) wide
- 4 mm (US size G/6) crochet hook
- dried rice
- tapestry needle
- compass

tension: 5 sts over 5 rows = 2.5cm (1 in)
finished dartboard dimensions: 33-cm (13-in) diameter

instructions

board

Mark and cut two 33-cm (13-in)- and one 10-cm (4-in)-diameter circles from the turquoise felt, and a 20-cm (8-in)-diameter circle from the navy felt. Mark and cut one 30-cm (12-in)-diameter circle from the stiff felt. (To draw a circle, use a pencil, string, and fabric marker. Tie one end of the string to the pencil and the other end to the fabric marker, making the string half the length of the circle you're drawing. Anchor the pencil in the centre of the circle you're drawing with one hand, and hold the string taut with the other hand. Mark the circle with the fabric marker, keeping the string taut and moving it around until you've made a complete circle.)

Centre the 20-cm (8-in) navy circle on one of the 30-cm (12-in) turquoise circles and baste. Centre the 10-cm (4-in) turquoise circle on top of the navy circle and baste it in place. Sew these two circles together, 0.25cm (⅛ in) from the edge, with matching thread.

Cut the following out of the rough side of the hook-and-loop fastener: one 4-cm (1½-in) pink square, six 6 x 4-cm (2½ x 1½-in) pink rectangles, six 4 x 4-cm (1½ x 1½-in) white squares. Baste the 4-cm (1½-in) pink square in the centre of the 10-cm (4-in) circle. Baste the white squares evenly around the navy circle, and baste the pink rectangles lengthwise around the outside turquoise circle, lined up between the white squares, as shown. Sew all the hook-and-loop fastener pieces onto the board with matching thread. Centre, and sandwich the stiff felt between the turquoise circles. Cut a 30-cm (12-in) length of C and double knot both ends to create an anchor. Centre each end of the yarn above a pink rectangle about 15cm (6 in) apart, and pin between the felt. Pin both circles together and sew 0.25cm ($^3/_{16}$ in) from the edge all around with matching thread, removing the pins as you sew.

darts

With A, make 6 dc in a magic ring, sl st in first ch to join.

Rnd 1: ch 1, 2 dc in each ch around, sl st to join – 12 sts.

Rnd 2: ch 1, [dc in next st, 2 dc in next st] around, sl st to join – 18 sts.

Rnd 3: ch 1, [dc in next 2 sts, 2 dc in next st] around, sl st to join – 24 sts.

Rnds 4–5: ch 1, dc in each st around, sl st to join.

Rnd 6: ch 1, [dc in next 3 sts, skp 1] around, sl st to join – 18 sts.

Rnd 7: ch 1, [dc in next 2 sts, skp 1] around, sl st to join – 12 sts.

Rnd 8: ch 1, [dc in next st, skp 1] around, sl st to join – 6 sts.

Fill with rice and knot securely. Hide ends on the inside. Make two more darts with A, and three more with B. With a compass, draw a 3-cm ($1^1/_4$-in)-diameter circle on the reverse of the soft white hook-and-loop fastener strip. Cut a hook-and-loop fastener circle for each dart and hand-sew to the back of each with white thread.

Toss a dart by cupping one in your hand with the hook-and-loop fastener towards the dartboard. Fling the dart forwards with your whole hand. This will help to propel the dart straight to the board without twisting and turning so that the hook-and-loop fastener sides face each other the whole time.

pin the tail on the donkey

materials

- yarn: Brown Sheep Cotton Fleece (80% cotton, 20% merino wool, 100g (3½ oz), 196m (215 yds)), 1 skein each of (A) Provincial Rose, (B) Limelight, (C) Truffle
- fabric: Robert Kaufman Kona Cotton (100% cotton), 45cm (45cm (½ yd)) Ivory; Floral Calico (100% cotton), 45cm (45cm (½ yd))
- wool felt in cream
- lightweight fusible interfacing
- tailor's chalk
- fabric weights
- sewing thread in pink and ivory
- stabiliser

finished board dimensions: 62.5cm (25 in) wide, 60cm (24 in) high
finished tail measurements: 12cm (5 in) tall, 3cm (1¼ in.) wide at the top

instructions

board

With the right sides together, fold the Ivory fabric in half. Use a measuring tape and chalk to mark 68.5-cm (27-in) height, and 34-cm (13½-in) width from the fold line. Cut along the chalk lines for a 68.5-cm (27-in) square. On the wrong side, mark 2.5cm (1 in) along three edges with chalk and connect the lines. For the top edge pocket, mark 7.5cm (3 in) along the edge and connect the chalk lines. Press the edges to the wrong side to the 2.5-cm (1-in) line. Flip the fabric to the right side and topstitch 1cm (⅜ in) from the edge on three sides with Ivory thead. Flip the fabric to the wrong side and fold and press the top edge to the wrong side to the 7.5-cm (3-in) line. Turn the fabric to the right side and sew 2.5cm (1 in) from the edge, making a pocket for the dowel.

donkey

The donkey pattern shown is the reverse of the end piece to make it easier to trace. Trace the donkey onto the liner paper that stays with the web of the fusible interfacing. Cut the excess interfacing around your tracing, but not the traced line. Set your iron to high, and iron onto the wrong side of the Calico fabric for a few seconds to hold in place. Cut the fused interfacing and fabric along the traced line. Peel off the paper backing, leaving the web stuck to your donkey. Make sure any wrinkles are pressed out of the Ivory backing and centre the donkey on the backing. With your hot iron, press for 10–20 seconds. Cut a piece of stabiliser bigger than your donkey and place behind the donkey on the wrong side of the fabric. Use pink thread and a sewing machine to sew a zigzag stitch about 0.25cm (⅛ in) wide, keeping stitch length as short as possible. Sew around the donkey, making sure your zigzag sits in far enough so the fabric won't easily come out.

see variations page 283

Enlarge to 1225% to make to actual size.

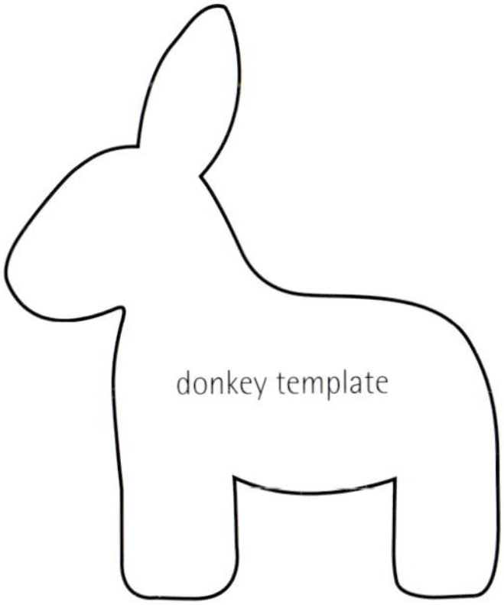

<u>tails</u>

Cut six 65-cm (26-in) lengths of A and fold in half. Make a knot about 2cm (3/4 in) below the fold. Tape the knotted end to a table or board to anchor it down, and divide the yarn into three sections of four strands each.

Braid the yarn until you have 9.5cm (3 3/4 in), and make a knot at the end of the braid. Trim off the excess, leaving a 5-cm (2-in) fringe. Cut a 2.5-cm (1-in) square out of cream felt. Place the felt behind the top knot and stitch the felt to the knot in the centre.

Repeat steps 1-4 to make two tails of each colour using A, B, and C yarns. Make more tails for a bigger party.

Use double-sided sticky tape to pin the tails on your donkey.

jacks

see variations page 284

materials

- yarn: Brown Sheep Wildfoote Luxury Sock Yarn (75% washable wool, 25% nylon, 50g (1¾ oz), 196m (215 yds)), 1 skein of Temple Turquoise
- 3.25 mm (US size D/3) crochet hook
- stuffing
- tapestry needle

tension: 6½ sts over 9 rows = 2.5cm (1 in)
finished dimensions: 9cm (3½ in) high, 9cm (3½ in) wide

instructions

centre piece

With 3.25 mm hook and yarn, make 8 dc in a magic ring, sl st in first dc to join. Dc in each st around until piece measures 9cm (3½ in) Stuff tightly and break yarn. Weave around the end and pull together, closing off the tube. Secure and weave in ends.

prong

With 3.25 mm hook and yarn, make 6 dc in a magic ring, sl st in first dc to join.
Rnd 1: ch 1, 2 dc in each st around, sl st to join – 12 sts.
Rnds 3–4: ch 1, dc in each st around, sl st to join.
Rnd 5: ch 1, [dc in next st, skp 1] around, sl st to join – 6 sts.
Rnds 6–11: ch 1, dc in each st around, sl st to join.
Break yarn with enough for sewing, and stuff firm. Make three more prongs.

With a tapestry needle, stitch the prongs one at a time around the centre of the 9-cm (3½-in) crochet tube in a cross. Weave in ends.

A set of jacks usually consists of ten jacks, but since these crochet jacks are much larger than normal, try making five. You'll need to buy a rubber ball to bounce.

sewn beanbag toss

see variations page 285

materials

- fabric: P&B Spectrum Solids (100% cotton), 45cm (1/2 yd) of Clementine; Moda (100% cotton), 25cm (1/4 yd) of Chicken Wire; Robert Kaufman Metro Living Big Circles (100% cotton), 25cm (1/4 yd) of Black; Lecien Dots, (100% cotton), 25cm (1/4 yd) of White on Grey Large Dots; Lecien Stripes (100% cotton), 25cm (1/4 yd) of Black Small
- grosgrain ribbon in grey, 2cm (3/4 in) wide, cut into four 38-cm (15-in) strips
- point turner or stick
- cardstock
- embroidery thread in pink and white
- dried beans or rice

finished board measurement:
50-cm (20-in) square
finished beanbag measurement:
12-cm (5-in) square

instructions

<u>fabric board</u>

Cut a 53-cm (21-in) square out of the Clementine fabric, using a tape measure and tailor's chalk to mark out the fabric.

Fold the fabric with the right sides together, line up two pieces of ribbon, and pin 1.25cm (1/2-in) from a corner. Repeat for the opposite corner. These will make ties for hanging up your fabric 'board'.

Sew three edges with a 1.25-cm (1/2-in) seam allowance, making sure to include the pinned ribbon edge. Clip all four corners, being careful not to cut too close to the seam, and turn right side out. Push the corners out with a point turner or stick.

Press the mat edges flat. Turn the open edge in 1.25cm (1/2 in), pin, and press. Topstitch 1cm (3/8 in) from the edge all around the square, beginning with the pinned edge.

Print the 12-cm (5-in) circle pattern onto cardstock. Measure and mark 19cm (7 1/2 in) from the centre top, bottom, and sides of the square to centre the circle. Place a few pins around the circle to keep the fabric from shifting. Place the circle in the centre and trace around with chalk. Measure and mark 1.25cm (1/2 in) around the outside of the circle.

Fold the centre enough to snip through both layers of fabric, and make all cuts through both layers. Cut triangles, starting from the centre and stopping at the first 12-cm (5-in) circle line. This will make it easier to cut the circle out evenly. Cut along the chalk line at the end of your snips to cut out the circle.

Make snips about 1.25cm (1/2 in) apart from the circle edge to the 1.25cm (1/2 in) line you made all around the circle. Fold these edges in, a section at a time, and press as you go until all the edges are turned in.

Pin around the edges and, with three strands of pink embroidery thread, backstitch 0.5cm (1/4 in) from the edge all around.

__beanbags__

With a tape measure and tailor's chalk, measure, mark, and cut two 6-in. squares out of each beanbag fabric.

Pin one pair of squares with the right sides together and sew with a 1.25cm (1/2 in) seam allowance around three edges. Clip the corners and turn right side out, pushing out the corners with a point turner or stick.

Fold in the open edge 1.25cm (1/2 in), and press. Fill each bag with one cup of dried beans or rice, and pin closed. Topstitch with white thread 0.75cm (5/16 in) from the edge. Repeat for the other three beanbags.

variations

crochet dumbbells

see base design page 239

circus strongman

Follow the 'crochet pirate' pattern on page 140 and change out the yarn colours to make a circus strongman. Crochet the legs with black yarn, and the body with the same amount of black for the trousers. Use tan yarn for the rest of the body and arms to make him shirtless. Make him bald and stitch a moustache on his face. Stitch muscle definition with a slightly darker thread on the chest. Stitch the arms on with a button at the shoulder join so that he can move his arms up to lift the dumbbells.

dumbbell rattle

Insert a jingle bell ball inside each end of the dumbbells to turn them into muscle-pumping rattles.

giraffe head rattle

Use yellow yarn and follow the crochet dumbbells pattern to make a giraffe head rattle. Insert a rattle inside the bulb, and stuff as you crochet. Stop crocheting at the end of row 24, loop yarn through the last 8 sts, and pull closed. Crochet two little yellow horns and stitch to the centre top of the head. Cut ears out of yellow felt and stitch to either side of the horns. Embroider eyes and a nose onto the face.

striped dumbbell

Use two colours of yarn and change colours every row to make fun striped dumbbells.

torch

Crochet a torch following the dumbbells pattern and using yellow yarn until the end of row 3 for the light, changing to red for the rest of the torch. Stop crocheting at the end of row 24, loop the yarn through the last 8 sts, and pull closed. Sew a small rectangular felt 'button' in the middle of the handle.

variations

knitted skipping rope

see base design page 240

red and white beaded skipping rope (pictured)

Make a classic red and white 'beaded' skipping rope just like the ones you used to use in school! Follow the skipping rope pattern and begin knitting with white yarn. Change to red after 7.5cm (3 in) of I-cord knitting, and continue changing colours every 7.5cm (3 in) until the end. Follow the rest of the skipping rope instructions to finish the rope, and omit the 3.5-cm (1¼-in) felt circles from the handles.

double dutch

Make two 5-m (16-ft) skipping ropes to swing at the same time to jump double Dutch. At least three players are required for this game.

tug of war rope

Use a thicker-weight cotton yarn or hold the yarn doubled to knit a tug of war rope. Be sure to add strong cording in the centre. Make the rope 15m (50 ft) long, and knit three cords to braid together for extra strength. Knot the braids tightly at the end to secure.

sausage links

Make sausage links by knitting 50cm (20 in) of I-cord and casting on 10 stitches for the cord. Use a reddish brown yarn, stuff as you knit, and tie the ends closed with yarn. Use yarn to knot the sausage every 10cm (4 in) to make your sausage links. This is a nice addition to the food on page 120.

ribbon stick

Make a ribbon stick for dancing by following the skipping rope handle instructions and extending the felt to be 38cm (15 in) long. Insert a dowel inside and stuff. Cut a felt circle the same diameter as both ends to close off the stick. Stitch a 40.5 x 5-cm (16 x 2-in) ribbon to the centre of one end of the stick.

variations

woven chequers

see base design page 243

chess

Follow the chequers pattern on page 243 to make the chess board, but enlarge the pattern to make the woven squares 5cm (2 in) instead of 2.5cm (1 in) Crochet 16 4.5-cm (1¾-in) squares per side, and embroider the different game pieces on top: (1) king, (1) queen, (2) rooks, (2) bishops, (2) knights, (8) pawns.

backgammon

Make a felt backgammon board by cutting a 38 x 23-cm (15 x 9-in) piece of felt for the base and border. Cut two 15 x 18-cm (6 x 7-in) pieces of felt in a contrasting colour and sew on top of the base piece so that there's an even border around and between the two pieces. Cut 2.5-cm (1-in)-wide x 7.5-cm (3-in)-tall triangles for each 'space', and make six for each top and bottom edge of the 15 x 18-cm (6 x 7-in) felt. Use a different colour felt for every other triangle and sew in place. Crochet circles, as in the chequers pattern, for the game pieces. Make 16 pieces for each player, and use a different colour for each set.

snakes & ladders

Follow the chequers instructions to make a snakes and ladders board. Embroider snakes and ladders connecting different spaces around the board. Crochet disk-shaped game pieces following the checker pieces pattern, and make a die from the needle felt dice instructions on page 260.

go

Make a Go game board with felt and embroider a 23-cm (9-in)-square grid with contrasting thread in the centre of a 25-cm (10-in) square. Crochet 40 black and 40 red circles, as in the chequers pattern.

knitted chequers

Follow the noughts and crosses board instructions on page 251, enlarging it to a 25-cm (10-in) square. Knit the board with red yarn and duplicate stitch the chequers with black yarn. Cut two layers of 2.5-cm (1-in) felt circles in red and black for the game pieces. Stitch two layers together for one piece, and make 12 red and 12 black pieces.

variations

knitted bowling set

see base design page 244

needle felt mushroom pins

Make six needle felt mushrooms using the needle felt toadstool pattern on page 203 to make a mini bowling set, and needle felt a 7.5-cm (3-in) ball for the bowling ball.

crochet pirate pins

Follow the crocheted pirate pattern on page 140 but omit the arms and legs to make pirate pins. Crochet a flat circle for the base and fill the bottom with dried beans for weight. Needle felt a 7.5-cm (3-in) ball for the bowling ball.

needle felt bocce

Make bocce balls by needle felting one 9cm (3½-in) ball for the jack, four 12.5-cm (5-in) balls in red, and four 12.5-cm (5-in) balls in blue.

woodland creature pins

Knit the fox from page 74 and its variations to create a set of woodland creature bowling pins. Fill the bases with dried beans for weight. Add stitch detailing to the needle felt bowling ball to make it look like a hedgehog.

'duck' pin bowling

Knit a set of ten ducks from the duck pattern on page 94 to make a set of little duck pins. Needle felt a 6-cm (2½-in) ball for the bowling ball.

variations

baby yoga mat

see base design page 247

yoga block

Follow the dominoes instructions on page 255 but cut the 66-cm (26-in) strip to 12-cm (4¾-in) long to make a yoga block. Use purple fabric for the block, and omit the crochet dots.

gingham picnic blanket (pictured)

Sew a baby picnic blanket with gingham fabric. Cut a 60-cm (24-in) square (or desired size), and make a rolled hem around the edges. Press the edges 1.25cm (½-in) to the wrong side, and 1.25cm (½-in) again to the wrong side. Turn the fabric over to the right side and topstitch 0.5cm (¼ in) from the edge. Embroider little red and black ladybirds on the blanket. You're ready for a tea party or a teddy bear's picnic!

road play mat

Sew a 76 x 101cm (30 x 40-in) play mat for toy cars and buses to drive on. Use green felt for the base, and stitch felt cutouts of roads, trees, bridges, and houses. Let your imagination go and add as many details as you like.

farm play mat

Sew a 76 x 101cm (30 x 40-in) play mat for the farm animals on page 106. Use green fabric for the base (for grass), and appliqué a pond, bushes, and a pigsty. You can use the dollhouse on page 148 as the farmhouse or convert it into a barn.

sensory play mat

Sew two layers of 101-cm (40-in)-square fabric to make a sensory baby mat. Place crinkly plastic between the fabric layers to create a different texture/sound, and sew bright colours and shapes on top of the mat for stimulation. Use textured fabrics or knit a bobble stitch section on the mat for texture.

variations

go fish!

see base design page 248

starfish
Make a starfish from felt for the fishing hook to catch. Cut two layers of felt and blanket stitch together. Stuff lightly and add a strong magnet inside before closing.

catfish
Knit a catfish to catch using the knit fish pattern on page 248 but knotting in some black whiskers with embroidery thread at the sides of the mouth and under the chin. Add a strong magnet behind the mouth, stuff, and sew closed.

angelfish (pictured)
Cut two layers of yellow felt to make an angelfish. Use the knitted fish as a base shape to refer to, and make two pointed fins coming from the top and bottom of the fish, with the points pointing towards the tail. Add blue vertical stripes to complete your angelfish. Insert a strong magnet behind the mouth and stuff before closing off.

pond play mat
Make a pond play mat for the fish to 'swim in' when you go fishing. Make your mat large enough to fit all the fish and the variations listed above. Use green felt for the grass base, and cut an oval pond to sew on top.

shoal of fish mobile
Follow the knit fish pattern and knit five fish in monochromatic colours to make a shoal of fish. Attach the fish to string and use the inside hoop of an embroidery hoop, as in the crochet airplanes mobile on page 50. String the fish so that they cascade down in descending order and colour.

variations

knitted & felt noughts and crosses

see base design page 251

knitted bingo

Knit a bingo board 18cm (7 in) wide and 20cm (8 in) tall, following the board instructions with a moss stitch border and duplicate stitch for the board lines. Make five 2.5-cm (1-in) rows across and five 2.5-cm (1-in) columns up and down. Stitch a star in the centre space as the free space. Stitch the word 'BINGO' at the top of each column. Make multiple boards and stitch the numbers 1–75 in a random order on the cards. Crochet the same game pieces as in the chequers instructions on page 243 to make bingo pieces.

sewn hopscotch mat

Sew a 1.8-m (6-ft)-long by 90-cm (3-ft)-wide hopscotch mat. Cut 30-cm (1-ft) square pieces of fabric for each block and appliqué them to the mat. Print out numbers onto 21.5 x 28-cm (8½ x 11-in) paper and use it as your pattern to appliqué the numbers onto the mat. Add a rubber nonslip backing to the mat if it's going to be used on hardwood floors or other slippery surfaces.

noughts and crosses potholders

Follow the knit noughts and crosses board pattern to make potholders. Duplicate stitch the grid lines, and duplicate stitch 'X's and 'O's in the spaces with orange yarn. This makes a playful kitchen accessory.

sewn noughts and crosses

Cut two 18-cm (7-in) squares from fabric to make a sewn noughts and crosses board. Embroider the grid lines on the top fabric and sew the pieces together with the right sides facing and a 0.5-cm (¼-in) seam allowance. Leave one end open and turn right side out. Turn the edges in 0.5cm (¼ in) and topstitch closed; continue topstitching along the rest of the edges. Make the felt 'X's and 'O's following the pattern to complete the set.

giant noughts and crosses

Multiply all quantities and measures by ten to make a giant noughts and crosses board and game pieces. The game board can double as a blanket.

variations

knitted sweatbands

see base design page 252

terrycloth sweatbands

Use terrycloth fabric to sew sweatbands. Cut the fabric to 10cm (4 in) and fold down to 5cm (2 in) for the height. Cut the fabric to the length needed as listed in the finished measurements for the headband and wristbands on page 252. Sew the long edge together with the right sides facing and turn right side out. Turn the short edges in and hand-sew together to form the bands.

flower headband

Knit a headband following the headband pattern. Add a crochet daisy from the peony variation on page 234 to thc hcadband and wear it to the side of the head.

superhero cuffs

Knit superhero cuffs to go with the superhero cape on page 159 following the knit wristband pattern. Use royal blue for the main band, and bright yellow yarn for the stripe. Embroider blue lightning bolts onto the yellow stripes. Sew yellow felt 'fins' protruding from both bands.

legwarmers

Knit legwarmers using rib stitch on straight needles. Measure the widest part of the calf and divide the number of centimetres (inches) by the number of stitches percm (in) according to the tension. Cast on about 5cm (2 in) shorter than the width measured. Rib stitch is very stretchy, so making it smaller will mean it stays up on the leg. Knit until the piece covers to just below the knee. Cast off and leave enough for sewing. Mattress stitch the long edges together to close up the back of the legwarmer. Knit another legwarmer to match.

striped sweatbands

Use two different-coloured yarns and change colours every two rows to make striped headbands and wristbands. Twist the yarn up the same side to carry the two colours along.

variations

sewn dominoes

see base design page 255

giant dominoes

Multiply all measures and quantities by three to make even bigger dominoes that can be used as pillows, floor pillows, or sofa pillows.

flashcards

Cut two layers of felt 10cm (4 in) wide by 20cm (8 in) tall and make flashcards. Sew stiff felt or interfacing between for structure. Sew or glue on felt pictures of objects such as the sun, clouds, a car and so on. Stitch the name of the object on the back of the cards.

building bricks

Follow the domino pattern and increase the width of the long strip by two to make plushie bricks. Use a reddish-brown fabric for the whole block and sew thin white felt strips along the edges to make the mortar. Make ten bricks to build a small wall or path.

mini skyscrapers

Follow the basic dominoes pattern and cut the 22 x 12-cm (8¾ x 4¾-in) rectangles in half lengthwise to make skyscrapers. Embroider little windows around the buildings, and make them different heights. Fill the base with dried rice or beans for weight, and use them for play with the Godzilla variation of the T-Rex pattern on page 96.

puzzle blocks

Sew six blocks following the domino pattern and lay them flat in two even rows. Embroider each block so that together they form one whole image when placed together in the correct order.

variations

cup & ball

see base design page 256

felt cup & ball

Make a cup using two layers of felt and interfacing in between for support. Cut a 6-cm (2½-in) circle for the base and a 9cm (3½-in)-high rectangle to fit around the circle. Stitch together to make a cup. Make a 15-cm (6-in) handle with one layer of felt and stuff. Cut a circle to close off the bottom and sew the other end to the base of the cup. Insert a dowel for support if necessary. Make a ball and attach, following the instructions for the crochet cup and ball.

crochet three cups magic trick

Follow the crochet cup pattern and make three cups in the same colour yarn. Crochet tightly to make the cups stiff. Needle felt a 4cm (1½-in) ball following the needle felt ball instructions on page 48 to complete the set.

stick & ring game

Follow the cup and ball pattern to make the stick and follow the instructions from the crochet ring toss on page 259 to make a small ring about twice as wide as the stick. Tie a string to the ring, and the other end to the middle of the stick, and make the string 30–38cm (12–15 in) long.

mini golf

Make a tabletop mini golf game by crocheting the cup and turning it on its side to knock the ball into. Needle felt a 5-cm (2-in) ball for the golf ball, and cut two layers of felt and stiff felt to sew in between, 38cm (15 in) long, to make the golf club.

crochet teacup

Follow the crochet cup pattern and add a 2-st-wide handle to the side to make a teacup. Make saucers about 2.5cm (1 in) bigger all around than the base of the cup by sewing two layers of felt together. Make three more teacups and saucers for a tea party set!

variations

crochet & felt quoits

see base design page 259

horseshoe toss

Follow the crochet ring pattern to make a horseshoe, but don't sew the ends together. Use grey yarn and insert a thick-tension wire, stuff and bend the crochet tube into a U-shape. Close off the ends, and make four horseshoes for the game. Make the ring toss stand and use as the stake for tossing horseshoes.

stacking ring toddler toy

Use the ring toss instructions to make a stacking ring toy for toddlers. Widen the centre peg so that the rings will fit snugly over it. Crochet six thick rings using rainbow colours, and make each one slightly bigger than the previous one so they sit from largest to smallest on the peg.

multiple pegs

Make multiple pegs for the rings to be tossed onto. Spread them apart to make the game a bit more challenging.

knitted ring toss

Follow the ring toss pattern to make the stand. Use the knit ring rattle pattern on page 47 to knit rings to toss. Increase the number of cast-on stitches to make the rings bigger. Knit multiple sizes of rings to make the game more challenging.

giraffe ring toss

Use the bowling pin knitting pattern from the bowling game, and embroider a giraffe's face onto it. Add horns and ears on top and use yellow yarn. This will be the 'stake' for tossing the rings onto. Make sure you crochet the rings large enough to fit around the giraffe.

variations

needle felt dice

see base design page 260

needle felt dice blocks

Use different-coloured wool to make a set of six needle felted dice blocks. Stack them together and knock them down!

sewn dice

Cut six 11.5-cm (4½-in) squares of red fabric and sew the edges together with the right sides together and a 0.5-cm (¼-in) seam allowance. Leave one edge open and turn the piece right side out. Stuff and invisible stitch closed. Cut 1.25-cm (½-in) white felt circles for the number of dots. Stitch dots to represent the numbers 1–6 on the cube. Repeat to make a second die.

twelve-sided die

Needle felt a 12-sided die by starting out with a ball, and flattening out 12 sides. Make each face a regular pentagon. Use white yarn to needle felt the numbers 1–12 on each face. Snip the yarn when you're finished with a number and needle felt the ends into the die.

alphabet blocks

Sew alphabet blocks using felt, and stuff. Cut out letters and corresponding objects for each letter, such as an apple for A, a banana for B, and so on for all 26 letters, and sew onto two sides of each block.

stacking puzzle blocks

Make three blocks that join up to make images when stacked on top of each other: try a giraffe, a clown, or a tree. Appliqué the images on in felt.

variations

crochet & felt darts

see base design page 262

lawn darts

Sew a 91.5-cm (3-ft) circle with three rings inside it to make a large lawn dart game. Sew beanbags from the beanbag toss game on page 268 as the 'darts' to toss onto the board. Embroider arrows on the beanbags to simulate darts.

sewn darts

Follow the crochet and felt darts instructions but use cotton fabric to make the board and pieces. Cut two 6-cm (2½-in) circles from felt to make the darts and sew them together with the right sides facing. Leave an opening, turn right side out, and fill with dried beans or rice. Make two sets of five darts in two different colours.

magnetic darts

Make a fabric slipcover for a cookie sheet and appliqué three circular rings in the centre to make a magnetic dartboard. Crochet the game pieces following the pattern for the crochet and felt darts and insert a strong magnet inside and close to one side next to the yarn before closing up.

clown face darts

Follow the crochet and felt darts pattern but cut out a clown face to sew onto the board instead of the rings. Sew a large red circle for a nose as the centre point. Use orange felt for the hair, and white for the face. Sew the same coloured hook-and-eye fastener onto the face and hair.

variations

pin the tail on the donkey

see base design page 264

pin the nose on the clown

Using the same dimensions for the fabric board, appliqué a clown without a nose in the centre. Cut red circles from felt for the clown's nose and use double-sided sticky tape to play the game. Make as many noses as you need for your partygoers!

pin the horn on the unicorn

Follow the pin the tail on the donkey instructions but shorten the ears to make a horse. Cut yellow felt triangles to make unicorn horns, and use double-sided sticky tape to play the game. Make as many horns as you need for the players.

pin the tooth on the narwhal

Enlarge the whale pattern on page 71 to make a narwhal to fit onto the board. Appliqué it slightly to the left of the board, to leave room for the tooth. Cut long, thin triangles from felt to make teeth to pin onto the narwhal. Use double-sided sticky tape to play the game.

hobby horse

Enlarge the donkey's head by 100 percent and add a neck to make a hobby horse. Cut two layers of fabric for the horse's head and neck only, with the right sides facing. Make the ears slightly smaller and cut them out of felt. Sew the head together, stuff, and add a thick dowel in the bottom before closing off. Sew the ears on and stitch eyes onto the face. Add yarn for the mane.

baby blanket appliqué

Use the donkey as a central appliqué for a baby's blanket. Make it a playful spin on pin the tail on the donkey by sewing fabric tails in different places around the blanket.

variations

jacks

see base design page 267

jacks mobile

Crochet five jacks and needle felt one 7.5-cm (3-in) red ball following the needle felt ball instructions on page 48. String the pieces around a 18-cm (7-in) inner embroidery hoop at different lengths.

jacks garland

Make ten jacks and one felt ball and string them together to make a fun garland for a children's game-themed party.

jacks wreath

Crochet 10–15 jacks and stitch together to make a fun jacks wreath. Add a couple of needle felt red balls to one corner of the wreath.

jacks toss game

Follow the beanbag toss pattern on page 268 and appliqué a red circle around the centre hole as the ball used in jacks. Crochet two sets of five jacks in two different colours to toss into the 'ball+.

pick-up sticks

Follow the tube crocheting of the prongs from the jacks pattern to make 25-cm (10-in) 'sticks' for a game of pick-up sticks. Insert a thin dowel in the centre as required for support. Crochet 20 sticks, and make sets of five of one solid colour. Crochet one stick with stripes to be the 'emperor' stick used to pick up other sticks.

variations

sewn beanbag toss

see base design page 268

feed the clown beanbag toss

Appliqué a clown's head onto the background fabric with the centre hole as his mouth for the beanbag toss game. Stitch felt eyes, a round red nose, and rosy cheeks to the face. Make a number of the fruits and vegetables and their variations from chapter 3, and fill with dried beans to make food to toss into the clown's mouth.

crochet balls (pictured)

To make three juggling balls, follow the crochet pattern below. Be sure to crochet tightly and with a smaller hook if necessary so there are no holes for rice to escape. Rnd 1: Make 6 dc in a magic ring; Rnd 2: 2 dc in each st around – 12 sts; Rnd 3: [dc in next st, 2 dc in next st] around – 18 sts; Rnd 4: [dc in next 2 sts, 2 dc in next st] around – 24 sts; Rnd 5: [dc in next 3 sts, 2 dc in next st] around – 30 sts; Rnd 6: [dc in next 4 sts, 2 dc in next st] around – 36 sts; Rnds 7–10: dc in each st around – 36 sts; Rnd 11: [dc in next 4 sts, dc2tog] around – 30 sts; Rnd 12: [dc in next 3 sts, dc2tog] around – 24 sts; Rnd 13: [dc in next 2 sts, dc2tog] around – 18 sts; Rnd 14: [dc in next st, dc2tog] around – 12 sts; Rnd 15: dc2tog around – 6 sts; Use a funnel to fill the ball with rice at the end before closing up.

apple toss

Follow the knitted apple instructions on page 111 to make five red apples and five green apples. Fill the apples with dried beans and use them for an apple toss game. Use different-sized baskets to toss the apples into to make the game more challenging.

puppy dog beanbag toss

Sew a puppy dog's head onto the background fabric and cut a hole for the mouth. Cut bone shapes from fabric and fill with dried beans for dog-biscuit beanbags to feed the dog.

index

KEY
Crocheted projects
Knitted projects
Felted projects
Sewn projects